Reading across Borders

Storytelling and Knowledges of Resistance

Shari Stone-Mediatore

Dedicated to the memory of my grandparents,
Ethel and Jack Stone

 First published in 2003 by
PALGRAVE MACMILLAN™
175 Fifth Avenue, New York, N.Y. 10010 and
Houndmills, Basingstoke, Hampshire, England RG21 6XS.
Companies and representatives throughout the world.

PALGRAVE MACMILLAN is the global academic imprint of the Palgrave
Macmillan division of St. Martin's Press, LLC and of Palgrave Macmillan Ltd.
Macmillan® is a registered trademark in the United States, United Kingdom and
other countries. Palgrave is a registered trademark in the European Union and other
countries.

0–312-29566–9 hardback 0–312-29567–7 paperback

Library of Congress Cataloging-in-Publication Data Available from the Library of
Congress

A catalogue record for this book is available from the British Library.

First Palgrave Macmillan edition: June 2003
10 9 8 7 6 5 4 3 2 1

Printed in the United States of America.

Contents

Acknowledgments

I owe my first thanks to Mary Rawlinson, Dick Howard, Don Ihde, and Anthony Weston, each of whom provided invaluable guidance and support when this work was in its most muddled stages. I am also grateful to Bernice Bild and David Ranney for helping me to keep my thinking grounded in practical issues and to Chandra Talpade Mohanty and Rebecca Steinitz for particularly thoughtful criticism.

Ohio Wesleyan University gave me the space to explore in my classes many of the ideas that made it into this book, and I thank my students at Ohio Wesleyan for discussing these ideas with me. I also thank Debbie Stone Bruell, a sister in the best sense of the word, for copied articles and nourishing conversation, and my parents, Shirley and Bob Stone, for homemade soup, expert house repairs, and constant support during the many years I worked on this book.

Most of all, I thank John Stone-Mediatore for his sound judgment, his inexhaustible generosity, his keen eye for questions I overlooked as well as value I was often at a loss to find, and, sometimes most importantly, his sense of humor and his music.

This book is dedicated to my grandparents, Jack and Ethel Stone, whose spirits still fill my world.

Abbreviations

Hannah Arendt

AR   A reply. *Review of Politics* 15 (1953): 76–85.

BPF   *Between past and future: Eight exercises in political thought*. New York: Penguin, [1954] 1968.

DU   The difficulty of understanding. In *Essays in understanding*, ed. Jerome Kohn.

HC   *The human condition*. Chicago: University of Chicago Press, 1958.

LK   *Lectures on Kant's political philosophy*, ed. Ronald Beiner. Chicago: University of Chicago Press, 1982.

MDT   *Men in dark times*. New York: Harcourt Brace Jovanovich, [1955] 1968.

NT   On the nature of totalitarianism. In *Essays in understanding*, ed. Jerome Kohn. New York: Harcourt Brace & Javonich, 1994.

OT   *The origins of totalitarianism*. New York: Harcourt Brace Jovanovich, [1951] 1979.

TH   *Thinking*. In *The life of the mind*. New York: Harcourt Brace Jovanovich, [1971] 1978.

TM   Thinking and moral considerations. *Social Research* 38 (1971): 417–46.

UP   Understanding and politics. *Partisan Review* 20 (1953): 377–392.

Paul Ricoeur

AS   Action, story and history: On re-reading *The Human Condition*. *Salmagundi* 60 (1983).

MT   The model of the text: Meaningful action considered as a text. *Social Research* 38 (1971).

TNi   *Time and narrative*. Vol. 1. Trans. Kathleen Blamey and David Pellauer. Chicago: University of Chicago Press, [1983] 1984.

Tnii   *Time and narrative*. Vol. 2. Trans. Kathleen Blamey and David Pellauer. Chicago: University of Chicago Press, [1984] 1985.

TNiii   *Time and narrative*. Vol. 3. Trans. Kathleen Blamey and David Pellauer. Chicago: University of Chicago Press, [1985] 1988.

Introduction

The Power of Stories

From Howard Zinn's classic *A People's History of the United States* to Central American popular-class testimonies, from "her-story" historiography to Arundhati Roy's story of families displaced by dams, historical and autobiographical narratives of experience have raised awareness of and gained sympathy for little-known social struggles. Recently, however, stories of experience have met with sharp criticism from unexpected sources. Feminists and poststructuralists have argued that we can no longer trust stories of experience to challenge ruling worldviews, for such stories are themselves constituted through ideological lenses. Stories that relate the experiences of marginalized groups may reveal the existence of difference or oppression, the argument goes, but such stories risk reinforcing the ideologically given categories of identity, difference, and separate spheres of life that structure narrative discourse as well as our own "experience."[1]

This book takes seriously recent critiques of narrative and experience, but it also seeks a way to engage productively narratives of marginalized people's experiences. I seek to reclaim such narratives because, while scholars have rightly become wary of appeals to such stories as "truth," our new distrust of experience-oriented narratives risks a dismissal of such texts that is just as epistemologically limiting and politically dangerous as the earlier positivism. In fact, despite academic critiques of experience, many social struggles, from welfare rights campaigns to fair trade coalitions, from the students against sweatshops movement to environmental justice advocacy, continue to rely on stories of experience to bring public attention to their concerns.[2]

Many Third World women, in particular, have found received theoretical discourses inadequate and have turned to experience-oriented writing to communicate their struggles against an array of patriarchal and neocolonialist institutions.[3] When scholars focus on criticizing "experience," we alienate our work from these practical struggles. We may address others' stories as sites for our deconstructive analysis, but we forfeit learning from them and building theories responsive to them.

Worse still, when we treat experience-based narratives as mere ideological artifacts, we reinforce the disempowerment of people who have been excluded from official knowledge production, for we deny epistemic value from a central means by which such people can take control over their own representation.[4]

When we dismiss stories of experience as ideological constructions, we not only undermine the authority of many marginalized voices but also overlook the importance of experience to critical social theory. As feminist standpoint theorists such as Sandra Harding (1991, 270–82), Nancy Hartsock (1983, 288–303), Chandra Talpade Mohanty (1991a, 33–38) and Dorothy Smith (1987, 49–55) have argued, people's daily experiences can inform and empower critical theory because such experiences are *only partly* determined by ideological processes. Everyday experiences also can react against, register the contradictions of, and ultimately constitute the motivation for intervening in ideological processes.

In affirming the epistemological value of stories of experience, I do not deny the dangers of positivism found in some appeals to experience by Michel Foucault ([1976] 1990), Judith Butler (1990, 324–25, 336–39), Judith Grant (1987), Gayatri Spivak (1988, 274–75; 1990, 19–20), and Joan Scott (1988, 4–7; 1991). Nonetheless, I argue that not all stories of experience lapse into positivism or allow for only a positivist reading. When, as is often the case with stories of marginalized experience, the stories reckon with contradictions or obscurities within experience or with aspects of experience that confound the logic of ruling discourses, such stories do not naively reinscribe received discourses; on the contrary, such texts can problematize the institutions and ideologies that shape all of our lives.[5]

Neither empiricist nor poststructuralist theories of experience can account for the subversive force of many marginal experience narratives. Empiricist and poststructuralist theories clearly differ: The former regard experience as indubitable evidence of reality whereas the latter emphasize the discursive construction of such "evidence." Despite their obvious differences, however, both schools presume that stories of experience are mere unreflective reports of spontaneous awareness. As a result, both obscure the capacity of writers to grapple with muted, contradictory, or even traumatized experiences. Moreover, both overlook the capacity of readers to attend to phenomena that are only intimated by metaphors or tensions within texts, phenomena that are not directly articulated because they defy our categories for representing experience.

Feminist standpoint theorists including Harding (1991, 270–95) and Smith (1987, 49–58) are more attentive to the complexity of experience and the critical force of thinking that starts out from experienced contradictions. Nevertheless, these theorists say little about the reading and writing practices by which we can transform obscure experience into critical knowledge.[6] Consequently, even feminist critics have been unsatisfied with the justifications for the marginalized standpoint that are offered by feminist standpoint theory.[7]

Given the limitations and confusions that burden even feminist and progressive understandings of marginal experience narratives, this book endeavors to present a more effective account of such narratives, one that can help scholars, teachers, and activists to realize the full value of such texts

Reclaiming Stories of Experience as *Stories*

My approach to rethinking the value of experience-oriented narratives is rooted in my own life experiences, in particular, my experiences of collecting, interpreting, and debating the relevance of experiential data. My activities have led me to treat experience specifically as *narrated* experience, for I have found that experience is meaningful to us largely by virtue of the way it is articulated in a narrative, that is, a pattern of identifiable actors and action-units that are qualified through metaphor and other poetic devices and that are related together within a coherent structure of beginnings and endings.[8] When, for instance, as a member of the Nicaragua Network, I tried to communicate the dangers of providing military aid to the Nicaraguan Contra, I found that data on Contra-related violence, which I found abhorrent, was not a cause for concern to people who presupposed a narrative framework in which the Contra were protecting freedom in a long-standing struggle of "Communism" versus "the free world." At the same time, when my own beliefs shifted—for instance, when I began to see multiple victims and oppressors in the Israeli-Palestinian conflict, or more recently, in the attack on the World Trade Center—my reorientation was due not only to new information that I had acquired but to my encounter with a new narrative pattern that enabled me to see the same set of affairs with greater clarity and subtlety.[9]

Likewise, when I collected data on the health problems afflicting video display terminal (VDT) workers, I saw that experience gains public recognition as "data" only when it fits standard analytic categories. When the repetitive stress injuries suffered by VDT workers did not fit the standard injury categories of worker compensation discourse, the workers could publicize their concerns only by telling stories, that is, by articulating their actions and sufferings within a creative but intelligible narrative logic.[10] As an intern for the Washington office of Amnesty International, I found that even seemingly self-evident, clearcut data depend on stories for their persuasive force. For instance, while Amnesty International takes pains to quantify and objectively report human rights abuses, they often present Congressional testimony in the form of stories, stories that invite listeners into a world in which data has moral and emotional impact and in which a set of options other than those defined by military, strategy-focused paradigms can be envisioned.

Phenomenology-influenced philosophers recognize this ineluctable "narrativity" of human existence and human thinking. Hannah Arendt (HC, 184–92), Paul Ricoeur (TNi, 54–64), David Carr (1986), Louis Mink (1987, 48–60), and Seyla Benhabib (1992, 126–29) describe how we experience events in terms of beginnings and endings, how we meaningfully communicate life events by recounting patterns of actors and actions, and how we consider the significance of possible actions by imagining them within narratives. As Ricoeur puts it, narratives articulate the "potential meanings" in life experiences, while life experiences provide the impetus to narrate (TNi, 74–76).[11]

Nevertheless, although some phenomenological theorists as well as our own daily lives affirm that we come to terms with worldly phenomena only by telling stories, the value of narrative to political thought remains largely unexplored. Empiricist social scientists dismiss narration as a "contaminant" of knowledge proper.[12] Poststructuralist theorists are more sensitive to the pervasiveness and inevitability of narrative in human thinking, but, like the empiricists, they tend to regard narration as a weakness that "undermine[s]" our claims to knowledge (Spivak 1990, 17–20).[13] And while the aforementioned phenomenologists address the distinct truth-content of narrative in valuable ways, they do not investigate the role of narrative in political thinking nor do they theorize a way to confront stories critically. In the absence of a thoroughgoing and critical account of the role of narrative in political thought, we continue to interpret our world in terms of stories, but we lack the theoretical apparatus to do so in a reflective and responsible manner.[14]

My central premise is that this inadequate attention to the relationship between narrative and political thinking underlies the present confusion over the epistemic status of marginal experience narratives. I propose that we can read, teach, and defend stories of experience effectively only if we clarify the contribution of narrative to political thought. We must examine how experience informs political thinking through the medium of narrative because we generally encounter, discuss, and invoke experience in narrative form. We must also examine the social practices by which narratives circulate, for experience becomes public knowledge through an exchange of stories in which specific people, in the context of historically specific social and cultural institutions, relay their views of events in a particular rhetorical style to a specific audience.

Based on my study of the writing and reading practices through which we understand historical experience, I argue that marginal experience narratives contribute to political thinking and political life precisely in their function as "stories," that is, as experience-rooted but creatively reproduced narrative texts whose meaning is realized in their interpretation by specific communities. Thus I share with the poststructuralists the belief that experience is always mediated by narrative discourse. Departing from both traditional epistemologists and poststructuralists, however, I argue that this narrative mediation of experience does not prevent experience from being a source of critical insight and mature political consciousness. On the contrary, some stories of experience stimulate and enrich political thought, as well as destabilize the more reductive, obfuscating narratives, precisely by the way the texts are constructed and read as stories. The task of this book is to theorize, so that we may pursue more effectively, those ways of writing and reading stories that contribute to critical thinking and liberatory politics.

The Opposition Between Story and Truth

In presenting marginal experience narratives as intellectually valuable *qua stories*, I challenge the long-standing opposition between story and truth. This opposition is presupposed by both empiricists who seek to eradicate narrative from knowledge proper and by poststructuralists who deny the possibility of knowledge on the grounds of its ineluctably narrative character. For the empiricists, the opposition between story and truth is rooted in Enlightenment epistemology which presumes the task of knowledge to be the representation of objects and thus the proper function of language to be denotation.[15] When readers in this tradition try to defend marginal experience narratives, they present the narratives as indubitable empirical truths. This defense is not adequate, however, because conservative and poststructuralist critics alike have had no trouble demonstrating that the alleged "truths" of marginal experience narratives are constituted by partial perspectives and rhetorical mechanisms.

While conservative critics contrast the alleged rhetorical "babble" of marginal experience narratives to the supposedly "more reasonable language" of orthodox historians (Kermode 1992, 33), poststructuralist critics recognize that no historian can avoid producing meaning through rhetoric. Thus poststructuralists rightly approach *all* histories as discursively constituted texts. Nevertheless, the poststructuralists retain the assumption that discursively constituted meaning is inherently spurious and ideological. As a result, they conclude (at least in the strong version of their arguments) that the narration of historical experience is thoroughly structured by ideological mechanisms and that all such narration therefore "reproduces rather than contests given ideological systems" (Scott 1991, 778).[16]

Marginalized Experience as Story

The opposition that both empiricists and poststructuralists have drawn between story and truth leads to a concomitant devaluing of both narrative and narrative-infused experience. Moreover, this depreciation of all things "contaminated" with narrative has a pernicious (even if not always intended) political effect; It specifically excludes *marginal experience* narratives from recognition as knowledge. While it is true that dominant experiences also have narrative form, narratives from dominant perspectives tend to be endorsed and repeated by powerful institutions, with the result that the narrative character of these representations passes unnoticed as they come to be accepted as "commonsense" knowledge.[17] In contrast, stories of marginalized experiences tend to conflict with "common-sense" knowledge and to enter public discussion explicitly as stories. This is not only because members of marginalized groups tend to have less institutional backing to present their stories as "truth," but also because a marginalized group's perspective on historical events usually differs from the perspective that has passed as the "general" perspective. When a group's perspective on events does not match the representation that has circulated as, for instance, "the American perspective," then they must acknowledge that their view is a particular group's story, not a general truth.

Marginal experience narratives also tend to show themselves to be stories insofar as they rely on personal anecdotes and informal records. Narrators of marginalized people's struggles often depend on such "lighter" sources because the people whose lives they narrate are rarely able to publish their views in official documents. In addition, people in marginalized positions tend to endure the effects of social contradictions for which data and statistics are often lacking. Statistics on phenomena such as toxic-waste-related illnesses, job-related repetitive-stress injuries, human rights violations suffered by imprisoned immigrants, families displaced by dams, or labor abuses suffered by women working in transnational industries are, of course, possible; however, large research institutions usually attend to such phenomena only after many personal stories are told.[18]

Finally, marginal experience narratives often require explicitly literary, creative styles because the analytic categories of "objective" historiography are inadequate to the experiences of people struggling against oppression. The standard categories of historical and legal discourse construe "actors" as discrete units, "actions" as the clear expression of an actor's will in the so-called public realm, and "events" as phenomena of the public sphere that are marked by a definite beginning and resolution. Such a narrative logic systematically occludes the kinds of experiences that are characteristic of the most marginalized people's struggles, for people in marginalized positions often experience discomfort with their social identity, shift between various group allegiances, endure the costs of public policies in their "private" lives, and resist social norms in gestures that fall outside official government channels or that unfold in incomplete, unpredictable ways (Alarcón 1990; Anzaldúa 1990a, xxii–xxvi and 1990b, 377–380; Harding 1991, 124–32; Lugones 1997; Mackinnon 1989, 184–194; Mohanty 1991a, 37–39; Smith 1987, 64–69; Stone-Mediatore 2000, 98–100). Such deeds and sufferings can be narrated adequately only when writers forego standard narrative categories and genre boundaries to respond to seemingly uncategorizable, contradictory experiences.

The Re-emergence and the Power of Storytelling

While narrators of marginalized experiences often must use informal sources, literary prose, and innovative narrative forms, not all narrators thematize this need for "storytelling." In the absence of a coherent theory of storytelling, many writers describe their work using empiricist metaphors such as "disclosing" or "documenting." Nevertheless, close attention to marginal experience narratives often reveals storylike elements that challenge the idea of objective representation. Marginal experience narratives often include, for instance, references to the subjectivity and particularity of the text's sources, creative descriptions of phenomena that cannot be subsumed under given analytic categories, and experimental forms that subvert "common-sense" ways of organizing the world.[19]

Although many writers do not theorize their unconventional narrative strategies, they need not do so in order to employ such strategies in ways that destabilize dominant discursive logics and highlight aspects of life that are occluded by those logics. Domitila Barrios de Chungara, for instance, whose work I analyze in chapter five, challenges the logic of the "private housewife" as well as the division between "personal autobiography" and "public history" when she presents testimony of her mother-and housewife-driven politics. Similarly, when Sk. Nazma relates the story of how she formed the Bangladesh Workers Solidarity Center in order to fight for back pay and better working conditions in garment factories, she not only mixes personal and political writing but also challenges the representation of "Third World women" as naturally docile, naturally suited to tedious labor. Through narrating their own activism, such women thus raise broader questions about the interests served by discourses that naturalize "identities" and "cultures" while they suggest the need to recognize multiply aligned Third World feminist subjects who are irreducible to the standard division between "traditional Third World" and "enlightened Western" people.

Other writers self-consciously pursue more "storylike" innovative and engaged narration in order to publicize marginalized experiences. When these increasingly numerous unabashed storytellers defy the norms of "objective" historical writing, they not only give voice to experiences that have been systematically occluded by dominant discursive logics but also throw new light on the structure of historical reality and historical knowledge. For instance, Gloria Anzaldúa (1990b) draws on her own experiences of cultural confusion to foreground the strengths of a mixed identity, while she also recasts "identity" as a heterogeneous, socially conditioned, and strategically chosen location. Arundhati Roy (1999) combines well-documented historical research with engaged and poetic stories in order to help readers appreciate the experiences of people who have been displaced by dams, while her unusual approach also challenges the logic of "expert" knowledge and market-defined values. Samuel Delany (1993) simultaneously uses and problematizes the categories "gay," "black," and "artist" in his memoir, thereby taking control over his own representation as well as adumbrating a gay subculture that defies our basic ways of conceptualizing subjectivity. Eduardo Galeano (1988) presents history in the form of poetically written historical vignettes that not only breathe life into moments of violence and resistance that have been buried in lesser-known documents and effaced in ruling narratives but, in so doing, recast history itself as undecidable and unpredictable, containing within the historically given possibilities for transforming history. And Susan Griffin (1992) artfully weaves together interviews with war survivors, her stories of collecting those interviews, and creative attempts to imagine others' lives, thereby exploding the notion of war as a specifiable "public event" while also challenging us to rethink history in terms of the personal, the emotional, and the bodily elements that have been excluded from history proper.

Neither traditional nor poststructuralist epistemologies recognize intellectual value in such literary, subjective, "storylike" representations of the world. Certainly, such stories do not provide the foundations of indubitable truth. Nonetheless, I argue that such stories, precisely by virtue of their artful and engaged elements, can respond to the inchoate, contradictory, unpredictable aspects of historical experience and can thereby destabilize ossified truths and foster critical inquiry into the uncertainties and complexities of historical life. Moreover, when writers such as Barrios, Delany, Anzaldúa, Griffin, Galeano, and Roy use their writing to explore unregistered or systematically obscured experiences of resistance to social norms, they do not just destabilize received representations of the world. In so doing, they also undermine the rationale for oppressive social institutions and facilitate broad-based resistance to those institutions. In effect, while we do not change reality merely by interpreting it differently, those stories that work with language to indicate the muted contradictions of everyday life, the diffuse agencies of multiply oppressed people, and the values and social relationships that ruling logics efface can nonetheless intervene in the processes that determine what gets recognized—and responded to—as real, significant, and possible.

This book is divided into two parts. Part one develops a critical account of the role of narration in political thinking. Hannah Arendt provides a rich resource in part one, for she developed her unique "storytelling" approach to political philosophy based upon her investigation of the kind of inquiry that is necessary in order to understand political phenomena. In chapter one, I draw on Arendt's phenomenology of the political world, as developed in *The Human Condition*, to sketch an account of political thinking as "storytelling." My Arendtian account of storytelling reconciles recent critiques of narrative discourse, such as those by Hayden White and Roland Barthes, with our ineluctable need for narratives in order to orient ourselves in the world.

Chapter two addresses the public role of narration, or storytelling. With reference to Arendt's "story" of Nazism in her book *The Origins of Totalitarianism*, I argue that storytelling can serve the public function that we can no longer entrust to "universal reason": the function of resisting political indoctrination and maintaining responsible public debate. Marxists, feminists, poststructuralists, and hermeneutic theorists have effectively discredited the Enlightenment notion of universal reason. Nevertheless, the concern from which that notion of reason arose—the concern for intellectual practices that counter prejudicial and complacent modes of political thinking—remains urgent in our world. In presenting Arendtian storytelling as one response to this concern, I do not claim that all stories promote critical thinking. I do argue, however, that we can resist the obfuscations and the stifling effects of dogmatic stories, whether Nazi narratives of race or Western narratives of progress, only with more historically sensitive, engaged, community-rooted, and creative storytelling.

If, as Arendt's study of Nazism indicates, stories can both encourage vibrant, critical debate and, at the other extreme, oversimplify history and thwart public discussion, then a responsible affirmation of storytelling must also suggest ways to evaluate stories critically. Certainly empirical accuracy is one important criterion for historical narratives. By itself, however, factual accuracy is not enough to distinguish between those stories that encourage and those stories that stifle critical political thinking. Indeed, some narratives forestall critical inquiry precisely by inundating readers with trivial facts.[20] Or, sometimes, "the facts" themselves have been manipulated by social institutions and merely reflect the logic of those institutions; for instance, insofar as the Nazis organized German society according to racial categories and executed those racial groups whom they deemed unfit to live, a factual story of German life might only "confirm" racist ideologies (Arendt OT, 349–50, 471–72).

In chapter three, I begin a discussion of how we might evaluate the extrafactual, "story" dimension of historical narratives with respect to their contribution to open and responsible public debate. My aim is not to impose on stories a rigid method or style but merely to clarify general features of responsible and debate-enhancing storytelling. I find useful resources for this project in Kant's theory of reflective judgment and recent Kant criticism. My turn to Kant will likely raise some feminist eyebrows, for Kant's theory of judgment is in many ways antithetical to the concern for human difference, emotional response, and stimulation of discussion that many feminist critics have found valuable in stories. Nonetheless, I show how certain progressive elements in Kant's theory resonate well with storytelling's aim to promote lively public debate. By critically appropriating Kant's standards of judgment and recasting these standards in light of the historically situated, the hermeneutic, and the engaged character of storytelling, I affirm a valuable impulse in our tradition—the impulse for community-accountable thought—while I renew this Enlightenment impulse in light of recent insights into the heterogeneous character of our communities and the situated and narrative character of our thinking.

Part two joins my Arendt-inspired theory of storytelling with contemporary feminist analysis in order to investigate how marginal experience narratives can contribute to a feminist democratic politics. I begin, in chapter four, with a study of recent feminist critiques of marginal experience narratives. I argue that poststructuralist critics such as Joan Scott present illuminating analysis of the way that ideological mechanisms structure the narration of experience; however, they ultimately oversimplify the relation between experience and language and consequently overlook the possibility of more subtle and subversive approaches to narrating experience. With reference to Howard Zinn's classic marginal experience history (1995), Samuel Delany's memoir (1993), and Arundhati Roy's controversial essay on India's big dams (1999), I show how experience-oriented writing is not only constrained by social and cultural institutions but is also a crucial means by which people can resist institutional control over how their identities and histories are represented.

Chapter five draws on transnational feminist analysis to situate storytelling within the context of far-reaching relations of domination and to examine the role of storytelling in resisting such relations. While various feminist and postcolonial theorists have affirmed the importance of marginalized experience as a starting point, or "raw material" for liberatory knowledge and politics,[21] I examine the crucial role that narration plays in transforming the raw material of experience into critical insight and power. Works by Gloria Anzaldúa, Chandra Mohanty, Uma Narayan, and Domitila Barrios de Chungara are particularly useful here, for these authors address both the complicity of ruling narratives with hierarchical social relations and the potential of strategically written marginal experience narratives to counter ruling ideologies and institutions. In light of these author's works, I present a case for stories that use language against the grain to explore tensions in everyday life and that situate the experienced tensions within a broader social context. I argue that such stories challenge the discourses that

naturalize social hierarchies while they open an imaginative space for us
to recognize alternative identities and ways of life. In so doing, they
facilitate the crossborder, multi-issue coalitions that are necessary in
order for us to confront effectively the transnational organizations that
increasingly govern our lives.

Chapter six addresses problems faced by readers and teachers of
marginal experience narratives. Many of us recognize a responsibility
to engage the perspectives of people who are more socially and culturally marginalized, but we have few guidelines for how to do so in an
effective and responsible manner. By examining what it can mean to
approach others' accounts of their struggles *as stories,* I elucidate a way
of reading that avoids appropriating others' claims yet still takes
responsibility to learn from others more critical perspectives on our
world. This hermeneutics of story reading helps to make meaningful the
call of feminist standpoint theory to "think from others' lives," for it
clarifies the intellectual and imaginative practices by which we can
transform, in a responsible manner, other people's stories of struggle
into a resource for our own critical knowledge.

Finally, I show how my study of storytelling elucidates the interrelated political and epistemological value of thinking from others' lives.
Neither Sandra Harding's presentation of the marginalized standpoint
as a means to "less false" knowledge (1991) nor her critics' attempts to
present the marginalized standpoint as a political rather than epistemological project[22] does justice to the unique value of thinking from
others' lives. In light of the foregoing theory of storytelling, I argue that
the value of thinking from others' lives lies not necessarily in creating a
more accurate representation of the world nor simply in taking the side
of the victim but in promoting more responsible public storytelling.
Such storytelling not only attends to historical facts but questions
received ways of interpreting the facts, explores aspects of the world
that are incongruent with received narrative frameworks, affirms our
responsibility for the way "sides," values, characters, and actions are
defined, and fosters democratic communities in which we continually
rethink our common histories and projects in light of each others'
stories.

As an educator concerned with preserving the classroom as a space
to explore ideas beyond the bounds of institutionalized discourses
and corporate-produced knowledge, I have developed this study of
storytelling, in part, to help me engage texts that provide avenues to
marginalized views but that do not look like what normally passes for
"knowledge." Texts such as those by Barrios, Anzaldúa, Griffin, Roy,
and Galeano do not fit under any rubric of professional knowledge, and

yet they open my eyes and the eyes of my students to the limits of our knowledge while they help us to discern ways of relating to one another and expressing our agency, which discursive norms efface. They also breathe life into critical theories, challenging us to test and deepen our theories of ideology, oppression, and liberation in light of the particular contours of our everyday lives. We can certainly be moved by stories to look at the world and ourselves in new ways without a theory of storytelling; however, when we theorize the intellectual value and historical role of stories, we can more self-consciously and self-critically cross disciplinary borders and reclaim stories as integral components of human thought. I hope this theory of storytelling helps others to scrutinize those stories that always already inform our thinking and to engage with those lesser-known narratives that are not objective truths but that nonetheless invite perspectives on our history and ourselves that offer hope for a more just and democratic future.

Part I

Hannah Arendt and the
Revaluing of Storytelling

Chapter 1

Political Narration after the Poststructuralist Critique

*Reality is different from, and more than, the
totality of facts and events, which, anyhow, is
unascertainable. Who says what is . . . always tells
a story. . . .*

—Hannah Arendt[1]

Everyday life attests to the centrality of stories in our thinking. We make sense of personal and world events alike by putting them in a story, and when we ask someone, "what happened?," we do not expect a mere list of facts but a pattern of identifiable actors and actions, related together within beginnings and endings. Recently, theorists of everyday life have affirmed this human need for narrative while some legal theorists, sociologists, philosophers, and historians have begun to pursue their work by telling stories.[2]

Despite the pervasiveness of stories in human thinking, however, current theories of knowledge recognize in stories no epistemological value. The Enlightenment theories that still inform mainstream conceptions of the social sciences view stories as subjective and rhetorical contaminations of truth.[3] Poststructuralist theories, although critical of the traditional commitment to a pristine truth, similarly identify narrative as a central means by which truth is "distort[ed]" and "undermined" (White 1975, 59; Spivak 1990, 20). When our epistemological theories deny the truth-value of narrative, this does not stop us from telling stories of world events; however, it does prevent us from telling and reading stories in the most reflective, most critical manner.[4]

Drawing on the work of Hannah Arendt, this chapter begins a critical account of the contribution of stories to political thinking. Such a theory must acknowledge the legitimate concern of Western epistemology to hold knowledge claims to critical standards. It must also, for that matter, address poststructuralist analysis of the way that narration produces meaning with language. At the same time, if this theory of storytelling is to help us narrate our world more deliberately and responsibly, then it must exceed both Enlightenment and poststructuralist epistemologies and must account for the power of stories to render our world intelligible. In her book *The Human Condition,* Arendt provides a fruitful beginning point for such a "post-poststructuralist" account of stories. Arendt here explains how stories respond to the essence of political phenomena even while stories are culturally informed, creative constructions. In using Arendt to defend the intellectual value of stories, I do not dispute poststructuralist analysis of the necessarily poetic and tradition-informed character of narrative discourse but I argue that, precisely by virtue of their literary core and their historical situatedness, stories are vital to understanding the depth and complexity of human phenomena.[5]

Narration Deconstructed

Modern Western epistemology has long regarded literary narration to be an obstruction to truth, but poststructuralists such as Hayden White (1966, 1973, 1975, 1980, 1982, 1984) and Roland Barthes (1989, 127–54) exceed their more orthodox colleagues in their critique of narrative. Not only explicitly literary works, they argue, but even seemingly objective documents construct their content through figurative language and narrative structure. Although White and Barthes address their analyses toward narratives in historiography, their analyses apply as well to the many academic, media, and popular representations of public events that have narrative form. In other words, their analyses of narrative discourse apply to all representations of real events insofar as those representations organize their content in terms of units of actors, actions, and places; they relate these units together within a pattern of beginnings and endings (which, unlike causes and effects, consist of unique sequences that cannot be predicted beforehand); they use poetic mechanisms to convey moral, emotional, and aesthetic qualities of lived experiences; and they have a meaning that lies not in an isolated conclusion but in the whole pattern of actors and actions.[6]

Barthes and White argue that, while narrative representations of real events often appear to represent reality directly, this appearance is deceptive: If the text appears to be rhetoric-free, this is only because, ironically, certain rhetorical strategies serve to mask the text's rhetorical construction. Historians produce this "reality effect," as Barthes calls it, by employing the same rhetorical techniques as those used by realist novelists. For instance, many historiographers, in the manner of realist fiction writers, avoid "shifters," that is, they omit any references within the text to the author, the audience, or the author's collection and arrangement of material (Barthes 1989, 127–40). They often refer to numerous concrete details that have no central role in the narrative but serve mainly to "confirm" that the writing follows reality as given (Barthes 1989, 138–39, 146–48). They also tend to use metaphors and narrative forms that are so customary in our culture that we do not notice their poetic functions (White 1966, 126–27; 1975, 61–63).

The point of White's and Barthes's analyses is not to reduce historiography to fiction nor to dispense with critical standards for the former. Even while both scholars address the historical text as a literary object, neither dispute that historiography also has an empirical dimension that should be regulated by rules of empirical accuracy and proper evidence. Nonetheless, they argue that an evaluation of the factual accuracy of individual statements "does not provide us with any way of assessing the content of the narrative itself" (White 1984, 22). In other words, the structure and metaphors of the narrative text generate a content that exceeds factual determination. Such language-generated "narrative content" is produced through rhetorical processes that are influenced by aesthetic, socioeconomic, and ideological factors (de Certeau 1986, 203–05; Mink 1978, 143–47; White 1975, 53–64; 1978, 3; 1984, 22; Barthes 1989, 133–48).

The Rhetorical Production of "Narrative Content"
Poststructuralist theorists identify specific ways that narrative mechanisms generate meaning and thereby construct what passes as "history." On the most basic level, individual sentences characterize the material that they seem to represent. Even seemingly factual statements about the historical world never simply report facts but embellish, evaluate, and endow the "facts" with factual status in the process of articulating them in language. They do so by virtue of the connotation of the words selected, the metaphors employed, even if these are taken-for-granted "dead metaphors," and the implicit assertion that the items reported are noteworthy (Barthes 1989, 138–39; Kuklick 1969, 316–27; Mink 1978, 146–67; White 1975, 60–63).[7] On a related but broader level, certain "controlling metaphors" provide a metaphorical theme to the narrative and thereby exercise a strong influence on the selection, organization, and presentation of factual material (White 1975, 62).

If statements of fact are inseparable from literary devices, this does not mean that fact is fiction. It does mean, however, that even empirically indisputable, evidence-backed statements present extrafactual meanings. Consider, for instance, a description of the bombing of Nagasaki in a recent acclaimed history of World War II:

> Originally destined for another target, the Nagasaki bomb was actually more powerful than the one dropped on Hiroshima, but primarily because of local terrain features caused less destruction and fewer casualties than the earlier one. It is, however, doubtful whether such details were known in Tokyo at the time or would have made any difference. The key point was that the atomic bombs were falling, that one plane with one bomb could now accomplish the effect of hundreds of planes dropping thousands of bombs at a time when the Americans were known to the Japanese to have enormous numbers of planes (Weinberg 1994, 890).

The lack of shifters together with the references to empirical details make the text appear objective; however, the content of the text is actually constituted by military metaphors. For instance, "target" construes a community as a faceless place on a military map destined for attack, while "casualties" presents deaths resulting from the attack in terms of "mishaps," things accidentally lost or destroyed.[8] The text's uncritical repetition of military metaphors not only generates a dehumanized, strategy-focused account of this bombing but also characterizes broader historical developments in terms of the controlling metaphor that underlies military discourse: the metaphor of a zero-sum competitive game in which one side's losses are the other side's gain. This game metaphor is implicit in the claim that American leverage over Japan is "the key point" about the bombing, for such leverage is "key" only if we presume that the events have the form of a competition between nations. The game metaphor also directs the text's focus toward geographic and strategic information, implying that impersonal data and national-level triumphs are the important stuff of history. The vague reference to casualties and a mention, on the preceding page, of fifty to eighty thousand deaths in Hiroshima acknowledge that the bomb killed many people. When, however, the text presents the death toll in a single dependent clause in a paragraph that focuses on military strategy, it accords such deaths little significance. To paraphrase Howard Zinn's comment on another classic history book, the text organizes the material in such a way that tells us, yes, that mass killing took place, but that this is not so important, that it should matter little in our judgments or actions.[9]

An additional way that historical narratives produce meaning, which is also influenced by the controlling metaphors, is through the identification of narrative elements: the actors, the actions, and the places. Such narrative elements, for instance, "the Americans," "the Japanese," "target," "dropping bombs," or "surrender," may seem to correspond to ontologically given entities. In reality, however, these narrative elements subsume myriad phenomena into what Barthes calls "units of content." The latter do not denote referents but divide phenomena into units that function as signifiers. The meaning that they signify is a function of the system of signifiers in our language as well as the way that the units are related to one another in a particular narrative. Realist histories take for granted the controlling metaphors and the accompanying "units of content" that are customary in their linguistic community and that are often standard for a particular field of historiography (Barthes 1989, 133–34).[10]

Weinberg's history of the second world war illustrates the impact of controlling metaphors and narrative units on the content of a text. The metaphor of a zero-sum game between nations that underlies Weinberg's text is standard for war histories and implies particular kinds of narrative units. Weinberg's actor-units, for instance, are defined in terms of discrete and unified nations, "the Japanese" and "the Americans," or a metonymy for the nations, "Tokyo" and "Washington." His action-units presuppose that such nations make rational competitive moves against one another, for instance, "defense," "strike," or "attack." Likewise, his place-units presume a proper place for war, for instance, "target" or "battlefield." Such units of content not only organize myriad data into coherent pieces but do so in a way that presupposes and reinforces the seeming rationality of war between nations.

The role of rhetorical devices in seemingly objective historiography is also evident in another classic and typical treatment of World War II: "In the week of 19–25 February 1944, 3800 heavy bombers of the VIII and XV A.A.F., escorted by fighters, attacked twelve targets vital to German aircraft industry, as far south as Ratisbon and Augsburg. Our losses were 226 bombers, 28 fighters, and about 2600 men; but some 600 German plans were shot down" (Morison 1965, 1028). Temporal, geographic, and technical details present a semblance of concreteness; however, the event qua meaningful event is constituted by narrative devices. Here, as in Weinberg's text, actor-units posit unified nations, action-units presuppose a rationality to "attack," and the conjunction "but," which links the two nations' "losses," presupposes and confirms the zero-sum nature of the competition.[11]

Finally, a narrative produces meaning by the way it relates the actor-and action-units together within an integrated whole. Typically, a narrative employs a consistent set of narrative units, encodes some of these as causes and some as effects, and groups various of these causes and effects together into "events." This creates a narrative with well-defined sections and sequences, even though such sections and sequences are not given in reality-in-itself (Barthes 1989, 134; White 1975, 58–60; 1984, 23–24). Even when a narrative follows rules of evidence and accuracy, the arrangement of the material into such a structured whole imposes literary meaning on a "welter of facts" and thus constitutes "a distortion of the whole factual field" (White 1975, 60). A narrative pattern distorts not simply by emphasizing certain facts rather than others but also by *adding* meaning. Depending on how the text identifies and arranges material, it can characterize the narrated event, as well history generally, as, for instance, a Manichean conflict, a single rationally developing process, or (as in postmodern literature) an undecidable, polysemic text (Barthes 1989, 137; White 1966, 126–29; 1975, 54–60; 1984, 23–25). Moreover, historical narratives can arrange the material so as to suggest one of literature's standard "story-types," such as comedy, tragedy, romance, or farce (1975, 54–60; 1984, 23–24) . When Western readers subconsciously recognize one of these story-types, the latter then serves as a conceptual model in light of which readers interpret particular historical incidents. Although the historian's comparison of the historical event to a story-type may seem to make history more comprehensible, "it is only more comprehensible by reference to the conceptual model," which is itself borrowed from literature and "exists quite apart from both the 'facts' and any explicit argument" (White 1975, 58).

The narrative structure that is most pervasive in Western historiography is that which Aristotle described in his analysis of tragedy and which has long been associated with narrative generally: the structure of a rise and then decline in tension that make up a clear beginning, a middle, and a resolved conclusion. White observes that histories of various kinds tend to follow this basic, taken-for-granted narrative structure. When they do, they characterize the outcome of the events narrated as a resolution of tensions. The message implicit in this narrative form is that historically successful institutions are rational and stable and that "the war is over," that is, that conflicts have been superceded (Vidal-Naquet, cited in White 1982, 135). On a metahistorical level, this narrative structure equates history with Progress in which we naturally and continuously evolve toward higher forms of life. Such a metahistory not only rationalizes the institutions that have succeeded in history but also, in presenting progress as inherent in the historical process, obscures the historical importance of criticism and protest (White 1966, 126–29; 1982, 127–28, 135–36; 1984, 20–24; Trinh 1989, 141–43).

White's Conclusions and Remaining Questions

By helping us to distinguish historical reality from rhetoric, White and Barthes provide valuable tools for demystifying history. The critical force of their analysis notwithstanding, however, their poststructuralist account of narrative is, in itself, incomplete and sometimes misleading. The strong conclusion that White and his readers often draw from his analysis—that narration imposes fictional meaning on an otherwise meaningless collection of facts—cannot account for the everyday importance of narration in helping us to understand our world.

Poststructuralist analysis of the productive character of narrative discourse need not, however, lead to the popular conclusion that narration has no epistemological value. When White argues that narration imposes literary structure on an unstructured historical reality, he presumes that "historical reality" means reality-in-itself, an objectifiable "welter of facts." He presents a compelling case that narration never directly represents such an objective reality; however, he never specifically disputes the value of narration for understanding historical reality as a phenomenon of human experience.[12] We need not reject entirely the contribution of narrative to historical knowledge, if we consider that "historical reality" encompasses more than objectifiable facts and that "historical knowledge" means more than the representation of such facts.

In various undeveloped but provocative remarks, White himself points toward such a rethinking of historical reality and historical knowledge. In these remarks (which become more pronounced in his later works) White argues that, although narration never represents objective truth, it can nonetheless offer "understanding" of "specifically human truth" (White 1984, 25 and 33).[13] Here White acknowledges that "truth" need not reside in "literal statements of fact" (1984, 21). The figurative elements of narrative, those elements that transform facts into a story, might have a different kind of truth-value than that of factual statements.

White turns to the hermeneutic tradition to examine the distinct kind of truth advanced by historical narrative. In light of this tradition,

White affirms that humans are always situated within history, so that we are part of the same historical continuum that encompasses the actions and texts that we study. This situation demands a unique kind of intellectual approach, "knowledge as understanding" (White 1984, 25). Unlike knowledge of objects, understanding of human works entails "carrying over," or "translating," meanings from one community to another. Such "carrying over" of meanings is a necessarily engaged process, for we belong to the same world as that of the work we study while our attempt to make sense of the work's meaning further relates us to that work. In addition, our tradition-given language plays an essential, not merely "contaminating," role in the process of understanding, for our language is the medium in which the past work's meaning is "translated" into our familiar world (White 1984, 25; Gadamer [1960] 1991, 295–311, 384–89, 395–99).

White is particularly interested in Ricoeur because Ricoeur specifically addresses the contribution of narrative to understanding. According to Ricoeur, narration transposes into an articulate form the human experience of living within time and of recollecting our experiences in terms of beginnings and endings (Ricoeur 1980). In his favorable discussion of Ricoeur, White modifies his own earlier critique of narrative and suggests that narration creates meaning—not in the sense of producing a fiction—but in the sense of encapsulating in language the interconnected pasts and presents of human experience (White 1984, 26–29). As White puts it, narrative "is an imaginary discourse about real events that may not be less 'true' for being 'imaginary'" (1984, 33). In other words, although the rhetorical dimension of historical narrative does not represent objective reality, it may nonetheless give form to structures and qualities of human experience.

When White invokes the hermeneutic tradition to address the specific sort of truth that narrative helps us to understand, he indicates an alternative to the seeming choice between viewing historical narration as objective representation or, at the opposite extreme, viewing narration as mere literary artifice. White, however, never elaborates on this distinctive narrative "truth." Nor does he reconcile Ricoeur's analysis of the suitability of narrative to human experience with his own earlier analysis of the distorting effects of narrative discourse. As a result, his suggestion that historical narration offers "understanding" of "specifically human truths" raises more questions: What is the character of this human truth that we understand through narrative? What kind of narrative process offers understanding of such truths? And, finally, if the aim of narration is not knowledge but understanding of the human world, then what is the character and value of such understanding?

Revaluing Narrative

The hermeneutic tradition, as White recognizes, provides a rich ɪ͡ source for examining the truth-value of literary language. Arendt's political phenomenology is also particularly relevant, however, for Arendt addresses the more specific problem of what it means to understand political phenomena through telling stories. By reading Arendt's work together with Gadamer's and Ricoeur's hermeneutic theories, I pursue the fundamental question that White leaves us with: What can it mean for creatively produced stories to offer understanding of historical reality?

I proceed (following a brief clarification of terms) by first explaining the structural affinity that Arendt traces between political phenomena and narrative discourse. I then examine the creative process, "storytelling," whereby the narrator transposes storylike political phenomena into written narratives. Finally, in light of Arendt's account of storytelling and Ricoeur's and Gadamer's hermeneutic theories, I explicate the specific kind of understanding that is made possible by stories.

A Note on Terms

Arendt is well known for her narrow, normative concept of the political, in which she identifies properly political actions as those actions that are achieved through discussion and cooperation and that enhance a discussion-based politics (HC, chapters 2, 24, 27). Throughout her work, however, Arendt also addresses political phenomena (and, likewise, the actions that make up such phenomena) in a broader sense: Political phenomena are all of those human-initiated phenomena, including those phenomena initiated by cooperative as well as coercive actions, that call for public debate about their meaning. "Political" in this broader sense marks a distinction from merely private matters as well as from matters that do not require discussion but can be treated by standard administrative procedures. (Arendt reserves the term "social" for the latter.[14]) The structural connections that Arendt draws between political phenomena and stories pertain to political phenomena in this broader, non-normative sense.[15]

Additional fine distinctions underlie Arendt's analysis of political phenomena. Arendt often shifts between the terms "historical" and "political" as if the two terms were interchangeable. We can make sense of this shifting if we consider that, with these two terms, Arendt implicitly addresses the same phenomenon under two different aspects:

Historical phenomenon designates a worldly phenomenon qua a phenomenon that is lived in a plurality of human lives; *political* phenomenon designates the same phenomenon qua a phenomenon of our shared world that appears in the public realm and that calls for public discussion of its meaning. In addition to this distinction between the phenomenon as it is endured in a plurality of human lives and the phenomenon as a common public affair, Arendt implicitly distinguishes both of these aspects of the present political phenomenon from the phenomenon that is conceptualized and remembered from hindsight. I use the term *event* to refer to the phenomena insofar as it is remembered, spoken about, and narrated from retrospect

The Affinity Between Life and Narrative
Arendt describes a structural affinity between political phenomena and narrative that begins to explain the importance of narration to political thought, yet without committing the reification of narrative language that White criticizes. Arendt first addressed the kinship between political phenomena and narrative when, in *The Origins of Totalitarianism,* she found "storytelling" to be the most effective approach to understanding Nazism and Stalinism. Her subsequent methodological essays and later book, *The Human Condition,* theorize the insights implicit in her earlier study. She argues in these later works that not only totalitarianism but all political phenomena call for narrative. Although causal analysis, chronicle, and non-narrative poetic description can all be applied to political phenomena, narration responds best to their inherently storylike structure (AR 777–81, HC 184–92, UP 388–90).

While Arendt emphasizes the kinship between narrative discourse and political phenomena, and even calls the latter "real stories" (HC, 185), she does not naively identify human life with written narratives. She argues, rather, that the narrative text and the appearing political phenomenon share similar features: Each consists of an integrated complex of interrelated elements; each relates these elements together in terms of unpredictable beginnings and endings; and each is essentially subjective, that is, their essence lies in their significance for experiencing subjects as well as the moral and emotional response that the phenomenon (or text) evokes in others. Narrative discourse exhibits these elements by virtue of its particular approach to language. For instance, unlike either theory or chronicle, narrative responds to the possibilities and constraints of language by naming actors and actions, relating these together within unique beginning-ending patterns, and using figurative language to convey moral and emotional qualities (this last trait is shared with poetry).[16]

Arendt finds storylike elements in political phenomena that are independent of narrative discourse and that are inherent in the structure of the political world. In her phenomenology of the political world, Arendt determines that specifically *political* phenomena—that is, phenomena that are of common concern and that call for public discussion to address their unique meaning—arise by virtue of certain enduring features of human life on earth. These basic features of the human condition include *natality,* which is the condition of being born as unique beings able to initiate new beginnings; *plurality,* which is the condition of living as distinct beings among others; and *publicity* (what I will call "publicness" in order to distinguish it more clearly from Arendt's other term, "publicizing"), which is the condition of sharing with others a common world that is not mere empty space but consists of all the objects, words, and institutions that relate and separate us within a "web of human relationships" (HC 184). As a result of natality, plurality, and publicness, phenomena appear in the common world that cannot be reduced to predetermined categories but demand collective inquiry into their unique and multifaceted meaning.

The same features of the human condition that give rise to political phenomena structure those phenomena in ways similar to narrative. For instance, due to natality and publicness, the phenomena begun by human action are structured as beginnings and endings that can be linked to one another from retrospect. This is so because actions that arise from human spontaneity and that unfold into the web of human relations cannot be reduced to causal laws, logic, or even an individual person's plan but constitute, rather, an unpredictable chain of actions and reactions (HC, 184–185, 190; UP, 388). At the same time that no incident can be predicted from the one before it, one can nevertheless, from hindsight, trace a particular incident to the incidents preceding it. For instance, as Arendt explains in *Totalitarianism* (which I analyze further in chapter two) the advent of Nazism was not inevitable and could not be expected; however, when we view Nazism from hindsight, we can trace it to the race-thinking, legal contradictions, and imperialist politics of the preceding century. Thus, similar to the events of a narrative text, the given turn of events does not constitute the only way that events could have developed, but we can nevertheless make sense of the conclusion from retrospect.

While natality gives rise to beginnings and endings, the complementary conditions of plurality and publicness structure actions as a web of interconnected individual experiences. This web of interrelated experiences arises first because, due to our condition of publicness, any action is performed "among and in relation to other acting beings" and

generates boundless reactions (HC 190). Even actions that are outside
of the public spotlight, or are only small gestures, can have widespread
repercussions. "This 'boundlessness' is characteristic not of political
action alone, in the narrower sense of the word . . . the smallest act in the
most limited circumstances bears the seed of the same boundlessness,
because one deed, and sometimes one word, suffices to change every
constellation" (HC, 190). When an action instigates multiple reactions,
a phenomenon arises that has broad public significance. At the same
time, due to plurality, this public phenomenon appears under "innu-
merable perspectives and aspects," for it is experienced by and appears
for people who inhabit different locations in a shared world (HC, 57).[17]
With respect to this dual structure of being-in-common and being-for-a-
plurality-of-distinct-perspectives, political phenomena are again analogous to stories; for stories, too, have a simultaneously pluralistic and
integrated structure insofar as they consist of diverse characters who
share a common set of affairs. Also like a story, the meaning of a
political phenomenon cannot be isolated in a conclusion but lies rather
in the whole web of interconnected actions and reactions. Arendt gives
poetic expression to this composite character of a political phenomenon when she describes it as a "constellation" (HC, 190). We can
identify a constellation's distinct elements but we can interpret its
meaning only by viewing all of the elements in their relation to one
another.[18]

Finally, a political phenomenon resembles a story with respect to its
fundamentally subjective status. A political phenomenon is essentially
for-human experience because, like a story, it consists of deeds and
sufferings in individual actors' lives. Furthermore, again like a story, the
political phenomenon is essentially subjective because it evokes moral
and emotional responses in other people and these responses are
integral to the meaning of the phenomenon. If we abstract a political
phenomenon from "the natural human reaction" it evokes, says Arendt,
then we rob the phenomenon "of part of its nature, depriv[e] it of one of
its important inherent qualities" as a phenomenon of the human world
(AR, 78–79).

Arendt's notion of a "natural human reaction" to a political phenomenon is clearly problematic given that different people often react
to the same phenomenon differently. Arendt's own account of plurality, which tells us that "everybody sees and hears from a different
position," implies that people will vary in their reactions to the same set
of affairs (HC 57). Moreover, as poststructuralist analysis of narrative
discourse indicates, different emotional and moral responses are elic-
ited by different ways of narrating the phenomenon. In her attempt to

defend her emotionally engaged approach to political inquiry, Arendt herself betrays the way that one's "natural response" to an event is shaped by narrative strategies. Using the British industrial revolution as her example, she claims that this phenomenon should arouse an indignation in response to its extremely unequal distribution of wealth and that such indignation is central to its meaning (AR, 78). This claim is compelling; however, it presupposes that we have configured the phenomena into a narrative that has divided the characters into classes who share the same historical context. The same indignation would not be evoked by a narrative that presented "Britain" as a single charac-ter-unit.

Nevertheless, even if we reject Arendt's claim that a political phe-nomenon compels a single, "natural" response, we can still accept the comparison here: A political phenomenon, as a constellation of deeds and sufferings in human society, resembles a narrative with respect to the importance of the response it evokes. Different people may respond differently to the same phenomenon, but the responses may still be integral to the phenomenon's meaning, if we allow that this meaning is itself perspective and context dependent, not fixed or universal. The same variability applies to the meaning of a narrative text, for literary critics generally agree that a narrative's meaning can vary for different readers, within certain limits. The interpreted meanings are not arbi-trary, so long as they are regulated by some interpretive guidelines. (In chapter three, I investigate the kind of guidelines we might apply to a storyteller's "reading" of a political phenomenon.)

Arendt's study of the narrative like structure of political phenomena finds support in the work of Ricoeur and Edward Carr. While Arendt addresses political phenomena, Ricoeur and Carr affirm the narrative structure of human experience generally. The latter two theorists differ from one another insofar as Carr identifies narrative structure with the structure of human life, whereas Ricoeur distinguishes the "inchoate narrativity" of life from the articulate narrative of written texts (Carr 1986; [1986] 1991, 18–52, 72; Ricoeur TNi 54–64, 74–81; 1980, 169–84).[19] Nonetheless, both Carr and Ricoeur agree with Arendt that narrative beginnings and endings cannot be "merely linguistic," for, insofar as we recognize these structures to be meaningful, they must at least resemble aspects of our experience that "need and merit being narrated" (Ricoeur TNi, 75).

Arendt and White

Arendt and White have obvious differences. Arendt emphasizes the narrative elements inherent in the human world, whereas White (apart from his discussion of Ricoeur) emphasizes the literary sources of narrative. Despite their different emphases, however, Arendt's conception of "real stories" is ultimately compatible with White's critique of narrative discourse. Even while Arendt argues that political phenomena share similar features with narrative discourse, she does not succumb to the positivism that White criticizes. She does not claim that political phenomena have any specific narrative structure. Neither does she mistakenly identify the structure and the metaphors of a particular narrative text with historical reality. She claims only that the events initiated by human action do not comprise a predictable casual chain but constitute rather subjectively meaningful deeds and sufferings that are related to one another as beginnings and endings, such that a storyteller can recognize human affairs as having arisen from prior affairs, when she selects one particular set of affairs to trace backward.

While Arendt's minimal claim about subjectively meaningful phenomena and interconnected beginnings and endings avoids naturalizing any specific narrative paradigm, it also leaves aside crucial questions that White raises for defenders of narrative. With his analysis of the productive character of narrative discourse, White challenges us to explain how we can justify the *specific* rhetorical construction of a specific narrative text. Historical phenomena may consist, in general, of subjective experiences related together as beginnings and endings, but any historical phenomenon lends itself to a plurality of possible narrative articulations, each of which is empirically valid but often has very different emotional and political implications (White 1975, 54–63; 1978, 84–99, 105–115; 1982, 134–37). Thus the question remains of how we can justify specific narrative strategies. Ultimately, we need to exceed Arendt's analysis (as I do in chapters three through six) in order to address this question of how to discriminate among different narrative strategies.[20]

Nevertheless, even if Arendt does not provide a justification for specific narrative strategies, she does begin to account for the importance of narration to our understanding of our world. She tells us that, insofar as narration uses poetic language to convey the subjective qualities of phenomena, insofar as narration does not follow fixed causal laws but traces beginning elements from the perspective of the conclusion, and insofar as narration relates together in one pattern a plurality of distinct actors and actions, narration helps us to confront the essentially subjective, the unique, and the dually pluralistic and whole character of political phenomena.

In her reflections on storytelling, Arendt offers further insight into the value of narrative. In particular, her reflections help to explain how the extrafactual dimension of narrative, the "narrative content" as White might put it, can be tradition-informed and creative and yet nonetheless offer understanding of the lived world.

Historical Narration as Story "Making"

Even while Arendt determines that political phenomena are inherently storylike, she recognizes that creative work is necessary in order to transform a political phenomenon into a written narrative. A political phenomenon may consist of a plurality of deeds and sufferings related together as beginnings and endings, but the subjective meaning of such actions and the way the actions "fit together and produce a harmony" never directly appears (Arendt TH, 133). Political phenomena, in other words, are like the ancient oracles described by Heraclitus: They are "manifest signs" (HC, 182). They are "manifest" insofar as they consist of nothing other than the incidents that unfold into the world, but they are also cryptic signs because their meaning is coherent only when they are "told as a story" (HC, 184). To tell a political phenomenon "as a story" is not simply to record but somehow to "translate" myriad deeds and sufferings (or traces and remains of these) into an articulate narrative.

An account of how a storyteller can create a story that never appears as such but that somehow is integrally related to the appearing event is key to defending the truth-value of narrative. Arendt does not theorize this creative process, but she points in a fruitful direction when she tells us that "it is not the actor but the storyteller who perceives and 'makes' the story" (HC, 192).[21] Her likening of storytelling to "making" is significant, for the latter has a precise meaning in her analysis of the basic human activities: *Making* exerts *work* on humanly processed materials so as to create useful products (HC, 136–73). Below, I explicate the sense in which storytelling is a kind of "making." I then draw on Ricoeur's analysis of poetic language to specify the epistemic value of such creatively made narratives.

The "Materials" of Storytelling

If storytelling is a kind of "making," then the storyteller, like the worker, relies on humanly produced "materials." Arendt's account of remembrance suggests that stories formed through remembrance constitute these "materials." "The meaning of what actually happens and appears while it is happening is revealed when it has disappeared; remembrance, by which you make present to your mind what actually is

absent and past, reveals the meaning in the form of a story" (TH, 133).
Remembrance-given stories are analogous to work materials insofar as
they are human reworkings, in this case, discursive reworkings, of
empirically given "raw materials," in this case, the "raw materials" of
experienced or witnessed actions. Arendt suggests that the narrator—
whether an academic, a journalist, or a lay person who narrates her own
past—needs remembrance-given stories just as much as the worker
needs physical building materials; thus, for instance, we have few
histories of the unique kind of "public freedom" realized by the French
Resistance because actors and witnesses quickly forgot that enigmatic
phenomenon and, without memories, "there simply was no story left
that could be told"(BPF, 6).[22]

Significantly, the "remembrance" that supplies historiography with
its stories is not mere memorization. It does not store and retrieve
isolated pieces of information but rather deciphers patterns that are
"invisible" and "put[s] them into words" (TH, 133).[23] Insofar as such
remembrance treats events of public significance and insofar its medium is language, it is not a mere individual but a cultural phenomenon.
Thus Arendt often equates remembrance with tradition (BPF, 5–6, 94,
261; TH, 133). Furthermore, as a cultural practice that works in
language, remembrance itself relies on a received linguistic framework.
This is why people failed to remember the French Resistance community of freedom in the first place, for they had no language with which to
name or conceptualize freedom as a "public" phenomenon (BPF, 5–6).

When Arendt locates the materials for historiography in remembrance-given stories, she challenges the presumed factual foundation of
historiography no less than White does. Since historiography was
established as an academic discipline in the United States in the
beginning of the twentieth century, it was legitimized as a profession, in
part, by opposing it to memory (Holt 1940; Higham 1963; Novick
1988, 1–41; Trinh 1989). On the surface, historiography's claim to be
memory-free seems plausible: Historians critically evaluate the reliability of documents and testimony, testing these documents against artifacts from the past that exist independently of anyone's memories.
Nonetheless, Arendt (like White) suggests a sense in which even "objective" historiography relies on memories. Insofar as historiography
presents not a mere collection of data but a humanly meaningful reality,
it tells a story. No amount of factual research can supply the story in
view of which facts are accorded significance. The stories that "[guide]
us through the vast realms of the past" are not given in the facts
themselves but are constituted, rather, through culturally situated and
creatively engaged remembrance (BPF, 94).

When Arendt claims that the historian depends on remembrance-given (or tradition-given) stories, she may seem to undermine historiography's foundation. She does not so much remove the ground from historiography, however, as she resituates historiography among the many cultural practices that transmit stories across generations. In Ricoeur's terms, she re-situates historiography within the "chain of speech" by which a community interprets its historical identity and which, as Carr notes, has its origin in our nonspecialized, everyday interest in our past (Ricoeur 1991, 131; Carr [1986] 1991, 3). In effect, she reminds us that "historiography," notwithstanding its methodological rigor, remains a form of remembrance-dependent storytelling. When we call this practice "remembrance" we stress its social and cultural situatedness, its interpretive dimension, and its practical origins. When we call it "historiography," we stress its knowledge-value and its public accountability. Despite the different names and emphases, however, all forms of storytelling, from everyday remembering of community events to professional historiography, are ultimately "grounded" on an endless chain of remembrance-given stories.

Arendt thus agrees with White that the historian can interpret facts only in light of extrafactual, culturally given narrative structures. She and White, however, pursue different implications of the historian's dependence on received narrative frameworks. White addresses the ideological effects of received narrative paradigms insofar as those paradigms influence the structure of our narratives in a way that is unnoticed and unjustified. Arendt does not ignore the ideological and obfuscating effects of certain narrative paradigms; she addresses such effects in her study of totalitarian ideology (which I examine in the next chapter). Her main concern, however, is that we need tradition-given stories in order to view historical phenomena in all of their richness of meaning. The danger of ideological narratives notwithstanding, we need stories handed down through "remembrance" (or tradition) in order to appreciate the full range of experiences and ways of living together that history has shown to be humanly possible. As Arendt puts it, "depth cannot be reached by man except through remembrance" (BPF, 94).

The "Work" of Storytelling

As a kind of making, historical narration not only draws on remembrance-given story "materials" but also "works" on these materials so as to render them more "useful." The discursive work that Arendt attributes to storytelling resembles the kind of narrative work that

White and Barthes analyze: Storytelling identifies units of actors and actions, uses metaphor and other poetic devices to convey the existential significance of the actions, and relates the actions together within an integrated pattern of beginnings and endings. Unlike White and Barthes, however, Arendt (and Ricoeur) argue that such discursive work is not mere distortion but can help a community come to terms with the significance for them of events in their past.

We can describe the work that Arendt (as well as White, Barthes, and Ricoeur) attribute to narration in terms of two basic kinds of work. First, narration performs the work of relating together within an integrated whole an ensemble of disparate elements (Arendt TH, 133; Ricoeur TNi, ix-xi; 1991, 7-11). White and Barthes emphasize the extrafactual and the indirect character of the meanings that are communicated through such narration. Arendt does not dispute the extrafactual character of narration, but she stresses instead the usefulness of a narrative pattern insofar as it "indicates where the treasures are and what their worth is" (BPF, 5). When a narrative relates actions together within a pattern of beginnings and endings, it may add meaning that exceeds isolated facts; however, it also provides the kind of framework that is necessary in order to identify and evaluate relevant information. In hermeneutic terms, the narrative pattern functions as the interpretation of the whole that guides our interpretation of the parts. I will call this narrative whole a *narrative matrix: narrative* because it is an objectifiable structure of interrelated narrative elements and *matrix* because it consists of meaningful content as well as a structure that can incorporate additional content.

The storyteller performs a second kind of "work" when she uses poetic language to convey the moral, emotional, and aesthetic qualities of a past phenomenon (Arendt BPF 261-62; TH, 98-109; Ricoeur TNi ix-xi; 1991, 7-11). This poetic work can be performed in one phrase or can be developed in descriptions throughout the story. In addition (as White and Barthes emphasize) poetic work is often achieved even when the language is not explicitly poetic. For instance, when Weinberg and Morison call parts of Japan and Germany "targets," they use a metaphor to characterize the designated places as objectified areas of military animosity. I will call a story's contribution to our understanding of the qualitative content of a phenomenon the production of a *story image: story* because it is not reducible to the narrative text but is realized as meaningful content as it is interpreted by specific communities and *image* because, like a visual image, it consists of an array of related qualities. "Image" here, however, does not refer literally to a mental representation of a visual picture but to the collection of moral, affective, and aesthetic qualities that a story helps readers to imagine in connection with a particular phenomenon.

In addition to making vivid the existential qualities of a specific past phenomenon, a story image can also provide a community with a shared, common-sense understanding of general moral and political concepts, such as "freedom" or "bravery." A story image plays this major cultural role when the phenomenon with which it is associated is a well-known historical instance of a moral or political ideal. In the United States, for instance, narratives of the early settlers' immigration to North America for religious freedom not only generate story images of the settlers' new freedom but also provide a general reference point with respect to which "freedom" has a commonly understood meaning in our country. Such narratives, when widely circulated, give North Americans a rich sense of what it means to live free from state interference in one's private life and thus help to solidify a shared political language and worldview. At the same time, however, such story images also limit cultural understandings of freedom; for instance, this conception of individual private-sphere freedom makes it difficult for North Americans to conceptualize or communicate the phenomenon that Arendt calls "public freedom."

Although story images often contribute to a shared political language and worldview, not all story images reinforce dominant ways of interpreting the world. As both Arendt and Ricoeur emphasize, narrators can challenge and recast received moral and political concepts when they creatively explore aspects of a historical phenomenon that escape conventional categories (Arendt UP; Ricoeur TNi, ix-xi; 1991, 7–11). Arendt demonstrates this ability of narrators to stretch our historical imaginations when, for instance, she traces the different meanings that "authority" and "freedom" have had in different historical contexts and when she uses oxymorons to describe the "inanimate humans" of the Nazi death camps (OT, 447).

Both Arendt and Ricoeur compare the work of narration in making palpable the existential significance of historical phenomena to the mental work that Kant called schematism (LK, 80–85, TNi, ix-x, 68).[24] According to Kant, we make determinative judgments, that is, we subsume particular phenomena under general concepts, by virtue of mental "schemata": representations in our mind that mediate between abstract categories and the sense impressions that we receive from empirical phenomena (Kant 1965, B177-B178). The story image plays a role similar to Kant's schema insofar as it, too, instantiates in our mind the meaningful content of a general concept and thereby allows us to identify sense data that we encounter in multiple situations as data that belongs to a general type of phenomenon, such as "freedom."

The narrative-generated story image, however, also differs from Kant's schema in ways that underscore the unique work of storytelling. Unlike like Kant's schema, and more like the empirically given exemplary particulars that Kant addresses in his theory of reflective judgment (1951, 196), the story image is not developed a priori but through reckoning with a specific historical phenomenon or traces of that phenomenon. Likewise, in the manner of Kant's exemplary particular, the story image is not an absolute, definitive standard for determinative judgments but serves only as a tentative guideline that makes vivid some (but not all) of the qualities that characterize a particular class of phenomena. Arendt notes that such historically derived, tentative guidelines are essential to the historical and political sciences, for general concepts in these fields are developed only by analyzing the particular phenomena that have appeared throughout history (LK, 84–85; BPF, 92).

Story images, finally, also differ from both Kant's schemata and Kant's exemplary particulars with respect to their roots in a tradition-given language. Unlike both of these conceptual aids described by Kant, story images are transmitted through a community's narratives and thus are conditioned by that community's language while they have their full force only for those who are familiar with that language and culture. The development of new story images is likewise anchored in a linguistic tradition, for storytellers articulate new nuances of meaning by working creatively with their received language.

The Truth-Value of Creatively Made Stories

The above account of narration as story making, if read together with Ricoeur's analysis of poetic language, can begin to explain the distinct truth-value of stories. When stories articulate narrative matrices and story images, they do not represent objects, but they can have the kind of truth-value that Ricoeur ascribes to poetic language. Although poetic language does not directly describe objects, it can "redescribe" the world: It can suggest "aspects, qualities, and values of reality that lack access to language that is directly descriptive" and can thereby help readers to view the world in a new light (Ricoeur, TNi, xi). Such a redescribed world has the status of "being-as." It does not exist as a nameable referent but neither is it purely linguistic. It is the world *as readers imagine it to be* when they consider the qualities that are suggested by the unconventional likenesses, the juxtapositions, and the unique configurations articulated in the text (TNi, xi, 77–81; TNiii, 154–55).[25]

In this view, the configurations and metaphors of a narrative text direct our attention in a way that moves us to consider aspects of a phenomenon that are not usually part of our consciousness. As Ricoeur puts it, the poetically written text offers "a new way of looking at things . . . an injunction to think in a certain manner" (MT, 558). It thereby guides us toward a richer, more self-conscious appreciation for nuances and possibilities of the lived world that we did not before notice or examine. If fictional language, too, can play this cognitive role, this does not make the poetically generated meanings any less real, for fictional stories are meaningful precisely because we can relate them to ways of being and qualities of life that are possible outside of the text (Ricoeur 1991, 5–11; TNi, xi, 74–81; TNiii, 154–79; MT, 543–44, 558).

The storyteller who narrates actual past achievements and crises with sensitivity to the specificity of those phenomena presents a distinct kind of "redescribed world." She presents a redescribed historical world that offers new perspectives on our own historical identity. Although these remain discursively created perspectives, or "ways of looking at things," such narrative-generated perspectives on our history have intellectual value. They help us to assimilate within our conception of ourselves and our community some of the yet uncodified, unnoticed elements of our heritage.

In sum, storytelling is a kind of "making" insofar as it draws on received discursive "materials"—that is, narrative matrices and story images that are given in past stories—and "works" on these materials— that is, rearranges received narrative matrices and redescribes actors, actions, and places—so as to provide a new way of articulating a political phenomenon as a story. As White and Barthes stress and Arendt also acknowledges, the story that a particular text presents is not given in the facts and is not the only story that could be told. It is produced through tradition-informed, historically situated, creative work and it is only one of many possible stories that someone might tell of the phenomenon. Nevertheless, this narrative work is not mere artifice or distortion. When the storyteller tells the event as a story, she draws our attention to certain relationships and qualities that are not given in the facts but that we might find to be relevant to the phenomenon as a phenomenon of our world. In effect, the story invites us to consider the meanings that we find to be pressing when we view the phenomenon in light of the conceptual resources that the story offers. The story is an invitation (as in Socrates's words to Crito) to "[l]ook at it this way."[26]

When we regard the narrative matrices and metaphors of a text as "ways of seeing" rather than attempts at objective truth, then the text need not be a definitive account of events in order to have epistemic value. In this view, the narrative text is not supposed to be definitive because it is not a representation but rather an imaginative guide whose meaning is realized as particular readers consider historical phenomena in its light. Readers have the responsibility to explore how well the orderings and comparisons presented by the narrative help them to appreciate aspects of the historical world that, although not visible as such, nonetheless characterize historical phenomena as human-initiated and subjectively meaningful phenomena.

Storytelling and Understanding

When narratives present "ways of seeing" that sensitize us to some of the richness and nuances of meaning in our world, they promote the achievement that Arendt and Ricoeur call *understanding*. Understanding has the intellectual value that I describe above, but it is not mere intellectual activity. Understanding, says Arendt, is "the specifically human way of being alive." It is a life-long process by which we strive to come to terms with a constantly changing and alien environment and "try to be at home in the world" (Arendt, UP, 377).[27] As I have noted earlier in this chapter, White (in his later work) affirms the distinct value of understanding, but he leaves vague the nature of understanding and its relation to historiography's more empirical dimension. Below, by drawing on Arendt, Ricoeur, and Gadamer, I clarify the relation of story-generated understanding to factual knowledge and explicate the sense in which stories make us "at home in the world."

Ricoeur: The Interplay of Knowledge and Understanding
In his theory of text interpretation, Ricoeur provides a useful model for conceptualizing the relation between understanding and knowledge in the historical sciences. Ricoeur himself does not focus on historiography but on the problem of interpreting written texts. With certain precautions, however, the interplay that Ricoeur describes between the subjective understanding and the objective explanation of a text can be compared to the interplay between the understanding-oriented storytelling dimension and the more empirical dimension of historiography.

In his theory of text interpretation, Ricoeur addresses the distinction as well as the interdependence of subjective understanding and objective explanation of a text. Basically, Ricoeur pursues the implications of Gadamer's idea that a text's meaning is fulfilled when it is "translated" into a language familiar to the reader. If a text's meaning is essentially its interpreted meaning for readers, says Ricoeur, then the written text is only a *potential* meaning that is not actualized until it is interpreted by a specific reader (1974, 90–93, 119–24). At the same time, the text itself constitutes an objective structure of signs that limits the range of valid interpretations. This subjective engagement with a text's meaning and objective analysis of the text's structure are joint processes. For instance, on the subjective level, we approach a text by trying to understand, in terms meaningful to our experience, specific parts of the text. Based on this understanding, we then guess at a meaning of the whole text. On the objective level, however, we must also check that our guessed-at interpretation accords with the objective structure of the text. This checking process indicates that some interpretations are simply not compatible with the given structure of the text. One can explain the inadequacy of such unacceptable interpretations (as teachers often must do) with reference to specific, fixed components of the text. At the same time, the unfixed, subjective elements of the text allow for a plurality, or a "specific plurivocity," of possible interpretations (Ricoeur MT, 530–51, 558; 1974, 121–24). Any teacher could most likely also confirm this latter phenomenon from experiences with unexpected but plausible student reactions to a text.

Ricoeur proposes that his theory of text interpretation provides a useful model for conceptualizing the relation between objective analysis and engaged interpretation in the human sciences. A human action, Ricoeur explains, is like a text insofar as the action has a subjective meaning that we instantiate only when we relate to our own world the kinds of "existential perplexities, human predicaments and deep-rooted conflicts" that the action exhibits (MT, 560). At the same time, as is the case when we interpret a text, we must check that our interpretation of the action's meaning is consistent with the written traces and physical remains that make up that action's "objective" structure (MT, 537–43, 560–62).

While Ricoeur proposes what he calls his "model of the text" as a general schema for the human sciences, Arendt throws light on the specific relevance of this model to the narration of political events. Based on her study of the structure of political phenomena and the kind of narrative work that such phenomena demand, Arendt develops an account of "interpreting" political phenomena that is strikingly similar to Ricoeur's model of text interpretation.[28] Like Ricoeur's text interpreter in his subjective task, Arendt's storyteller confronts a political

phenomenon whose subjective meaning for an audience is only potential, or in her words, "invisible." The storyteller actualizes this meaning
when she articulates it in a form that is intelligible to her community. To
do so, she must approach the phenomenon in an engaged manner so as
to gain a sense of its moral and emotional significance in terms vivid for
her. At the same time, like the text interpreter in his more objective task,
the storyteller must check that her interpretation is consistent with the
objectifiable structure of the "text," in this case, the documents and
artifacts that make up that phenomenon's traces and remains. While
such fixed signs regulate storytelling, they also (like the objectifiable
structure of a written text) allow for a plurality of plausible interpretations. Thus a political phenomenon's story can be told and re-told
without exhausting its meaning. In this view, the narration of a political
phenomenon has an objective dimension that must conform to standards of evidence and accuracy. At the same time, insofar as narration
helps a specific community to come to terms with an event's meaning
for them, it also demands engaged and creative interpretation that aims
at understanding and that exceeds empirical determination.

Gadamer: Understanding as Reconciliation with Reality
While Ricoeur addresses the interplay between objective explanation
and subjective understanding, Gadamer focuses specifically on understanding. Gadamer helps to provide a systematic account of the kind of
lifelong and world-orienting understanding that is the aim of Arendtian
storytelling. Although Gadamer (like Ricoeur) directs his analysis
primarily to written texts, his analysis throws light on the character of
understanding, more generally. Most importantly, Gadamer elucidates
the sense in which understanding reconciles us to strange phenomena,
yet without reducing those phenomena to familiar categories.

Gadamer describes the understanding of a text as work that generates a "fusion of horizons" between the reader's world and the world of
the text. The reader creates such a fusion by attempting to subsume the
text within a framework of meaning that is informed by his familiar
worldview. In turn, however, he must also revise his projected framework of meaning as he tries to account for elements of the text that resist
assimilation into his framework. He continually modifies his presumed
conceptual framework as he seeks to make sense of more and more of
the text's strange elements ([1960] 1991, 295–311). This interpretive
task is endless due to the alterity of the strange text as well as the
constantly changing character of the reader's own world. Nonetheless,
although never complete, such interpretive work advances the reader's
understanding, for it enriches his sense of the range of meanings that the

text encompasses while it also expands his own worldview as he revises that worldview in light of the text (Gadamer [1960] 1991, 295, 306–307, 546–547).

The Specific Kind of Understanding Achieved through Storytelling

Analogously to Gadamer's reader, who seeks understanding of a written text, Arendt's storyteller extends the boundaries of her worldview as she tries to understand the complex meanings of a historical phenomenon. As the storyteller attempts to subsume traces and remains of the historical phenomenon within an intelligible narrative, she may encounter aspects of that phenomenon that resist her familiar narrative resources. If the storyteller pushes the limits of her received narrative resources in the attempt to make sense of the vexing, seemingly unthinkable aspects of the past phenomenon, then she begins to include that phenomenon within her historical imagination as well as to revise and enrich the latter.

We might call the specific kind of "fusion of horizons" that a storyteller makes possible a "fusion of stories," for the storyteller subsumes the phenomenon to be understood within a specifically narrative framework of meaning; that is, she articulates a narrative that relates the distant phenomenon to stories of the more familiar world. Such a narrative bridge to a strange phenomena does not entail merely integrating that phenomena within a known sequence of causes and effects, for this would only locate the strange event in a causal chain, leaving its meaning alien to us. Neither does such a narrative fusion, at the opposite extreme, posit an absolute context of meaning, a "universal history," in which to define the event once and for all, for such a dogmatic narrative would ignore the different interpretive frameworks that different historical locations and narrative strategies make possible. Unlike both causal analysis and universal history, the storyteller's "fusion of stories" is a historically contingent, language-dependent connection to the past. It is achieved when the storyteller applies her received narrative matrices and story images to a strange phenomenon while also adapting and extending those narrative resources to respond to the alterity of the phenomenon. Arendt pursues precisely this approach in her story of Nazism. For instance, she makes the lived character of the death camps palpable to readers by describing the camps in terms of our familiar image of hell, yet she also challenges us to rethink "hell" as a situation *on earth* in which living beings were treated "as if what happened to them were no longer of any interest to anybody, as if they were already dead" (445). She also traces the unthinkable atrocities of Nazism to their beginnings in the imperialism and the citizenship-dependent rights of the modern nation-state, thus recalling our familiar narrative matrix of modern Europe but also highlighting the less visible, contradictory aspects of the nation-state's history. (I examine Arendt's story of Nazism more closely in the next chapter.) Through her narrative, Arendt thus relates the seemingly alien phenomenon of Nazism to familiar stories of our world, while she also stretches the limits of our familiar stories in attempt to come to terms with Nazism.

Like the fusion of horizons described by Gadamer, a fusion of stories can connect us to the past in a way that is intellectually stimulating, not dogmatic, although the latter is always a danger. Ricoeur clarifies this distinction between a dogmatic and a critical-minded interpretation of the past. He reserves the term *Tradition* for the transmittance of a belief about the past (or past work) whose truth we take for granted and whose claim we abstract from its relation to various competing traditions (TNiii, 217).[29] He coins the term *traditionality* to describe a more modest claim: a claim about the meaning of a past work that one proposes to be true, at least in relation to one's own historically located hermeneutic work. Unlike an appeal to Tradition, a proposed interpretation of a past work engages the reader in the interpretive process, for such a claim presents itself as revisable. In addition, when an interpreter presents her interpretation of the past work as a form of traditionality, she recognizes that she can traverse the distance between past and present worlds but that she can do so only through her own historically situated interpretive work; thus she leaves to each community the responsibility to reinterpret the past work in terms of their own historical and cultural contexts. Finally, when text interpretation is pursued as a form of traditionality, the interpreter recognizes the contingent character of her own conceptual framework and thus engages in the kind of testing process that Gadamer associates with genuine understanding; she projects her worldview onto the text to be understood while she also tests, revises, and "fractures" that received worldview as she explores suppressed and unnoticed elements in the past work (TNiii, 217–23, 227).

Storytelling encompasses a similar range of dogmatic and critical forms. Similarly to appeals to Tradition, a story that presents itself as a universal, fixed truth creates "chains fettering [us] to a predetermined aspect of the past" (Arendt BPF, 94). When, however, in the manner of traditionality and in accord with genuine understanding, a storyteller presents her narrative not as an absolute truth but as one way to reckon with the meaning of past phenomena, and when she allows the strangeness of the past to destabilize her received narrative resources, then her story cultivates an experimental approach to history, allowing the past to "open up to us with unexpected freshness and tell us things no one has yet had ears to hear" (BPF, 94). In addition, when a storyteller acknowledges that her narrative renders the past event intelligible by virtue of her own historically located discursive work, then she reminds us that historical narratives are always historically contingent, tentative interpretations, not definite truths. The ultimate responsibility for assimilating, building upon, or rejecting such proposed narratives lies with each reader.

In sum, when a narrative promotes understanding of historical phenomena by creating a fusion of stories between strange and familiar worlds, that narrative helps us to assimilate within our worldview the odder elements of our history while it encourages us to rethink and revise our worldview in response to those oddities. Such understanding, Arendt reminds us, is unending, for our world is infinitely complex and always changing, as are we, ourselves. Although never complete, the process of trying to understand strange historical phenomena is nonetheless necessary in order for us to face up to the depth of meanings that make up our heritage and to orient ourselves in the world.

Thus, if understanding makes us "at home in the world," it does not necessarily make us comfortable with or accepting of the world as given. On the contrary, when a storyteller modifies her received narrative resources in response to the strangeness of specific historical phenomena and when she presents her story as only one historically contingent proposed interpretation of that phenomena, then her story makes us at home in the world only to unsettle our familiar sense of "home" and to emphasize our responsibility to examine our home's darker corners. Ultimately, storytelling makes us at home in the world not so as to make us complacent with the world as we have known it but so as to enhance our responsiveness to the full range of hopes and dangers that are possible in our midst.

The Productive Role of Storytelling

When stories make past events understandable as part of our history, they resemble the third, final element of *making*: They add a new "durable product" to the world. Stories create a "durable product" in the sense that they endow fleeting phenomena with a lasting form, thereby transforming phenomena that are experienced in a plurality of lives into publicly recognized history (Arendt HC, 173).[30] Arendt calls this "production" of history the *publicizing* of a phenomenon. Political phenomena are always already public in the broad sense that I have called publicness: They appear in a shared world and affect many people. When political phenomena are narrated, however, they gain the additional quality of *publicity,* that is, public acknowledgment as part of our common history (HC, 50).

When Arendt emphasizes the more compelling reality that phenomena acquire upon being publicized in a story, she echoes Husserl's insight that our experience of the world's reality depends on our experience of others who seem to encounter the same world.[31] Going beyond Husserl, Arendt recognizes the need for interpretive activity in order to share and confirm lived experiences. She identifies storytelling as the central means by which we communicate and thereby mutually confirm our experiences. "For us, appearance—something that is being seen and heard by others as well as by ourselves—constitutes reality. Compared with the reality which comes from being seen and heard, even the greatest forces of intimate life—the passions of the heart, the thoughts of the mind, the delights of the senses—lead an uncertain, shadowy kind of existence unless and until they are transformed, deprivatized and deindividualized, as it were, into a shape to fit them for public appearance. The most current of such transformations occurs in storytelling" (Arendt HC, 50). Although Arendt claims that un-narrated phenomena "lead an uncertain, shadowy kind of existence," her point is not to deny the force of un-narrated experiences. She recognizes that such experiences can be intense for those who endure them, for instance, the French Resistance fighters "knew well enough the meaning of what they did," even though they could not name it, and the inmates of death camps had a lived knowledge of the camps' horrors, regardless of whether or not the camps were publicly acknowledged (BPF, 6; OT, 439). When, however, these events are told in a story and received meaningfully by an audience, then actors as well as later generations can experience them differently, as if they had greater certainty.

White correctly warns that the power of storytelling to transform lived phenomena into publicly recognized history is dangerous. Especially when we forget the limits and revisability of our stories, storytelling risks reifying one narrative construction of history and confusing it with history, per se. Arendt reminds us, however, that we must risk narrating our world, for only when we narrate historical phenomena can we not merely passively endure them but (at least begin to) thoughtfully and collectively confront them (HC, 208). Women's consciousness-raising groups in the 1970s were not motivated by

Arendt, but they demonstrated precisely this power of stories to turn obscure, "shadowy" experiences into collectively addressed public issues (Mackinnon 1989, 86–95).[32]

In effect, while White provokes us to consider how narratives convey "specifically human truth" through "imaginary language," Arendt elucidates the character of such narrative-generated "truth." On the one hand, she confirms that the "truths" offered by narrative are neither certain, fixed, nor separate from us. On the other hand, however, she recasts this seeming limitation as an intellectual and political virtue; for precisely as historically situated, engaged, creative, and tentative constructions, stories orient us in a world of multifaceted, humanly begun, and subjectively meaningful phenomena. Such stories do not substitute for theory or empirical data; however, when stories use language creatively to throw new light on familiar worlds, when they explore possible ways to assimilate strange phenomena within our historical imagination, and when they give coherence, albeit a tentative, open-ended coherence, to unique historical phenomena, stories achieve what theory and data cannot. Stories keep us mindful of the myriad, often untheorized significances of historical dramas while they affirm our role as actors and interpreters in the unfolding of those dramas.

Chapter 2

The Public Role of Storytelling

A revolution may well put an end to autocratic despotism . . .   *will never produce a true*   *of thinking.*

—Immanuel Kant[1]

How can we j   lating violence,
gross inequali   refugees make
the need for re   easingly urgent.
Moreover, as critics   affirmed, responsible moral and political   of each one of us is
crucial to a free society, for   res not only appropri-
ately structured institutions bu   iduals who question received doctrine and participate t   fully and responsibly in
public life.

Enlightenment theorists thought that "universal reason" would be our ticket to mature political deliberation and a responsible public sphere. In recent years, however, the universal reason that was supposed to counter prejudices and stipulate the conditions for objective moral truths has been discredited. Marxists, feminists, and poststructuralists alike have shown that the supposedly innate, self-grounded, and principled reason that Kant hoped would overcome prejudices is itself neither universal nor unprejudiced. On the contrary, this reason presupposes a culturally specific metaphysics that denigrates women, non-European cultures, and the traits associated with them, while it denies moral significance to all of the "subjective" and "contingent" elements of our world that many believe are integral to human life. In the end, appeals to "universal reason" may only mask the prejudices of those who claim its power, allowing the allegedly "rational" people to judge others while shielding their own practices from scrutiny.[2]

If we can no longer trust public reasoning to "universal reason," neither, however, can we dismiss the legitimate concern behind the search for such a reason. The concern for critical and community-accountable modes of reasoning remains urgent as world events increasingly call for our moral deliberation while political leaders are all too ready to replace public discussion with moral clichés and catch phrases. Without an alternative conception of mature and responsible public reasoning, critics expose the prejudices of universal reason only to face another, equally threatening danger: the undermining of the public sphere with moral formulas and political complacency.

This chapter examines how the practice that Arendt has called "storytelling" can foster responsible public debate, yet without appeals to a specious universal reason. When people tell and read "stories," in Arendt's sense, they perform the kind of critical praxis that Kant assigned to reason: They subject received beliefs to "free and open examination" (Kant CPR, 9n.). They do so, however, without presuming transcendent principles or an Archimedean standpoint. Especially in a world in which diverse communities must learn to live together, judgments that appeal to alleged universal principles are dangerous, for they enable some people to presume a moral high ground while they demonize others. By contrast, storytelling, as Arendt envisions and practices it, takes responsibility to "judge," or present an evaluative knowledge claim about, others' actions; however, it does so only by trying to understand the people who are judged (which is not the same as forgiving them[3]) and situating them within the storyteller's world, thereby bridging the moral divide between communities and bringing the storyteller's own world under critical review.[4]

Clearly not all stories promote responsible public debate. As Arendt herself emphasized in her book *The Origins of Totalitarianism,* some narratives foster only rote, prejudiced modes of thought. The dangers of ideological narratives notwithstanding, however, Arendt's account of totalitarianism indicates that we can better realize the mature public debate called for by Kant as well as contemporary thinkers if we do not try to rid public debate of stories but instead tell more stories. In light of Arendt's work, I argue that we resist dogmatic and obfuscating narratives and maintain responsible political discussion only by practicing more experience-attentive, explicitly engaged, and innovative political narration.

The Problem of Responsible Moral Judgment

Arendt is not the only scholar to seek a path between a specious moral universalism and an irresponsible moral relativism. Like Arendt, post-

Enlightenment theorists, including Seyla Benhabib (1992) Richard Bernstein (1991), Lisa Disch (1994), and Satya Mohanty (1997), caution against making presumably authoritative moral and political judgments, yet remain committed to judging our world. These post-Enlightenment scholars ask how might we judge responsibly, notwithstanding the impossibility of universal principles or an objective standpoint from which to judge.

Benhabib's work in moral and political theory (1992) and Mohanty's work in literary criticism (1997) offer representative and lucid responses to the problem of a post-Enlightenment moral judgment. They each examine how we might theorize an open-minded, self-scrutinizing, and broadly accountable judgment, yet without denying our own situatedness in history, bodies, and language. Although approaching the problem from distinct disciplines and with distinct concerns, Benhabib and Mohanty arrive at similar conclusions about the possibility of a broadly accountable mode of judgment.[5] Both determine that we can salvage moral universalism without positing a universal structure of reason if we simply accept that all of us have the ability to act in and evaluate our world. This minimal assumption, they argue, makes theoretically conceivable an inclusive judging community whose interactive deliberations would form the basis for a broadly accountable way of reasoning.[6] In this view, the norms of respect for each person and recognition of each person's autonomy are not self-grounded principles of reason but are rather conditions that we must strive to realize in order to achieve and sustain the judging community, or, as Benhabib puts it, the "ongoing moral conversation" (1992, 38).

Based on their visions of the judging community, Benhabib and Mohanty also rethink "objectivity." Objectivity, in their analyses, is not the standpoint of a transcendent reason but the temporary achievement of a historically specific community insofar as the community judges in a manner that is responsive to the concerns of all members. Such an achievement requires social conditions that are conducive to an exchange of views as well as social and interpretive skills, in particular, skills in considering other people's perspectives (Benhabib 1992, 4–9, 34–55; Mohanty 1997, 140–41, 198–200, 232–34, 242–51).

Arendt and the Practice of Responsible Judgment

While post-Enlightenment scholars theorize a more defensible "public use of reason," they nonetheless leave vague the everyday practices by which ordinary people can pursue such situated critical reasoning.[7] In her own "story" of Nazism, Arendt enacts one such practice; that is, she demonstrates one practice by which academics as well as lay people can pursue a situated but responsible engagement in public life.[8]

Arendt's attention to the more practical elements of responsible judgment is not surprising, for she confronted the failure of Enlightenment morality on an immediately practical level. Having lived through the early years of Nazi Germany, she saw first-hand that the principle of "inalienable human rights" had little power to influence people when those people subscribed to a different set of principles. Having seen many of her countrymen and colleagues participate in Nazism, she knew from experience that the Enlightenment principles of equal respect and moral responsibility could not stop people from killing their neighbors (Arendt OT , 440–58; Disch 1994, 94–97, 113–14). She likewise witnessed the hollowness of "universal" moral principles when the Nazis constructed a social order that defied those principles and destroyed the autonomous person that those principles presupposed (Arendt OT, 438–47). In her presence at the Nuremberg trials, she saw, too, how an appeal to transcendent principles can insulate the judge's world from criticism: When the four Great Powers judged the Nazis by appeal to universal norms, they elided Nazism's connections to their own world while they overlooked the fact that their own nations protected "human rights" only for citizens (and not always all citizens) so that, in effect, "no such thing as inalienable human rights existed" (Arendt OT, 269).[9]

At the same time, having grown up in Germany among Germans, Arendt also knew that "the Nazis," despite their monstrous actions, were also human beings who belonged to the same world as herself. Driven by the immediate issue of how to respond to both the horror and the human core of Nazism, Arendt did not present a comprehensive theory of impartial knowledge or democratic institutions. Instead, she focused on the more specific problem of how to face up to the reality of Nazism. In effect, she sought to condemn Nazism's atrocities, yet without labeling Nazism "radical evil," for this would fail to address Nazism's human character and it connection to her own world.

The Origins of Totalitarianism *as Responsible Judgment*
Refusing a moral high ground, Arendt addresses the moral challenge of Nazism in an unusual approach that she calls "an analysis in terms of history" (AR, 78) or later, more modestly, "my old fashioned storytelling" ("Action and the Pursuit of Happiness," cited in Vollrath 1977, 160).[10] Whatever we choose to call her approach, the crucial point is that Arendt's book *The Origins of Totalitarianism* narrates the connections between Nazi and Stalinist totalitarianism and our own world. The

narrative makes clear that a meaningful analysis of Nazism and Stalinism cannot leave unscathed the Western world's own moral and political institutions. As she puts it, "If it is true that the elements of totalitarianism can be found by retracing the history and analyzing the political implications of what we usually call the crisis of our century, then the conclusion is unavoidable that this crisis is no mere threat from the outside" (Arendt OT, 460).

In her original title for the book "The Elements of Shame: Anti-Semitism—Imperialism—Racism," Arendt highlights the continuity between modern European history and totalitarian regimes as well as the shame this implies for all of us.[11] Unfortunately, however, the title that the publisher gave to the book as well as much of the book's favorable commentary, including the praise from *The Foreign Affairs 50-Year Bibliography* quoted on the back cover, gloss over this fundamentally inward-looking focus. Her publishers would rather read the book as a study of the totalitarian "other" than as a study of our own history. They would rather emphasize the book's more scientific elements, describing it as an analysis of "origins" (the publisher's term) and as "preparing the way for a whole series of studies of totalitarianism" (the *Foreign Affairs* jacket blurb), than confront the book's more unconventional "storytelling" elements that challenge the West's own ideological premises and analytic categories.

In contrast to the publisher's title and jacket blurb, Arendt makes clear from her first pages that she critically examines the Western world's own institutions and ideologies. In her preface, for instance, she describes her project as an attempt to comprehend our century's darker moments. She sought to comprehend, in particular, two world wars, terror-run states, death factories, and an aftermath of unprecedented homelessness. Comprehension of these events, she explains, does not mean excusing or accepting them but rather "examining and bearing consciously the burden which our century has placed on us—neither denying its existence nor submitting meekly to its weight. Comprehension, in short, means the unpremeditated, attentive facing up to, and resisting, of reality—whatever it may be" (OT, viii). Such comprehension avoids the twin wrongs of "reckless optimism and reckless despair" (OT, vii). While the former trusts time to improve the situation, the latter passively submits to the destructive processes. By contrast, an approach that seeks comprehension treats terror-run regimes and death camps as at once threats to the foundations of Western civilization and as phenomena whose human elements we can begin to understand and thereby more effectively resist.

Arendt probably was not surprised when her critics charged that *Totalitarianism* lacked theoretical distance, scientific grounding, and standard theoretical categories.[12] In her view, these disciplinary conventions only obstruct our engagement with Nazism's specificity and its challenges to our own worldviews. In an attempt to respond meaningfully to phenomena such as a race-based legal system and state-orchestrated death camps, Arendt availed herself of existing social and political theories; however, she also drew on literature, biography, and testimony in order to treat events in their specificity, their strangeness, their moral intensity, and their situatedness within our world. The resulting bricolage of historical and social analyses, biographical sketches, innovative metaphors, and open-ended narration does not pretend to offer definite knowledge. It does, however, have value as a "story": a narrative in which someone concerned about her community's future traces new patterns of beginnings and endings, and articulates new metaphors, so as to help her community come to terms with disturbing or unappreciated aspects of their heritage.

Arendt's story of Nazism differs from both typical historiography and typical political science. Unlike conventional historiography, which is structured in terms of temporally bounded events or eras, *Totalitarianism* is organized in terms of ongoing and overlapping totalitarian "elements." The chapters follow elements such as modern antisemitism, race-thinking, and power-oriented politics through their multiple connections to modern forms of terror and ideology. At the same time, the book differs from typical political analysis insofar as it treats these elements not as general political forms but as historically specific developments that eventually "crystallized into totalitarianism" (AR, 78). For instance, *Totalitarianism* does not presuppose a general political category, "antisemitism," but instead examines the specific kind of antisemitism that emerged from the Jews' relation to other social groups and from hierarchies within Jewish communities in nineteenth- and early-twentieth-century Europe.

Arendt's element-organized but historically sensitive approach throws light on the historical conditions from which Nazism arose, yet without presenting Nazism as either alien or inevitable. When, for instance, Arendt traces Nazi antisemitism to the conditions in prewar Europe that made many Germans antagonist toward Jews, she shows Nazi antisemitism to be neither arbitrary (as in the scapegoat theory) nor inevitable (as in the theory of an eternal antisemitism) but comprehensible in terms of the social conditions from which it arose. This approach allows critics to hold Germans responsible for their actions, as the antisemitism is understood to be a human response to history rather than a natural instinct; at the same time, this approach recognizes that Nazi racism is not unique because similar social conditions can prompt race hatred in our own world. Perhaps most importantly, when Arendt treats the conditions that gave rise to Nazism as beginning elements rather than causes with necessary effects, she leaves the prospects for Nazi forms of racism in our own future undecided, dependent on how we choose to respond to social conflicts.

By tracing Nazism to beginning elements, Arendt also makes some historical sense of Nazism, yet without reducing Nazism to familiar conceptions of Western history. For instance, she pursues the historical beginnings of Nazism's race-based law and expansionist politics. When she finds these beginnings within European history, she brings Nazism closer to home but also reveals "pre-totalitarian" elements in the latter. These elements include a European race-thinking that reduced human beings to "animal species" (OT, 234); policies of "national self-determination" that left hundreds of thousands of people without a state to represent them (OT, 280–302); declarations of "human rights" that were protected only for citizens, so that precisely when people, such as refugees, fell back on nothing but their humanness, they lacked "the right to rights" (OT, 300); democracies that extolled representative government but in which the majority of citizens remained alienated from political life (OT, 311–14); nations that proclaimed respect for all humans but that treated as inferior or placed in internment camps those same groups who were persecuted by the Nazis (OT, 269, 288); and powerful, globally influential institutions that disempowered individuals, leaving "modern men [unable] to live in, and understand the sense of, a world which their own strength has established" (OT, viii). By situating Nazism within modern European history, Arendt thus not only makes Nazism more comprehensible but also makes our own history more strange. Her story reveals that the same global reach that makes Western nations so powerful also disempowers people, that the acclaimed doctrine of "inalienable human rights" remains a mere abstract declaration, and that "national law" at once affirms the principle of law and restricts "legal equality" to citizens (OT, viii, 270–302).

Arendt uses a second strategy characteristic of "storytelling," poetic language, to pursue comprehension of Nazism. Recognizing that Nazism and its beginning elements must consist of humanly possible modes of being, even if these actions and sufferings seem unimaginable to most readers, she supplements objectifying political theories with testimony, literature, political documents, and memoirs. She reads the latter not simply for the information they report but also for hints of how the writers experienced themselves and their worlds. She conveys such between-the-lines experiences to readers with new metaphors and provocative reconfigurations of familiar phrases. For instance, in her study of imperialism, she engages not only major political and economic theories but also the letters of Cecil Rhodes and T. E. Lawrence as well as the philosophy of Thomas Hobbes. Examining the subtexts of these works, she describes how Rhodes and Lawrence exhibit, and how Hobbes unwittingly anticipates, the contradictory implications of imperialism for Europeans themselves. Ironically, when European imperialism flexed its muscles across the globe by turning politics into the accumulation of power and public life into administration, it also generated a *disempowered* European individual who experienced himself as a mere "cog in the power-accumulating machine" (OT, 146). Accordingly Lawrence, despite his key role in British international politics, "never lost his awareness that he had been only a function and had played a role" and that the most he could contribute to history was by "push[ing] the right way" (OT, 220, and Lawrence cited in OT, 220). Likewise, if Rhodes believed "he could do nothing wrong, what he did became right," this expressed not only his vanity but also his identification with a larger, inexorable process of expansion (Millin, cited in Arendt OT, 215). Similarly Hobbes, in theorizing the state that corresponds to bourgeois accumulation of wealth, anticipates not only the reduction of politics to an endless process of generating power but also the destruction of individual significance that such a politics implies. If we cannot comprehend German submission to Nazism, suggests Arendt, we might consider "the poor meek little fellow" of Hobbes's state, who, in "a Commonwealth based on the accumulated and monopolized power of all its individual members" is left "powerless, deprived of his natural and human capacities" to think and act (OT, 146).

Arendt addresses even the Nazi death camps as a humanly comprehensible and historically close phenomenon. While she insists that we should be able to understand the camps, she also recognizes the difficulty of doing so. The massive crimes committed in the camps, she admits, include actions that surpass anything we know by the term "crime." While she quotes extensively from David Rousset's testimony of life in the camps, she warns that even such eyewitness accounts cannot convey the camps' full horror, nor can photography relay the reality of the camps to those of us who have not endured them (OT, 442–46, 459). Ultimately, she renders the death camps "human" only by problematizing familiar conceptions of human life. For instance, in order to make humanly comprehensible a situation in which "the whole of life was thoroughly and systematically organized with a view to the greatest possible torment," she compares the camps to levels of hell (OT, 445). Although her critics view this metaphor as amateur subjectivism, in fact, the comparison skillfully invokes a culturally familiar image of organized torment, hell, and creates an oxymoronic description of hell on earth that at once connects with and stretches our imagination of existential possibilities.[13] Continuing the metaphor, the camp inmates are "living corpses," people stripped of individuality and spontaneity and lost to the outside world (OT, 447). Arendt's vexing descriptions not only challenge received notions of "human nature" but also throw a disorienting light on our current world, for they indicate that "anything is possible" and that we cannot take for granted the existence of human dignity and individuality in our own community (OT, 459).[14]

By telling the story of Nazism, Arendt thus critically evaluates Nazism while also allowing Nazism to present lessons for the present. The lessons are not easy ones. As Arendt puts it, the history of antisemitism, imperialism, and totalitarian demonstrates "that human dignity needs a new guarantee which can be found only in a new political principle, in a new law on earth, whose validity this time must comprehend the whole of humanity while its power must remain strictly limited, rooted in and controlled by newly defined territorial entities" (OT, ix).[15] In her call for a new approach to protecting human dignity, Arendt anticipates the more radical feminist and postcolonial voices today. Anticipating critics such as Jaqui Alexander and Chandra Mohanty (1997b), Arundhati Roy (1999), Teresa Hayter (2002), Judith Butler (2002), and Susan George (2002), Arendt calls for governments that are more closely connected to specific populations and for moral commitments to "dignity," "equality," and "autonomy" that treat these neither as the exclusive rights of citizens nor as innate human properties but as goals that we must continuously struggle for by constructing the social and political conditions that enable us all to live together on equal and dignified terms. If Arendt's radical challenge to fundamental modern institutions and values passes unnoticed by many of her commentators, this may be because we are so accustomed to the idea that the globe is divided into discrete nations and that humans have inborn autonomy that we have difficulty even recognizing when arguments challenge these assumptions.

Totalitarianism may not lead all of its readers to a radical questioning of fundamental presuppositions of modernity. Still, the book's story of Nazism should at least discourage us from a naive nostalgia or utopianism. When we see that Nazism and Stalinism emerged from

developments within our history and are revealing of historical possibilities, we can no longer presume a strict opposition between terror-
run regimes and "the free world." We can no longer presume that our
nation-state system and our ideals of rights and dignity can prevent
large-scale atrocities within our own society. The lesson is not that we
must reject our tradition altogether but rather that "[w]e can no longer
afford to take that which was good in the past and simply call it our
heritage, to discard the bad and simply think of it as a dead load which
by itself time will bury in oblivion" (OT, ix). In effect, her story
impresses on us that we cannot leave our destiny to a presumed progress
inherent to our history but must face the limitations of our received
moral principles and political institutions and must actively explore
better ways to protect the dignity of all people.

Ideological and Critical Thinking

> *[H]ow much and how correctly would we think if*
> *we did not think in community with others to*
> *whom we communicate our thoughts and who*
> *communicate theirs to us!*

—Immanuel Kant[16]

In the last chapters of *Totalitarianism*, Arendt focuses specifically on
the form of thinking that makes possible terror-run states. Arendt's
study of "ideological thinking" anticipates the community-situatedness
of reason that Benhabib and Mohanty theorize. While Benhabib and
Mohanty analyze the kinship between responsible reasoning and vibrant community life, Arendt describes a specific historical instance of
the dependence of reason on community discussion: She traces the
breakdown of critical reasoning under Nazism to a breakdown of
community life in prewar Germany. Even if Arendt exaggerates the
extent to which lack of community discussion impaired people's ability
to think, her study identifies the political and epistemological dangers
of isolated, overly abstract modes of thought while it throws new light
on the relations among experience, critical thinking, and community.

Ideological Thinking and Loneliness
Nazi Germany abounded with the opposite of Kant's free exercise of
reason. Many people accepted the ludicrous proposition that Germany
would rise to world power were it not for a small group of Jews. Many

willingly brought innocent friends to executioners. Many extolled the supremacy of an "Aryan" race to which they themselves (as is the case for many Germans) did not belong.

When Arendt traces the existential conditions that made possible such widespread and seemingly irrational adherence to Nazi doctrine, she finds that these conditions were not so much the "[l]aziness and cowardice" that Kant, in his famous inquiry into the nature of enlightenment, blamed for retarding critical thought (1988b, 54). She finds (more in accord with Kant's lesser-known reflections on the public character of thinking[17]) that widespread Nazi indoctrination was facilitated by the lack of communicative relations in prewar Germany. In particular, she determines that economic chaos and social disintegration in prewar Germany resulted in widespread loneliness in which people were alienated from almost all communicative and trusting human relationships. When prewar Germans could not discuss surrounding events with others, and especially when those events were as unprecedented and confusing as the massive unemployment and inflation that destroyed the whole class of small businessmen, they could not fully process their perception of events and the roots of the economic crisis thus remained obscure and fragmentary. In addition, when few people engaged in public inquiry into the meaning of political events, the community could not revise their "common sense" political language to respond to changing circumstances. If so many Germans took seriously the absurd story of a Jewish world conspiracy, despite the Jews' evident decline in power, this irrationality was due, in part, to social conditions that prevented people from sharing and confirming their perceptions and that made people desperate for some "certain truths" that could replace the lost stability of the experienced world (OT, 308–24, 350–52, 362, 474–77).

"The Tyranny of Logicality"

Dogmas and formulas . . . are the ball and chain of our permanent immaturity.

—Immanuel Kant[18]

In addition to studying the social conditions in prewar Germany that made people susceptible to following political dogma, Arendt examines structural elements internal to Nazi doctrine that thwarted critical inquiry and promoted specifically *ideological* thinking. By ideological, Arendt (following Kant) refers to complacent, uncritical thought.

Arendt's study of "ideological thinking" does not substitute for Marxist or Nietzschean analyses of ideology; it does not replace analysis of
how ideologies falsely generalize particular interests or how ideologies
reify social and cultural constructs. Arendt does, however, complement
these analyses. She adds to current theories of ideology insofar as she
describes how the logical structure of an ideological doctrine can thwart
free and meaningful thought by isolating thinking from community
discussion of historical events, while the same logical structure can
foster complacency by obscuring the historical role of human judgment
and action.

Like other critics of ideology, Arendt recognizes that ideologies are
not false in a simple empirical sense. Ideological doctrines may accord
with "the facts" but still deceive insofar as the doctrines abstract
historically contingent facts from the factors that produced them and
thereby present social "facts" as if they were accidental or natural
occurrences (Arendt OT, 456–59; Marx 1997, 287–89). Likewise,
warped political doctrine may "function as true" (as Foucault puts it,
1980, 131) when people believe it or when social institutions organize
the world to fit the doctrine (Arendt BPF, 252–54; NT, 350–52). Nazi
institutions, for instance, *created* a society in which food rations,
employment, and even guilt and innocence were determined by race,
thus producing the "truth" of racial hierarchies. Even the Nazi claim
that certain "races" were "unfit to live" was, in a sense, confirmed
when Nazi death camps systematically executed those people (OT,
349–50, 362–63, 470–72).

While Arendt recognizes the dangers of ideologies that sanctify or
naturalize a socially constructed world, she does not identify this as the
crux of ideological thinking. More fundamental to Nazism's threat to
free thinking, she argues, is a certain logical form: a strictly deductive,
independent-from-the-experienced-world logic that unconditionally compels the thinker's adherence. Arendt's critique of the "tyranny of
logicality" may seem to be directed against logic per se. However, it is
actually a critique of beliefs about *history* that substitute logic for
attention to historical phenomena. Racist doctrines, for instance, explain all of human history in terms of logically necessary natural
processes (OT, 470). Arendt's insight is that historical thinking becomes rote, shallow, and irresponsible when we replace thoughtful
reflection on historical existence with strictly logical analysis.

Strictly deductive thinking about the historical world is naive and
dangerous, first, because it operates independently of the specifics of
historical life (UP, 386–87). Once the initial premises are accepted,
deductive thought generates itself, ordering facts into a logical system

"with a consistency that exists nowhere in the realm of reality" (OT, 471). Nazi doctrine, for instance, consists of an abstract, untestable first premise: natural competition among races. Once we accept this first premise, it follows logically that identity is decided by race, that some races are less "fit" to succeed than others, that the elimination of those races is intended by nature, etc. Such strictly deductive analysis leaves no room for people to reflect critically on the concepts of "race" or "nature" in light of the complexity of specific historical phenomena. While ideologies operate independently of experience, the more effective doctrines borrow from experience even when they oversimplify it. For instance, the Nazi premise of racial competition was compelling, in part, because it spoke to actual antagonism among differently situated social groups. At the same time, Nazi doctrine abstracted this antagonism from the complexity of social life and presented it as if it were an eternal, all-subsuming "natural law": the law of competition among races. Such a presumably fixed, transcendent law is so general and overarching that it resists refutation by any particular incident (OT, 470).

A purely logical doctrine also deters people from studying the particulars of historical life because such a doctrine maintains its consistency by positing a "hidden truth," such as the "Jewish conspiracy," beneath the surface of perceived events. In this way, such doctrines reduce experienced reality to a mere facade and ultimately impoverish experience itself, for they produce "a mentality in which reality . . . is no longer experienced and understood in its own terms but is automatically assumed to signify something else" (OT, 471). Moreover, a strictly deductive form of historical thinking again elides the complexities of historical life because it proceeds without community discussion. Logic, Arendt points out, is the one mental activity that one pursues entirely alone. Such a solitary thinker confronts historical phenomena from only a limited perspective and easily ignores those limitations (UP, 387).

Finally, strictly deductive belief systems treat all of history as the inexorable development of a single idea and thereby obscure our responsibility to judge and respond to historical events. The Nazi idea of natural competition among races, the Bolshevik idea of class struggle, as well as the modern Western idea of progress each participate in this deception, for they each present history as the logical and necessary unfolding of an abstract idea. When, by contrast, we confront the ambiguities and complexities of specific historical phenomena, history appears less certain, more open to our own judgment and action. Acknowledgment of this uncertain, indeterminate character of history marks the distinction between legitimate social theory and ideology.

Whereas social theories describe the frameworks in the context of which people act and create history, ideologies posit "laws" of historical motion itself. Ideologies thus replace historically grounded reflection on our various possible futures with acceptance of an inevitable destiny (OT, 349–50, 362–63, 462–73).

Experience, Community, and Critical Thinking
Arendt's study of Nazi ideology casts a new light on the relation between experience and critical thinking. It suggests that, if thinking is to be critical in the sense of subjecting received premises to examination, if thinking is to be free in the sense of originating new premises, and if thinking is to be responsible in the sense of acknowledging its own historical effects, then it must reckon with the complexity and the indeterminacy of historical life. Historical experience, in this view, is the fulcrum of critical thought. Unlike in modern epistemology, however, experience here is crucial not by virtue of its "certainty" but, on the contrary, because its nuances, ambiguities, and unpredictability continually challenge any "certain" historical truths.

Arendt likewise recasts critical thinking as a collective practice, for if critical thinking must attend to historical experience in its obscure, unfixed, polysemic dimensions, then it is best pursued with others who can challenge, augment, and complicate our beliefs. In this view, community life is integral to "individual" critical thought. The community may circulate dogmas and formulas but it also provides the forums that are necessary in order for us to confront historical life in its full richness and complexity. Thus vibrant, responsible political debate requires more than enlightened individuals. It requires public spaces in which we can exchange our diverse perspectives on the world. Likewise, it requires intellectual practices by which we can communicate truth claims while also acknowledging the partial and tentative character of our claims, for only when we can present claims about the historical world without claiming logical necessity or absolute truth can we "think in community with others" and thereby compare political doctrine to historical reality in all of its plurality, ambiguity, and indeterminacy.[19]

Storytelling and Participatory Politics

In her later works, Arendt theorizes the relations among experience, community, and critical thinking that are implicit in *Totalitarianism*.

These works, which include "Truth and Politics," "The Archimedean Point," *Lectures on Kant's Political Philosophy,* and "Imagination," address the problem of truth in the political field. Because the works focus on epistemological issues, Arendt's editor, Ronald Beiner, argues that the works move away from Arendt's earlier practical concerns and toward a new concern with "disinterested reflection" (Beiner 1982, 91). I would argue, however, that the works remain motivated by political concerns insofar as they theorize a "truth" that is compatible with a discussion-based politics. In essence, the works continue Arendt's longstanding concern to resist elements of totalitarianism, for they investigate the kind of thinking that can sustain a participatory public sphere. Moreover, although Arendt does not specifically address storytelling in the later works, storytelling is precisely the kind of tentative, interactive knowledge practice that the later works argue is crucial to a participatory politics.

"Objectivity" versus Community-Situated Knowledge

In her later works, Arendt presents a case for community-situated, explicitly partial, and tentative knowledge practices. These works accord with contemporary critiques of "objectivity" insofar as Arendt, similarly to Marxist critics, poststructuralists, and feminists, argues that the Enlightenment goal of timeless and bias-free knowledge of our world is unattainable. Not only does our social location and language always bias our understanding of the world, but our knowledge claim in turn affects the world by influencing what our community treats as "true" and "real." Anticipating Benhabib and Satya Mohanty, Arendt draws on an undervalued element *within* the Enlightenment tradition— Kant's notion of publicity—in order to demonstrate that "objective" claims about political phenomena are not only untenable but politically dangerous. In *Perpetual Peace,* Kant explains that a legitimate political claim should be able to be openly expressed in public (1988a, 125–30). Taking seriously the public character of political truth-claims, Arendt determines that distance from public affairs is not an epistemic and political virtue but a liability, for when a theorist tries to escape his social location by rising above public affairs, he avoids the public exposure and the community testing that are necessary in order to keep knowledge publicly accountable (LK 41–49; BPF, 241–47). In addition, because claims to objective knowledge are "not between men but above them," such claims facilitate coercive power relations in which some people make decisions and others simply follow (Arendt BPF, 247).

Within her critique of objectivity, Arendt also points toward the possibility of noncoercive knowledge claims. We can present evaluative knowledge claims about the political world without exercising coercion, she suggests, if our claims are situated within political communities, in the relations "between" people. Taking their cue from Arendt, scholars such as Satya Mohanty (1997), Benhabib (1992), and Disch (1994) theorize various models of community-situated moral and political reasoning. Their theories suggest how we might legitimate knowledge claims or develop responsible models of public decision making in the absence of universal principles. Arendt addresses an issue that is fundamental to each of their theories: the everyday practices in which people formulate community-situated, noncoercive claims about the political world. Storytelling is central to these practices.

A Community of Storytellers

Storytelling, as Arendt described and practiced it, constitutes an ideal medium in which to present noncoercive, community-situated beliefs about political phenomena. Unlike theories that oversimplify historical reality in the attempt to explain it, stories promote further inquiry into the nuances of the phenomena narrated. When storytellers, whether writers or lay people, use language creatively to indicate enigmatic or uncodified experiences, such as when Arendt describes the paradoxical disempowerment of individuals that accompanied power-centered imperialist politics, such stories turn public discussion to the subtleties and perplexities of specific historical phenomena. Stories thereby promote a genuinely critical and responsible political deliberation that resists the fatalism and abstraction of ideological thought. Arendt calls this historically sensitive and open-minded kind of thinking "between-past-and-future thinking," for it unhinges "the future" from the momentum of a seemingly determined past while it re-anchors our visions of the future in a continual engagement with the complex significances of our past.

Stories also encourage critical and inclusive political discussion because stories, at least when they present themselves as stories, make a claim about the world without ending debate. When someone tells a story *as a story,* that is, as a historically located person's attempt to render intelligible distant phenomena, she does not replace one total explanation of the world with another. Instead, she invites her community to try to understand the particular historical perspective that her way of organizing and describing events makes possible. Such a perspective is always partial and always only one way of telling the story; however, so long as this inherent partiality is acknowledged, it is not a shortcoming but a virtue, for it stimulates reconsideration, retelling, and supplementation from other standpoints.

Storytelling also engages its audience in the interpretive process because its task of understanding a strange phenomenon (as I explained in chapter one) is never complete but must be endlessly pursued by each one of us. A story contributes to this lifelong task when it articulates images and a narrative matrix that relates a distant phenomena to a more familiar world. Significantly, such narrative bridges to strange phenomena do not define those strange events once and for all but offer discursive resources for readers' own further imaginative work. Thus a story, when recognized as such, it is not an endpoint but a point of departure from which readers can explore the lived significance of strange affairs and can consider how their own lives might be situated within the web of actions and reactions that make up those affairs.

Storytelling, as Arendt describes it, not only encourages each reader to engage creatively with history but also fosters the kind of interactive public inquiry, or civic culture, that Arendt as well as contemporary theorists identify as crucial to participatory politics. Arendt, like Benhabib and Mohanty, makes clear that a civic culture in which people confront each other as participants in public life does not demand a universal human nature nor a general will. It requires only our commitment to develop publicly accountable "common sense" understandings of phenomena that "everybody sees and hears from a different position" (HC, 57). Storytelling promotes the kind of intellectual skills and attitudes that are essential to such a civic culture. When a story asks us to imagine the deeds and the sufferings of its characters, the story does not presuppose that we share a common consciousness with the characters. The imaginative shift of perspective called for by a story requires "only" that we try to make sense of the character's tale and consider how that tale might accord with, or challenge, our familiar narratives of our world. Although this does not require identification with others, it does require open-mindedness, humility, and hermeneutic skills, the same kind of skills that make possible a discussion-based public sphere.

At the same time that story reading cultivates appreciation for others' perspectives, storytelling allows us to present our own views without preempting discussion. When we tell a story as a story, we confront our audience as co-storytellers, people who will continue the narrative from their own perspective. Such regard for others as co-storytellers counters the tendency of ideologies to identify and judge people according to predetermined categories. Whether these are racial, sexual, or citizenship categories, rote categorization of people prevents us from responding to people as individuals and prepares us for excluding whole groups of people from basic rights and respect.

Enlightenment humanism counters such objectification of human beings with the principle of universal respect. As Arendt points out, however, this moral principle has little impact when a doctrine such as Nazism counterposes it with its own internally consistent, alternative principle, such as the principle of racial hierarchies.

Storytelling provides a means other than "universal principles" for resisting the objectification of people. When we share stories, we speak not from "above" but from within a community of storytellers. We address our audience as fellow storytellers, people who have perspectives of their own to contribute to the ongoing narrative. When we exchange stories, we also learn about how we both resemble and differ from one another. We thereby resist ideologies that absolutize and demonize human differences. A community of storytellers thus learns to listen to one another as individuals and cannot so easily categorize one another or impose on one another a predetermined agenda.

Finally, storytelling promotes civic culture insofar as it affirms every person's responsibility to contribute to political discourse. Storytelling enjoins everyone in political discussion because, in a community of storytellers, critical thinking is not reserved for the disinterested "expert" nor for the poststructuralist critic who cynically deconstructs others' truth claims. Instead, all of us who narrate particular historical experiences and offer our stories for public consideration can promote historically grounded critical assessment of received narratives. Likewise, when we understand ourselves to belong to a community of storytellers, we recognize that we are each responsible for the pasts we own up to, the heritages we claim, and the futures we foreground in our own continued storytelling.

Not all stories, of course, realize this potential contribution of storytelling to inclusive and responsible political debate. Nazi narratives had no such virtues. Nonetheless, Arendt teaches us that we best resist the obfuscations and the stifling effects of ideological narratives not with story-free "truth" but with more avowed "storytelling," that is, storytelling that forgoes professional detachment and standard analytic categories in order to reckon with the complex historical and human significances of specific phenomena. Although such storytelling does not replace general theories or empirical data, it does test the limits of received theories and categories, bring overlooked phenomena under discussion, and encourage the mutual exchange of perspectives that is vital to a participatory politics.

If storytelling plays this crucial public role, then we advance responsible public debate not by somehow ridding political thinking of stories but only by telling and reading stories in a more self-conscious, self-critical manner. The following chapters investigate how we might do so.

Chapter 3

Toward a Critical Theory of Stories

The Arendtian account of storytelling that I have presented in the last two chapters helps to justify the narrative work that is now increasingly common across the disciplines. In effect, while various legal scholars, philosophers, sociologists, and historians have begun to pursue their work through telling stories, Arendt helps to explain why we need such stories: Although not a replacement for theory or empirical data, stories have an irreplaceable function of their own insofar as they sensitize us to yet untheorized human and historical significances of political phenomena while they promote continual, inclusive discussion of those phenomena.

Not all stories, however, contribute to the historically sensitive, open-minded, interactive thinking that is storytelling's potential achievement. Arendt herself knew too well that many stories promote only "double-talk" that "does not disclose what is but sweeps it under the carpet" (MDT, viii). Conventional standards of evidence and accuracy cannot, in themselves, distinguish the more obfuscating from the more politically and intellectually stimulating stories, for many stories of historical events that are empirically accurate nonetheless distort the event's human significance and preempt further discussion.[1] Given the distortion and the stifling effects of many—even empirically valid—stories, proponents of storytelling must not only affirm storytelling's potential value but must also articulate ways to evaluate stories critically. Without critical standards relevant to the extrafactual story dimension of our representations, we cannot systematically distinguish between those stories that obstruct responsible political discussion and those stories that promote the critical thinking and discussion-based politics that, for Arendt, are storytelling's hallmark.

This chapter begins to articulate critical standards suited to storytelling. My aim is not to impose on stories a rigid method. I aim merely to begin a discussion of some general characteristics that mark those stories that, whatever their specific content or method, live up to Arendt's vision of intellectually stimulating, community-enhancing storytelling. I find resources for articulating such standards in neglected elements within the Western tradition, namely, in Kant's theory of reflective judgment. This theory, which Kant presents in his *Critique of Judgment,* offers a critical model that is suitable to storytelling insofar as Kant's principles of reflective judgment, *enlarged thought* and *communicability,* call for us to test our prejudices and to anticipate communication with others. These two goals resonate with the intellectual and political aims of Arendtean storytelling.

At the same time that I attempt to appropriate Kant's principles of reflective judgment, I recognize that Kant's principles cannot be applied to storytelling without substantial revisions. In his theory of judgment (as in his theory of reason), Kant presumes a single, ahistorical human consciousness while he reduces all human differences and emotions to distracting contingencies. As a result of these assumptions, his principles of judgment are in certain respects antithetical to the sensitivity to human differences, emotional life, and historical context that Arendt and many contemporaries find valuable in storytelling. Nevertheless, these serious limitations in Kant's theory notwithstanding, I argue that the spirit, even if not the letter, of Kant's theory reflects well the aims of Arendtean storytelling. By critically appropriating Kant's principles and reformulating them in the light of the task of storytelling, I revive the progressive impulse in our tradition for self-critical, community-situated thought while I use this critical tradition to articulate a more responsible account of storytelling.

Storytelling and Kant's Principles of Judgment

My turn to Kant's theory of judgment to develop standards for storytelling might surprise contemporary proponents of storytelling and Kant himself, but not Arendt. In her *Lectures on Kant's Political Philosophy,* Arendt argues that, although Kant presents reflective judgment as a theory of aesthetic judgment, his model of judgment applies as well to the exercise of *political* judgment in a participatory public realm. I take only a short leap from Arendt's application of reflective judgment to the field of political judgment when I apply reflective judgment to the field of political *storytelling.*

When I apply reflective judgment to storytelling, however, I also revise Kant's theory in ways that Arendt failed to do. In particular, Arendt never addressed the ahistorical, apolitical character of Kant's model of judgment. Because Arendt accepted Kant's model of judgment uncritically, Arendt's editor, Ronald Beiner, argues that Arendt leaves behind her attention to practical life when she follows Kant. When Arendt turns to Kant, says Beiner, she finally resolves the tension between the practical and the contemplative aspects of judgment by "opting wholly for the latter [contemplative] conception of judgment" (1982, 139). Ultimately, he says, Arendt's concern in her Kant lectures "is no longer a theory of *political* judgment"; that is, although Arendt examines judgment in its application to political events, she no longer (as she did in her earlier work) conceives of judgment as an activity of political actors. Instead, says Beiner, Arendt's Kant lectures (like Kant, himself) treat judgment as if it were an activity of solitary spectators (1982, 138).

I agree with Beiner that contemporaries need to exceed both Kant and Arendt in order to address more fully the practical character (and, I would add, the narrative character) of political judgment. However, I consider this rethinking of political judgment in terms of its practical and discursive aspects to be more of an *extension,* not a rejection, of Arendt's intriguing reading of Kant. To be sure, Kant in many ways presented judgment as a solitary, purely contemplative task. But this is not the side of reflective judgment that Arendt embraces. On the contrary, Arendt highlights those elements in Kant that situate the spectator within a judging community and that unite the actor and the spectator in one person; for instance, she says that, for Kant, "[s]pectators exist only in the plural" and that the "spectator sits in every actor" insofar as the actor considers the public significance of his or her activity (Arendt LK, 63).[2] Clearly, Arendt did not turn to Kant in order to recast judgment as a solitary, apolitical activity. She turned to Kant, rather, because Kant articulated critical standards that are compatible with a focus on particulars and with an interactive public realm. If her appropriation of Kant is limited, this is not because (as Beiner claims) she allows Kant to lead her away from practical life. The problem is rather that Arendt only begins to adapt Kant's theory of judgment to the political field. She never completes this task.

Below, I continue the project that Arendt begins. After briefly reviewing the relevant material in Kant, I examine how Kant's principles of judgment can apply to political judgment and, likewise, to political storytelling. Going beyond Arendt, I then examine the limits and dangers of Kant's principles. My final section suggests how we might revise Kant's principles so that they respond better to the historically situated, practical, and discursive character of political judgment qua storytelling.

Kant's Theory of Judgment

Kant presents his theory of reflective judgment as a response to the problem of validity in aesthetic judgment. Our judgments about beauty, Kant recognizes, cannot be objective. We cannot judge artworks (as Kant thought we could judge action) by a predetermined, universal standard, for the beauty of each artwork is unique. Neither can we abstract from our subjective response to the artwork, for the essence of beauty lies in our experience of it. Nonetheless, Kant argues, our aesthetic judgments can exceed mere personal taste. Our judgments can have general validity if we reflect on our subjective response in accord with the maxim of *enlarged thought:* We imagine how other people might view that same artwork; then, upon comparing our judgment with the possible judgment of others, we test and set aside our individual biases (in particular, we set aside our emotional attachment to the artwork's charm and our interest in the object's existence). We thereby approach a "universal standpoint" on the artwork that we can expect to be "communicable" to everyone (1951, 132–38).

Notwithstanding serious limitations in Kant's theory (some of which I address below) Kant's model of judgment offers an enduring insight: Not only rule-governed thought but even experience-based, particular-focused thought can be held to critical standards. Kant's maxim of enlarged thought describes how, in the absence of universal principles, we can move beyond the biases of our immediate, personal response. The broadening of perspective demanded by enlarged thought does not entail a mere survey and tally of the views of people on the street, for this would merely exchange our prejudices for the prejudices of others. Instead of such a survey approach, enlarged thought demands that we think for ourselves "in the place of everyone else" (1951, 136); that is, we imagine ourselves viewing the phenomenon from the standpoint of others and then we take responsibility for the judgment that we subsequently develop.[3] When Kant identifies the mark of such enlarged thought as *communicability,* he emphasizes the potential community accountability of our claims, even when they cannot be strictly objective (1951, 47–49, 135–38).

Reflective Judgment as Political Judgment

In her Kant lectures, Arendt affirms the broad relevance of Kant's theory of reflective judgment. She boldly presents Kant's theory of judgment as his political philosophy. Whether or not Kant would agree, Arendt makes a good case that reflective judgment presents a model of critical standards that is suitable to the political field.

Reflective judgment is relevant to political inquiry, first, because political judgment presents problems of validity similar to those presented by aesthetic judgment. When we judge the meaning of a political phenomenon (as when we judge the beauty of an artwork), we must consider the subjective response that the phenomenon, as a human phenomenon, evokes in us. Kant's maxim of enlarged thought, which directs us to take into consideration the possible reaction of others, allows us to respond subjectively to a phenomenon's moral and emotional content and yet still evaluate it in a rigorous and publicly accountable manner (LK, 14, 84–85; AR 78–79).

The maxims of enlarged thought and communicability are also suited to the political sphere insofar as they promote discussion and sociability among a diverse population. The goal of communicability promotes sociability with one's neighbors because it requires not only self-consistency but the ability to communicate one's view to others. In addition, unlike claims to objective knowledge, which tend to stifle discussion, a judgment that claims communicability invites further discussion. Arendt emphasizes the sociability that is implicit in Kant's principles when she describes enlarged thought as "train[ing] one's imagination to go visiting" (LK, 43). Like the right to visit other countries that Kant espouses in *Perpetual Peace,* the imaginative "visiting" of enlarged thought affirms a sociability within us that does not require us to think like everyone else but only to leave our familiar location and situate ourselves, temporarily, in the place of others.[4] Read in this way, enlarged thought and communicability promote broad discussion and sociability, yet without presupposing a common will or a homogeneous population. In effect, when we view the world from others' standpoints and anticipate communication with others, we recognize that others have views different than our own, while we still try to develop a judgment that we could openly present to them.

Arendt highlights these favorable political implications of "communicability" when she associates communicability with Kant's criterion of political rightness, *publicness.* Publicness is the ability of a political claim to be presented openly to the general public without defeating its purpose (Kant 1988a, 125–30). Although Kant presented publicness as a strictly formal principle of reason, Arendt relates this principle to the political goal of an open, participatory public realm (Arendt LK, 41–49).[5] Reading communicability and publicness in light of each other, Arendt notes that both standards place moral value on the publicizing of opinions, while they associate evil with "withdrawal from the public world" (LK, 49). Likewise, both standards imply care for public spaces in which ideas can be freely aired. This concern dovetails with the political aim of storytelling to maintain a participatory, discussion-based politics.

Reflective Judgment and Storytelling

Arendt does not address storytelling per se in her Kant lectures. Nonetheless, if we take seriously her earlier claim that we grapple with the human essence of a political phenomenon only when we tell it as a story, then the political "judgment" to which she refers in her lectures must have narrative form. In fact, the elements of Kant's model of reflective judgment that Arendt highlights—the focus on particulars, the subjective engagement, and the community situatedness—are those same elements that she values in storytelling. Insofar as Kant's principles of judgment are suited to political judgment, they are suited, in particular, to political judgment in the form of storytelling.

Kant's principles of judgment are relevant to storytelling, first, because they describe how we can judge responsibly even when we base our judgment on subjective experience and even when we lack general standards. These are precisely the conditions under which storytelling operates. For instance, when Arendt defends her storytelling approach to Nazism and Stalinism, she argues that storytelling is appropriate because it responds to events in terms of their inherently subjective content and their uncategorizable "phenomenal distinctness" (AR, 78–79; UP, 382).[6] In fact, her description of storytelling echoes Kant's account of reflective judgment: Kant describes reflective judgment as a process in which "the imagination in its freedom awakens the understanding," that is, our concepts are not predetermined but emerge as we reckon with particular phenomena (Kant 1951, 138); Arendt describes storytelling likewise as an activity that "proceeds from facts and events instead of intellectual affinities and influences" (Arendt AR, 80). Thus, insofar as Kant designs his principles of judgment to apply to engaged, particular-focused activity, these principles are tailor-made to storytelling.

In addition, Kant's principle of communicability is relevant to storytelling because the storyteller, unlike the presumably objective theorist, admits that she works from within the historical world that she narrates. She also admits that she has a practical goal: to help her community make sense of past phenomena in terms that resonate in their world and to stimulate further discussion of the phenomena. Such a community-situated, open-ended project cannot be held to standards of certainty or objectivity. It can, however, be held to the criterion of communicability, for the latter requires neither transcendence of perspective nor distance from the public world but only a consideration of diverse perspectives. Communicability is not only compatible with storytelling's socially situated, engaged approach but is vital to its aim of promoting open, inclusive discussion.

The Limits of Kant's Principles

Arendt highlights the virtues of Kant's principles of enlarged thought and communicability, but she does not address the limits of these principles. I here identify ways that Kant's principles fail to do justice either to the complexities of political judgment qua storytelling or to Kant's own aim of community-accountable thought. This critical analysis prepares the way for me to revise Kant's principles so that they retain Kant's community-minded spirit but respond better to the challenges of political judgment.

Pronouncing Judgment or Telling a Story?

If we apply Kant's principles of judgment to the political field, we need first of all to address a structural difference between aesthetic and political judgment. Kant's art critic reflects on his perceptual experience of an object, arrives at a judgment in his mind, and then pronounces his judgment. The critic who judges the meaning of a political phenomenon, however, pursues a more language-dependent, hermeneutic task. Hermeneutic work is demanded by the nature of the political phenomenon because, unlike Kant's artwork, the political phenomenon is not a perceptual object but rather a boundless chain of lived deeds and sufferings (Arendt HC, 190). Thus the political phenomenon does not exist as a single entity until a critic selects a particular set of incidents to interpret as an "event." Moreover, this political event not only generates a perceptual and affective experience for the critic but is *in itself* a collection of lived experiences. Such experiences appear for the critic only as signs of their lived reality. The critic encounters such signs as appearing actions or, more likely, physical traces and written representations of those actions. She must therefore "translate" such appearing signs into a language that signifies their "invisible" lived qualities. While the critic may respond emotionally to the appearing political phenomenon, her response presupposes her interpretation of signs of the phenomenon qua lived phenomenon.

Furthermore, if we accept Arendt's earlier account of the storylike structure of political phenomena (the account that she presents in her book *The Human Condition* and that I analyze in chapter one), then the critic who interprets the meaning of a political phenomenon interprets this in specifically *narrative* language. In effect, the political critic's

"judgment" consists of the entire written narrative, for when the critic
is a storyteller, her response to her subject matter "does not primarily
reside in the explicit value judgments" but is "an aspect of the narrative
itself" (Benhabib 1990, 186). For instance, when Arendt judges Nazism
and Stalinism in *The Origins of Totalitarianism,* she identifies actors
and actions, relates these together within a narrative pattern, and
describes these in analytical as well as literary prose. Arendt's "judgment" as well as the events that she judges gain articulation only
through the narrative. Thus, if we want to apply Kant's principles of
judgment meaningfully to political judgment, then we must exceed
Kant and must examine what it can mean for these principles to guide
hermeneutic work and to be exhibited by a narrative text.

Imagination or Actual Dialogue?

In addition to the need to reformulate Kant's principles of judgment in
the context of narration, any attempt to apply Kant's principles to
political judgment must also address problems internal to Kant's
theory. These problems burden Kant's original theory of reflective
judgment, but they become particularly apparent when we apply the
theory to the political field. As I have noted, Kant formulated enlarged
thought as a purely imaginary process because he wished to avoid the
problem of the critic simply exchanging his views for the views of
others, without taking responsibility for those views. While Kant's
concern for active and responsible thought is certainly a legitimate one,
his assumption that a critic could cancel his own biases by simply
imagining other standpoints is problematic. As feminist theorists have
argued, a critic does not confront views radically different from his own
unless he engages with actual other people of different social and
cultural locations. In Benhabib's terms, the critic must engage with
"concrete others" in order to genuinely test his own views (1992,
158–68). The challenge of genuinely enlarged thought, therefore, is for
the critic to broaden his views in light of the actual views of others, yet
while still somehow thinking for himself and taking responsibility for
his own beliefs.

Political judgment presents an additional complication because the
political critic has two levels of "other standpoints" to investigate. If a
standpoint (to paraphrase Arendt) is "the place where one stands, the
conditions to which one is subject" (LK, 43), then a political phenomenon itself consists of a collection of standpoints. The political critic
must therefore investigate not only the views of other spectators but
also the historically specific standpoints that *make up* the political
phenomenon.[7] An investigation of such historically specific stand-

points requires extensive practical work, such as physically traveling to other people's communities, learning other people's languages, and listening attentively and patiently to (or carefully reading) other people's stories.

When Kant formulates enlarged thought as a mere imaginary exercise, he overlooks the practical work needed to engage the standpoint of historically specific others. Moreover, he risks silencing those people whose actual views play no role in his model. This was probably not Kant's intention, as he developed his model out of the legitimate concern for broad-minded and responsible thought. Nevertheless, when Kant proposes that a theorist can achieve enlarged thought by means of a mere thought experiment, he risks authorizing the theorist, or the "expert," to speak on behalf of an entire community—even when that theorist has never actually interacted with any community members. In addition, when Kant presumes that enlarged thought can be achieved through imagination, he obscures the need for practical struggle to create the social and cultural conditions that are necessary for a genuine exchange of diverse views. The social conditions necessary for a genuine exchange of views might include, for instance, literacy and education programs that empower people to tell their own stories or publicly supported radio and history projects that foster the recording and dissemination of diverse historical perspectives.

My point here is not that we should do away with imaginative perspective taking but rather that imagination, by itself, in not enough. Imagination does not substitute for the practical work of listening to concrete others. Nor does it substitute for the social task of creating public spaces in which those who have been excluded from official knowledge production can publicize their own stories. "Enlarged thought" can be applied meaningfully to political judgment only if we ensure that the critic's imaginative work does not replace but instead supplements and enhances actual public discussion.

Painless Visiting or Disorienting Travel?

What happens . . . when a scholar changes
perspectives within scholarly narration without
changing social position?

—Carole Anne Taylor[8]

In addition to the practical work of investigating historically specific standpoints, enlarged thought ultimately demands some imaginative work, also, in order for the critic to understand the lived significance of other people's situations. Even with respect to the imaginative component of enlarged thought, however, Kant oversimplifies the imaginative task. When Kant (and Arendt following Kant) proposes that we think for ourselves "in the place of everyone else," he assumes that we can imaginatively transfer our thinking mind to the social and cultural location of others. Arendt recognizes the need to cross social and cultural boundaries in our imaginative perspective taking, for she notes that standpoints "differ . . . from one class or group as compared to another" (LK, 43). But can we really leave behind our own class, race, gender, and culture when we "visit" the standpoint of another? Recent analysis of subject-positions indicates that we cannot so easily, even in imagination, detach our thinking minds from our social standpoints.[9] Everyday language also registers the difficulty of cleanly separating our social standpoints from the rest of our selves: We call social positions "social *identities.*" The result of this close connection between our social standpoints and our innermost selves is that when we try to "visit" the standpoint of another we inevitably bring along extra baggage; that is, we inevitably harbor assumptions bound up with our own social and cultural standpoint.

Arendt unwittingly illustrates these dangers when she tries to use Kant's model to "visit" the perspective of someone who lives in a slum. If Arendt (in the skeptical words of one her commentators[10]) "make[s] visiting sound so easy," then this is because, despite her intentions, she never really leaves the comfort of her "home," that is, her own standpoint-related worldview. Seeking to imagine the perspective of a slum dweller, Arendt considers herself—a German Jewish North American professional—living in a slum. She never considers how the slum might be experienced by people of different social and cultural backgrounds. An Afro-American man with minimal formal education or a Salvadoran woman without full citizenship, for instance, would each experience the slum differently than someone of Arendt's social position. They would each be treated differently by welfare agencies, job agencies, cab drivers, and policemen, would see different images of people like themselves in the media, and would face different possible ways of earning money, and different kinds of threats to their personal safety. Arendt's conclusion, that the slum exhibits "poverty and misery," does express the negative character of the slum; however, it fails to do justice to the myriad and profound ways that living in a slum may affect some people's basic experiences of themselves and their world.

Perhaps even more importantly, insofar as Arendt carries with her into the slum her own standpoint-related assumptions, she fails to appreciate how the slum can throw into relief the limits of her own worldview. For instance, viewing the slum from her middle-class perspective, Arendt determines the slum to be a place of mere victimization, the opposite of home and the absence of creative energy. This interpretation of the slum presupposes that "home" is a place of unequivocal comfort and that "action" is the clear public expression of one's will. She can take for granted these notions of home and action because they belong to the worldview of the dominant culture.[11] If, however, we take seriously the perspective of someone who lives in a specific slum, someone for whom the area, notwithstanding its deprivations, is also a place of heritage, community, and resistant activity, then we would likely see a richer view of the slum as well as of home and action. For instance, when residents of Chicago's infamous Cabrini Green public housing project organized resistance against the city's plans to tear down the "slum" that was their neighborhood, they challenged the dominant culture's (and Arendt's) simple opposition between slum and home and between social marginalization and historical action.[12]

North American and European feminists who seek to address the perspectives of Third World women often fall into a similar trap. Despite our intentions to globalize our perspective, many of us unwittingly retain our accustomed theoretical reference points. We reduce women in other countries to our own "objective indicators," such as literacy and fertility rates, or we judge women in terms of a concept of "agency" that presumes agency to be the purview of public actors and successful organized movements. As a result, we wrongly reduce the women we seek to learn about to mere passive victims, failing to understand the specific kinds of struggles and resistant activities that many women pursue. We also overlook how the perspective from Third World women's lives challenges the neutrality of our own interpretive frameworks and categories (Alarcón 1990, 357–64; Lugones 1987, 9–12, 17; Mohanty 1991b; Taylor 1993, 58–69).

I emphasize these difficulties of "visiting" another standpoint not to suggest that we should give up thinking beyond the constraints of our own standpoint. My concern is rather that, when we pursue the perspective of another, we must be mindful of the ways that our own standpoint constrains our understanding of the other's world. If we want to begin to resist these constraints, then we must forgo the comforts of our familiar worldview. We must be prepared to confront the disorienting, unsettling views of ourselves and our world that genuine engagement with another standpoint entails. In addition, if one of us from the dominant culture who has grown accustomed to epistemic agency considers the perspective of someone from a more marginalized social location, we must be ready to meet challenges to our own epistemic authority; for the other's perspective may reveal that our taken-for-granted authority is actually a privilege that is built on the exclusion of others' voices (Alarcón 1990, 359–64; Lugones 1987, 9–12, 17; Smith 1987, 19–36, 56–57, 74–77; Taylor 1993, 60–73). Grappling with such challenges to our own ingrained presuppositions, self-image, and epistemic authority demands more emotional and intellectual work than either Kant or Arendt acknowledge.

Individual or Community Prejudices?

Kant's model of judgment is also limited because, despite Kant's championing of prejudice-testing, Kant ultimately does not say enough about how we can test our most deeply held prejudices. Kant formulates enlarged thought so as to test individual biases; however, philosophers have since shown that our most entrenched biases are not individual but community wide. Hermeneutic theorists, for instance, explain that culture-wide, tradition-given prejudices structure a community's language and constitute the very medium in which people apprehend the world (Gadamer [1960] 1991, 573).[13] Marxist theorists offer further insight into the development and force of community-wide presuppositions. When the more socially powerful groups have greater control over the institutions that produce and distribute knowledge, those groups can widely disseminate their views and present their views as if they were universal truths. Such socially produced "common sense" beliefs inform academic and popular discourses and, consequently, affect the whole community's way of thinking. Such beliefs thus tend to remain unnoticed and untested, even when we consider the perspective of many different people (Marx 1997, 438–40; Harding 1991, 287, 311; Smith 1987, 19–20).

Community-wide, language-embedded prejudices present a particular challenge for enlarged thought. In the context of such prejudices, a critic must somehow scrutinize presuppositions that are pervasive in her society and implicit in her language. In the case of political judgment, such prejudices also take the form of narrative matrices and story images that structure "common sense" history. Thus enlarged thought, for the political critic, demands that the critic be able to reflect critically on the basic narrative resources that prefigure her interpretation of events.

Superceding or Confronting Differences?

Finally, if we apply "communicability" to political judgment, then we must rethink this standard so that it does not require that the critic somehow supercede particular perspectives and practical interests. In Kant's account, the communicability of an aesthetic judgment is based on its abstraction from individual biases such that the judgment is "valid *a priori* for everyone" (1951, 32, 35). Such a "universal standpoint" on the artwork is possible because aesthetic value (in Kant's account) consists of the pleasure that an artwork produces in our mind by virtue of the harmony of the artwork's formal qualities with the structure of our basic cognitive faculties. Since these cognitive structures (according to Kant) are the same for everyone, everyone will experience the same pleasure in an artwork, so long as they attend to aesthetic form and set aside their emotional reaction to the artwork's content as well as their practical interest in the artwork's existence. Insofar as the critic focuses exclusively on the contemplative pleasure he receives from the artwork's form, his judgment will be at once aesthetically sound and universally communicable (1951, 38–46, 132, 135).

Whether or not Kant's notion of a bias-free universal standpoint makes sense for aesthetic judgment, it is certainly not sensible for political judgment. When someone judges a political phenomenon, she cannot set aside particularities of perspectives but, on the contrary, must attend closely to the different ways that differently situated people experienced the same phenomenon. Attention to such differences of perspective is crucial here because a political phenomenon, as Arendt explains in her political phenomenology, is a shared phenomenon "that everyone sees and hears from a different position" (HC, 57). It is a public occurrence that comprises a constellation of deeds and sufferings in a plurality of individual lives. Thus a political phenomenon is fundamentally multifaceted and differences of perspective are essential to its meaning. Furthermore, the variation of experience across different standpoints is systematically determined by social and political institutions that are themselves constitutive of the political world. Thus a political critic cannot abstract from the differences among differently situated actors' (and spectators') experiences of a political phenomenon without destroying the fundamentally heterogeneous structure of the phenomenon. Although Arendt elides the importance of systematically determined differences of perspective in her Kant lectures, she foregrounds precisely such differences in her historical work. For instance, when she narrates the modern nation-state's commitment to "the rights of man," she highlights the uneven effects of this agenda for national citizens and refugees: It guaranteed the former legally protected rights while it excluded the latter from the community of legal equality (OT, 269–302). This difference in the way that different social groups experience "the Rights of Man" is crucial to Arendt's analysis, for it marks the uneven application of law that Arendt identifies as one key "pre-totalitarian" element in Western Europe. Arendt also recognizes the importance of systematically determined variation of experience across different standpoints when she claims that "indignation" is central to the meaning of the British industrial revolution; for this indignation stems precisely from the wide discrepancy between the way that working-class and upper-class people experienced the same historical developments (AR, 78).

While the storyteller must attend closely to standpoint-related differences of perspective on the historical phenomenon that she narrates, she must also acknowledge the way that her own narration of events affects politics in the present. In other words, unlike Kant's art critic, who remains in the intellectual realm, the storyteller is at once an intellectual critic and a political actor. She is a critic insofar as she studies historical phenomena from retrospect, but she is a political actor insofar as her way of telling the story contributes to contemporary debates over the community's identity and projects. In light of this contribution of stories to political discourse, Arendt emphasizes the general political function of stories: Stories can bring more aspects of political phenomena under discussion and can thereby sustain a vibrant, participatory public life. In addition to this general public role of stories, however, any story is also political in the more partisan sense of affecting power relations. This is so, first, because even when a story encourages inclusive, critical-minded public discussion, some groups have a greater interest than others in promoting open discussion. (Some groups have an interest in restricting discussion, as history has shown too well, most recently, for instance, with Campus Watch, a group that seeks to silence teachers who criticize Bush administration policy.[14]) Furthermore, even stories that foster lively public discussion can be written in a plurality of ways, and different ways of telling the story promote attention to different people's concerns and interests.

Given the diverse experiences that make up a political phenomenon and given that any story will privilege some people's experiences and concerns over others, no story can present a neutral "universal standpoint" on a political event. The challenge in applying "communicability" to political narration, therefore, is to consider how a story might be widely communicable to a diverse public, even when that story inevitably serves the interests of some parts of the public more than others. Finally, if we apply "communicability" to storytelling, then we must rethink this standard as a standard that reflects not only epistemological but also political aims, in particular, the aim of sustaining a debate-centered, participatory politics.

Toward Communicable Stories

Certainly, Kant did not formulate his principles of enlarged thought and communicability in ways adequate to storytelling. Nevertheless, a story of a public event must exhibit some type of "enlarged thought" testing of biases and some type of "communicability" with others if it is to promote the historically sensitive thinking and the inclusive, lively public debate that Arendt values in storytelling. The challenge is for a story to promote the spirit of enlarged thought and communicability—test prejudices and anticipate communication with others—even while the story confronts community-wide, language-rooted prejudices, attends to the radical otherness of the perspectives it tries to understand, and acknowledges the irreducible differences within its community as well as its own inevitable partiality.

With the aid of two skillful storytellers, Arendt in *The Origins of Totalitarianism* and Susan Griffin in *A Chorus of Stones: The Private Life of War* (1992), I identify some narrative approaches that meet this challenge. I describe these narrative approaches as ones marked by "enlarged thought" and "communicability," for they exhibit and they likewise promote in their readers the open-mindedness and the public accountability that Kant's principles affirm. When, however, I invoke Kant's principles to describe Arendt's and Griffin's texts, I not only renew Kantian themes of prejudice testing and community accountability, but I also recast these themes in light of post-Enlightenment insights into the depths of our prejudices and the heterogeneity of our communities.

Difference-Sensitive "Visiting"

Arendt and Griffin, notwithstanding the uniqueness of each of their writing styles, meet the challenge for a more difference-sensitive, more discussion-enhancing kind of perspective taking in similar ways. Both authors use elements in their familiar world as a starting point for imagining specific elements of distant worlds. At the same time, both also warn against oversimplifying the imaginative task, for both thematize their difficulties in trying to make sense of other people's lives. Likewise, both closely examine the testimonies of others while they also attend to the gaps and incoherencies in those testimonies. In so doing, both Arendt and Griffin provide readers with points of entry into strange worlds, yet they do so without either reducing those worlds to familiar places or asking readers simply to mimic others' testimonies, as if those testimonies could provide us with certain truth. Neither do they skirt the challenges that strange perspectives can present to our own authority and worldviews.

In *Totalitarianism,* for instance, Arendt pursues understanding of Nazism in a manner very different from her painless mental excursion into the slum. In this historical work, Arendt describes her attempt to comprehend the other's world as a challenging, endless project that casts a disturbing light on her own heritage. For instance, seeking to understand the Nazi death camps as a human phenomenon, she peruses historical records, including survivors' memoirs and government documents. At the same time, she does not simply summarize these texts as if they offered straightforward information. Instead, she combines quotations from these texts with reflections on the near impossibility, for anyone who has not lived through the concentration camps, of imagining the camps' lived reality (OT, 440–47). She also highlights the camps' shocking character by describing them in jolting, oxymoronic prose; the camps were a place of "living corpses," a place where human nature was systematically destroyed and "inanimate men" were led "like ghastly marionettes" to their execution (441, 453, 455). We can gain some comprehension of these seemingly unthinkable monstrosities, she says, but only if we confront them as part of our own world, traceable to elements within our own history. Thus, without glossing over its horror, Arendt situates Nazism in relation to Western European history, tracing its beginnings to European imperialism, race-thinking, and exclusionary national law. In this way, Arendt calls on us to understand life under Nazism while she makes clear that the attempt to do so will raise difficult questions about our own world.

On the surface, Griffin pursues a project very different from Arendt's. In *A Chorus of Stones,* Griffin rethinks recent wars in light of their emotional, bodily, and interpersonal dimensions. These elements of so-called "private-life," she suggests, have been omitted from history proper at the expense of distorting our understanding of historical phenomena as well as perpetuating the practices of denial that sustain institutionalized violence. To recover these suppressed aspects of history, Griffin collects stories from an array of individuals whose private lives have intersected with recent wars, including, for instance, scientists who worked on the atom bomb, Japanese atom bomb survivors, North American and German soldiers and generals, and workers who mined and processed weapons-grade uranium in ignorance or in denial of the long-term health effects on themselves and their children. Her style is as radical as her content. She strategically interweaves stories of historical actors with tales of her own research, bits of historical and scientific data, present-tense imaginative reconstructions of historical experiences, and first-person accounts of her attempts to compare her own life to the lives of historical characters.

Despite Griffin's highly literary, personal style, however, Griffin's approach to perspective taking echoes Arendt's. Like Arendt, Griffin demands that we confront the uncomfortable views of ourselves that accompany any genuine attempt to understand another's standpoint. While Arendt asks Western readers to understand Nazism in light of its connection to their own Western European heritage, Griffin asks us to address the denials, the self-deception, and the emotional numbing that run through war by examining similar phenomena in our own communities and own lives. She begins, for instance, with a confession that is at once more personal than anything in Arendt's historiography and analogous to Arendt's joint investigation of Nazism and familiar history: "I am not free," Griffin admits, "of the condition that I describe here" (1992, 3). She proceeds to confront not only secrets and denials that underlie state violence but also "many closely guarded family secrets that I kept, and many that were kept from me" (3). This personal examination is integral to her historical analysis, for such introspection (similar to Arendt's re-examination of her own history) allows her to make some human sense of seemingly alien affairs.

For instance, Griffin explores the standpoint of World War I ground soldiers through creating a collage of historical and personal stories: tales of specific soldiers who suffered shell-shock, a fictional exploration of a soldier's internal struggle with military discipline, and reflections on her own aphonia following her parent's divorce. This multivoiced narrative does not equate the soldiers' difficulties with Griffin's childhood trauma, for the various stories remain distinct. Each of the stories also remains fragmented, an incomplete reckoning with the human experiences of battle or family breakup. Nonetheless, Griffin's imaginary explorations and her scrutiny of her own trauma provide guideposts to understanding the paralyzing effects of shell-shock; in terms of the theory of storytelling I presented in chapter one, her reflections offer "story images" of emotional distress and physical paralysis that sensitize us to experiences that official narratives as well as our own

everyday consciousness would rather overlook. As these images make
the debilitating effects of shell-shock more comprehensible, they also
bring into focus the stranger, less comfortable aspects of Griffin's (and
perhaps our own) home life.

In another painfully honest passage, Griffin recounts her efforts to
make sense of Heinrich Himmler's extreme antisemitism. In the process, she compares Himmler's antisemitism to her own grandfather's
attempt to define himself in opposition to Jews (1992, 129–37). Again,
Griffin does not reduce one man's story to the other's; rather, she shows
how honest probing of her familiar world unearths common themes
with a seemingly alien world. Her work encourages readers to use
stories from their own lives to gain insight into the standpoint of others
while it warns of the self-exposure and self-criticism that such comparisons entail.

Griffin also follows Arendt insofar as she practices extensive historical research, while at the same time she acknowledges the elusiveness
and the incompleteness of the tales that she researches. For instance,
when she recounts her interviews with Japanese survivors of Hiroshima, she attends not only to their words but also to their silences and
times when language fails them. In her report of Ota, a man who was
severely wounded by the bomb and who had laid for days with other
swollen, maggot-ridden, bleeding, half-alive bodies, Griffin emphasizes
his difficulties in telling the story: "'Now to speak of it,' he told us, 'is
almost unbelievable'" (1992, 102). As Ota described being reunited
with his sister thirty-two years after the explosion, "he touched his
throat and said he was not able to speak" (104). Similarly, when Griffin
interviews Yoko, a woman left orphaned by the bomb, she recounts not
only her story of how she lost her family in the aftermath of the
explosion but also her "mimed gestures of shyness and fear," the
lingering effects of suffering that cannot be verbally shared, suffering
that Griffin can only begin to imagine by comparing Yoko's experiences
to memories of her own broken family (97–98).[15]

With their engaged and inward-looking approaches and their self-
consciously experimental prose, neither Arendt nor Griffin pretend to
offer conclusive knowledge of other lives. Instead, they both make clear
that their stories are historically situated, creative explorations of a few
aspects of another's affairs. On the one hand, such stories serve as
provocative invitations to other worlds, encouraging us to continue
exploring in our own imagination what it would be like to experience
another's world. On the other hand, their research-intensive and yet
still inconclusive stories remind us that imagination is only one element
of the difficult practical work of reckoning with another person's

standpoint and that, at best, we can gain only partial and tentative understanding of that standpoint. The authors underscore this caution when they show their own struggles to make sense of historical documents and testimonies and when they reveal those texts to be themselves incomplete reckonings with sometimes unspeakable experiences. Their narratives thus encourage both imaginative perspective taking and concrete research of others' testimonies while they also affirm the need for humility and tentativeness in our resulting interpretation of other's affairs. Their openly experimental styles and qualified claims likewise imply the need for public spaces in which others can criticize our narratives and tell their own stories.[16]

Testing Community-Wide Prejudices

I have argued that Kant's approach to prejudice testing is inadequate because it addresses only individual prejudices, whereas the most trenchant and influential prejudices are those that are endemic to the community. Community-wide prejudices are not easy to test. Gadamer, however, suggests one way that we can test, even if not disregard, community-wide prejudices. In his Heidegger-informed theory of text interpretation, Gadamer, in a deliberate departure from Kant, argues that we cannot possibly rid our thought of prejudices. Prejudices are constitutive of our received language and, moreover, such language-rooted prejudices provide a framework of meaning without which we could not make sense of human works. Thus we cannot help but approach a text by projecting onto that text anticipated meanings, or "foremeanings," that are informed by our culture's language-transmitted ways of understanding the world ([1960] 1991, 265–85).

Despite Gadamer's anti-Kantian affirmation of prejudice, however, Gadamer implicitly continues and strengthens Kant's project of testing prejudices when he describes what it means to understand a text. Genuine understanding of a text, says Gadamer, proceeds with *methodological consciousness*. Methodological consciousness does not require that we approach a text free of bias; however, it does demand that we remain open to the specificity of the text "so that the text can present itself in all its otherness and thus assert its own truth against [our] foremeanings" (Gadamer [1960] 1991, 269). Like Kant's maxim of enlarged thought, Gadamer's notion of methodological consciousness describes how we can test our prejudices without assuming an Archimedean standpoint. Exceeding Kant, methodological consciousness tests and revises our language-rooted, culture-wide prejudices. We can test and adjust (even if we cannot set aside) the language-transmitted prejudices that underlie our reading of a text, says Gadamer, if we are "sensitive to the text's alterity" and attend to how the text before us resists the meanings that we impose on it ([1960] 1991, 269).

Storytellers can practice their own kind of methodological consciousness insofar as they thematize the tradition-given narrative resources that inevitably prefigure their interpretation of historical events. To do so, they must neither ignore nor reject received narrative paradigms but must find ways to test those paradigms with respect to specific historical phenomena. Although this is no easy task, both Arendt and Griffin demonstrate possible ways to pursue such "narrative methodological consciousness." In *Totalitarianism,* for instance, Arendt tests the limits of the dominant paradigm of "progress." This paradigm presents history as a continual and inexorable advancement of reason and morality that culminates in modern Western neoliberal institutions and that is threatened only by forces external to Western civilization. Significantly, Arendt does not simply exchange the narrative of progress for an equally reductive narrative of doom but instead explores the limits of the progress scheme for understanding Nazism and Stalinism. As she tries to understand Nazism and Stalinism by situating them within Western European history, she begins to destabilize the progress paradigm, for she reveals "pre-totalitarian" elements that exist within the presumed pillars of progress; for instance, within modern self-governed nations, she reveals the presence of persecuted minorities and homeless refugees who have no nation that represents them; within the jurisdiction of modern national law, she reveals noncitizens who are excluded from legal equality; and, within our acclaimed global institutions, she identifies a politics that reduces public life to the expansion of power. Her attempt to negotiate the history of Nazism and Stalinism with the history of progress thus retains familiar bearings of Western history, such as national law, national self-rule, and global interconnectedness; however, her story also challenges us to rethink these centerpieces of Western history in light of historical developments that resist the "progress" paradigm.

Arendt likewise both acknowledges and problematizes the Enlightenment worldview when she invokes the norm of "human dignity" to assess the dangers that totalitarianism presents. With her appeal to "dignity," Arendt accepts that she and her readers are situated within an Enlightenment interpretive framework that allows her to identify "dignity" as something of value in human life, something that our institutions should strive to protect. At the same time, however, when she foregrounds instances of the destruction of human dignity within our own heritage, she challenges the Enlightenment interpretation of dignity as an innate human property that Western institutions une-quivocally affirm (OT, ix, 274–302, 447)

In her own way, Griffin also tests preconceived narrative frame-works. In particular, she tests the standard narrative matrix that structures histories of war. This standard narrative matrix presumes that war begins with a public declaration of hostilities, ends with a victory for one side, takes place on a (masculine) battlefield, and is structured as a zero-sum competition between unified nations. Griffin tests these assumptions by interweaving within her history of recent wars elements of "private life" that have interfaced with these wars. When (in Gadamerian fashion) she engages this personal experience "in all its otherness" and allows it to "assert its own truth against [our] foremeanings," she does not simply replace the political with the personal but destabilizes basic cultural presuppositions about war. For instance, Griffin problematizes the battle-centered focus of the stand-ard representation of war when she follows individual lives as they move in and out of battlefields. She follows with Gadamerian sensitiv-ity the troubled family lives of Appalachian mineworkers who lost sons to the second world war, the psychological turmoil of a Russian immigrant who, upon returning to the states after a special forces unit in Vietnam, engaged in criminal activity and murder, and the physical and emotional trauma of a U.S. Marine Corps officer who was subjected to clandestine radiation testing by the U.S. military and who the Pentagon denied had participated in any tests when he fell ill to leukemia. Griffin shows these phenomena to be integral to the public events we call war, and yet they defy the nation-based "characters" and the treaty-marked "conclusions" that have structured our interpreta-tion of war.

In addition to complexifying the actor-units and the boundaries of the standard war narrative, Griffin also problematizes the rules of "objectivity" that underlie the conventional narrative. The standard narrative of war (in accord with historical discourse, more generally) is structured by rules of objectivity that dictate a focus on impersonal "public" events and an exclusion of emotional, bodily, and otherwise "subjective" aspects of life. By strategically recuperating the subjective elements that "objective" historiography excludes, Griffin indicates the gendered and the political character of this exclusion. For instance, in one passage, Griffin mixes standard historical classifications with unspoken, unclassifiable moments of battle. On the one hand, she identifies the World War I soldier that she narrates in conventional terms: The individual is "Captain Arthur Agius, 3rd Battalion, Royal Fusiliers, 56th Division" and the context is "the Battle of the Somme."

On the other hand, however, she defamiliarizes these standard historical markers when she places "Captain" and "Battle" in the same paragraph with a description of Aguis's limp body and his uncontrollable crying upon the death of his friend (1992, 244). By leaving Aguis's affective responses to battle and the standard battle categories in tension with one another, Griffin problematizes both the cultural ideal of the brave soldier and the presumed "objectivity" of war historiography, for she indicates how both of these ideals presuppose the active censoring of "feminine" elements that pervade the battle experience.

Elsewhere, Griffin highlights the politics of "objective" war narratives by exploring more closely the experiences that lie behind "shellshock" and the discursive operations that censor such experiences. When she examines the existential conflict that the battlefield paralysis of soldiers indicates but that the rules of public language and objective historiography systematically efface, and when she thematizes this effacement, Griffin reveals the complicity of war historiography with the rationalizing of war and the suppression of dissent. In one passage, for instance, Griffin examines the muted character of a soldier's experience with reference to Elaine Showalter, who explains that shellshock "is *a silent complaint* against masculinity": It is a somatic reaction against masculine norms of discipline and bravery that is silent, in part, because our public language does not allow men to be characterized in terms of "feminine" speechlessness and powerlessness (Griffin 1992, 239, her emphasis).[17] Griffin gives voice to this censored experience through a fictional recreation of the kind of struggle against social norms that might leave a soldier immobile and speechless. She shifts from third-to second-person voice as her imaginative journey becomes increasingly vivid.

> At the sight and sound of flying shrapnel, bullets, explosions, his flesh shrinks, his head ducks, his whole body cowers, even though he rails at himself, calling himself *coward, poltroon, sissy.*
>
> Not the idea of death but a wall of flame, not the abstract notion of sacrifice but the bodily knowledge that just under your foot, as you take your next step, there may be a mine. . . .
>
> You are caught then between these two, forced into a no-man's-land between the social body and the body you were born with which is too much like a woman's body. If you turn in one direction you betray the honor of your gender. You are, as Homer said, unmanned. But your body of birth will not obey. Refuses movement. . . .

But your mind will not admit its complaint. You cannot put what you are feeling into words. You were among the bravest, after all (239).

By imaginatively reconstructing the bodily and emotional impulses that overwhelm abstract ideas of sacrifice and that lead the soldier to shrink and cower in the face of bullets, and by inviting us to imagine ourselves in the soldier's situation, Griffin not only theorizes but helps to make palpable the experiences that the terms "battle," "soldier," and "sacrifice" only obscure. In addition, by thematizing the private language, such as "sissy," that is available to register the muted experiences, she highlights the misogyny that maintains both military discipline and the banishment of "private" experiences from public discussion. Finally, by exploring the soldier's paralyzing conflict between his intuitive aversion to battle and his internalized male norms, a conflict that objectivity historiography can, at best, call "shell-shock," Griffin reveals the biases inherent to "objective" historical discourse. She indicates that a discourse that refuses recognition to emotional and bodily life implicitly legitimizes war by making war appear "masculine" and silencing dissent.

When Arendt and Griffin foreground tensions between received narrative paradigms and specific historical phenomena, they pursue enlarged thought further than Kant himself, for they destabilize not mere individual biases but language-rooted, community-wide prejudices. At the same time, they do not simply debunk social prejudices but also engage historical phenomena in such a way as to point toward richer, more nuanced conceptual frameworks for our future storytelling. This revision and refinement of our community's narrative resources resonates with Kant's goal of prejudice testing while it also fulfills the aim of Arendtian storytelling to expand and invigorate public discussion of our history in light of the complexities of specific historical phenomena.

Confronting the Social Production of Prejudices

Ultimately, we can test community-wide prejudices effectively only if we confront their social production and social effects. Marx and Marxist-oriented feminist standpoint theorists emphasize that the prejudices that prevail in a society are those that are circulated by dominant social groups and that rationalize dominant social institutions. No one escapes the influence of such ruling beliefs; however, dominant social groups benefit from ruling beliefs while the more marginalized groups endure the contradictions of those beliefs and the institutions they rationalize in resulting practical conditions in their lives; for instance, many workers remain impoverished under "prosperity," the poorest populations, often communities of color, live by the pollution left by "progress," and women tend to mediate between spheres of life, such as "nature" and "culture," that dominant worldviews and institutions separate. We can therefore best test the limits of ruling beliefs if we view the world from the standpoint of people who daily confront those limits and the contradictions of those beliefs (Dichiro 1996; Harding 1991, 10–12, 119–33, 149–52; Hartsock 1983; Marx 1997, 287–300, 438–40; Smith 1987, 49–100). I pursue feminist standpoint theory and its relation to storytelling further in chapter six. Here my point is simply that standpoint theory offers yet another guideline for enlarged-thought storytelling: Stories can better test community-wide prejudices if they narrate historical events from the perspective of socially and culturally marginalized lives.

The challenge for enlarged-thought storytelling is to use the standpoint from marginalized lives to test dominant beliefs and yet still respect Kant's concern not to passively repeat others' views. Griffin demonstrates one way that this can be done. Griffin focuses on lives that have suffered the concealed costs and contradictions of military institutions; however, she narrates these lives in a manner that prevents readers from simply mimicking these people's stories as "truth." Her unabashedly literary, engaged prose and her open-ended collage of story fragments makes clear that the text offers no single, neat truth for easy repetition. At the same time, the strategically composed narrative does indicate historical and thematic interconnections among various individuals' affairs and invites readers to further investigate these connections. When a reader pursues these connections, she will not find a certain historical truth, but she may gain critical insight into prevailing social beliefs; for instance, if a reader pursues the connections Griffin sketches between militarism and systematic violence against emotional and interpersonal life, she will likely encounter contradictions in the identification of the military with "security"; and, if a reader pursues the similarities that Griffin traces among the kind of attitudes and values that sustain military practices in different nations, she will likely encounter gaps in the Manichean logic that would have us identify with an all-good side that is defined in opposition to an all-evil enemy. Although not in themselves a coherent worldview, such gaps and contradictions in ruling beliefs encourage readers to rethink their received worldview in light of new problems and perspectives. In this way, Griffin uses the perspective from marginalized lives not to ground certain truths but to encourage readers' own "enlarged-thought" testing of received truths.

Communicability in Light of Differences

Finally, we must ask how a story can be widely communicable, even when the community comprises a plurality of perspectives and when a story can never represent every perspective equally. In her analysis of political decision making, Lisa Disch suggests a form of communicability that is compatible with irreducible differences of perspective and inevitable partiality. Disch asks how a political decision can be accountable and communicable to a diverse public, even if it is not politically neutral. Recognizing that no policy decision can resolve all conflicts of interest, Disch argues that a decision can nonetheless exhibit "communicability" (or, as she prefers, "publicity") if the decision publicly acknowledges its partiality. Specifically, the decision should include a public record of different groups' varying interpretations of the situation as well as a record of how the decision will affect diverse groups (1994, 210–20). In this way, different standpoints are publicly recognized, even if they are not all equally served by the final decision. In addition, unlike policy decisions cloaked in the rhetoric of "general interest" or "universal principles," those decisions that publicly acknowledge their partiality and exclusions will reveal their temporary, imperfect status and will thus encourage further discussion (1994, chapter 7).[18]

Disch's model of difference-sensitive communicability can be adapted to storytelling. Like the policy decisions of concern to Disch, a story cannot transcend differences of perspective. A story can, however, demonstrate sensitivity to how differently located people experience the same event. Such a story, analogously to Disch's policy decision, is accountable and communicable to a diverse public, even if it is not neutral. Stories are particularly suited to this difference-sensitive communicability, for stories treat the diverse experiences of different characters who share a common context. Arendt demonstrates this potential sensitivity of stories to standpoint-related differences when she distinguishes the effects of nation-state building on citizens and on stateless people. Griffin shows how stories can also address differences within units that have been considered a single entity; for instance, she traces conflicts between soldiers and generals and she relates tales of people who have been exploited as military test victims by their own government. In general, a story can be communicable, in Disch's revised sense, if it attends to differences of experiences both across and within social groups. A communicable story must also allow for the possibility of additional perspectives on the event that the narrator has not anticipated, which it can do by acknowledging the contingent and revisable status of its own character-units.

Most importantly, a story that is genuinely communicable to a diverse public must anticipate radically different notions of what counts as "the event." For just as social and political problems (as Disch observes) are defined differently by differently located people, a political "event" will have different boundaries and encompass different characters and actions, depending on who you ask. Although Arendt overlooks this matter in her Kant lectures, she recognizes the vagueness of event boundaries in *The Human Condition* when she describes a political phenomenon as a "boundless chain" of actions and reactions. A story can acknowledge the multiple possible ways of delineating "the event," but only if it shows the constructed and revisable status of its entire narrative composition, including its character and action-units, its beginning and ending boundaries, and the kind of material that it recognizes as historically important.

Arendt and Griffin illustrate two possible ways that a story can denaturalize its own narrative construction and thereby solicit further discussion of what counts as "the event." When Griffin creatively juxtaposes historical and personal narratives in a collage that resists reduction to any single narrative or any closed set of characters, she underscores the plurality of ways that the narrative can be configured while she invites readers to narrate additional connections between war phenomena and instances of emotional alienation, denial, or violence in their own lives. In her own way, Arendt also emphasizes the openness of historical narratives and history itself to our interpretive activities. When Arendt structures her history of Nazism in terms of "pre-totalitarian elements," elements that run through various times and places but that she traces back far enough only to make sense of her current world, she makes clear that the way we delineate historical events is a function of our own present-minded concerns. She also indicates our role as interpreters and actors in the unfolding of events: The book's ending, she says, is really "a new beginning," a beginning that "is identical with man's freedom" (OT, 478–79). This concluding remark is meaningful because freedom and responsibility are woven into the fabric of the narrative insofar as Arendt judges past events with a view to helping us understand and respond to the possibilities those events imply for the present.[19]

Feminist advocates of storytelling consider a story's encouragement of active participation and response from readers to be a central virtue of storytelling. Disch emphasizes that "[n]o story can be told 'once and for all' because every telling engenders new contests over the meaning of the event" (1994, 104). Hilde Lindemann Nelson notes that even dominant, authoritative stories contain spaces for other stories "to weave their way inside," for "it is in the nature of a narrative never to close down completely the avenues for its own subversion" (1995, 34). If, however, all stories "leave opportunities" (as Nelson puts it) for retelling, not all stories (as Nelson is also aware) encourage such discussion and retelling. More often than not, narratives of public events are written in an impersonal "realist" style (a style that I analyze in chapter one) that effaces the text's rhetorical construction and presents the narrative as if it were a mere copy of reality. When the media, the government, and other powerful knowledge-producing institutions employ this style, and especially when they construct the event in similar ways, then that particular narrative construction of the event seems all the more natural. Far from soliciting retelling, such a narrative forestalls other ways of narrating the world.

The standard of communicability offers one way to register the dangers of dogmatic narratives and to distinguish them from Arendt's ideal of storytelling. This standard reminds us that a story that presents itself as authoritative, neutral, and rhetoric free may seem objective; however, insofar as such a story attains its "objectivity" by denying its interpretive core and suppressing the multifaceted and undecidable character of the phenomena it narrates, such a story lacks *communicability,* for it obscures the tentative character of its own interpretation and preempts further discussion of the events. The standard of "communicability" thus provides one way to register the failure of those stories that are empirically accurate but unduly deterministic and politically stifling. At the same time, this standard allows us to recognize the distinct value of those stories that promote the open mindedness, the continual exchange of views, and the sense of historical responsibility that Arendt and contemporaries value in storytelling.

As reformulated here, the standards of "communicability" and "enlarged thought" ask us to evaluate critically the rhetorical construction of any story of a public event. They direct us to the story's formal and stylistic construction, not in order to measure the story against a single valid style or to reduce the story to a predefined genre but to examine how well that particular way of telling the story promotes critical and inclusive public debate. These standards (as I have reformulated them in the context of storytelling) also tell us that a story promotes such debate and thus lives up to Arendt's vision of politically and intellectually stimulating storytelling, insofar as it makes explicit its historical and imaginative work, insofar as it presents familiar narratives in their tension with unfamiliar perspectives, insofar as it uses systematically obscured standpoints to destabilize "common sense" truths, insofar as it thematizes it's own interpretive choices, in short, insofar as it presents itself as a historically situated story. These guidelines do not guarantee that a story will be politically neutral. They do, however, remind us that no story is neutral and that, rather than neutrality, a story should strive to advance open-mindedness, self-criticism, historical sensitivity, and broad democratic participation in the stories we tell of ourselves and our world.

In this account, the narrative dimension of our representation of public events is neither arbitrary nor absolute truth but is an intervention in public debate that is accountable to standards of communicability and enlarged thought. The following chapters build upon this theory of storytelling to investigate the most effective way to read and defend stories of marginalized people's experiences.

Part II

Counter-Narratives and Cross-Border Politics

Chapter 4

The Problem of Experience

This chapter begins my investigation of stories that present the experiences of people in marginalized groups. Once considered a radical alternative to master narratives, stories that present the experiences of women, workers, and racial and sexual minorities are now suspect, even among progressive scholars. Feminists and poststructuralists no longer trust marginal experience narratives to critique ideology because they have seen how people's "experiences" of their identities, desires, and perceptions are, in fact, constituted through ideological processes. Thus, many argue, when we try to counter ideological representations of the world with appeals to oppressed or exploited people's "experiences," we in fact reproduce the ideological mechanisms that structure experience, position subjects, and maintain social hierarchies (Butler and Scott 1992b; Grant 1987; Haraway 1990, 200–02; Mohanty 1982; Scott 1988, 4–7, 18–24, 56–60; 1991; Spivak 1988, 274–75).[1]

All of us who read, teach, or write experience-oriented texts need to come to terms with this critique of experience. On the one hand, given the continued importance of marginal experience narratives to feminist, labor, and Third World struggles, we cannot abandon experience-oriented narratives, either as writers or readers. On the other hand, we cannot ignore the warnings of recent critics who find appeals to experience fraught with naive empiricism.

In order to prepare the way for a theory of marginal experience narratives that can explain their value in light of recent criticism, this chapter examines the problems that burden the narration of experience. I then investigate the possibility of surmounting these difficulties. Specifically, I investigate elements of nonempiricist, genuinely critical uses of experience in three representative marginal experience narratives: a memoir by Samuel Delany, *The Motion of Light in Water: Sex and Science Fiction Writing in the East Village* (1993); Howard Zinn's classic social history, *A People's History of the United States* (1995); and Arundhati Roy's innovative essay on the human and environmental effects of India's dams, "The Greater Common Good" (1999). Based on my reading of these texts, I identify elements of "experience" and "narration" that both empiricist and poststructuralist theories of marginal experience narratives overlook and that a theory of such narratives adequate to both their dangers *and* their critical potential must address.

The Critique of Experience

Feminist theory has been at the forefront of investigations into the value as well as the dangers of "experience." On the one hand, feminist consciousness-raising groups and scholars including Temma Kaplan (1990), Nancy Hartsock (1983), Catherine Mackinnon (1989), and Dorothy Smith (1987) have demonstrated the importance of "women's experience" to critical theory and practice. They have used accounts of women's experience to mobilize feminist solidarity, bring public attention to women's concerns, and expose the gender biases of supposedly neutral knowledge and policy.[2]

On the other hand, feminists of various schools have problematized the attempt to use "women's experience" to build a genuinely transformative knowledge or politics. Feminist epistemologists, for instance, have warned that we cannot rely on experience to counter ideology because experience itself is formed through ideological processes. Even visual experience, Donna Haraway argues, although it manifests itself as the simple reception of an external reality, is actually an effect of "active perceptual systems" that enact "specific *ways* of seeing" that are informed by culturally conditioned expectations (1988, 583). Furthermore, as feminists in the Marxist tradition emphasize, the "reality" that we encounter is a product of human history, but everyday experience tends to confront such historical reality as if it were mere fact. As Sandra Harding puts it, "our experience lies to us," presenting culturally determined behavior and historically contingent social arrangements as if they were an eternal and natural reality (1991, 286).

Additional problems arise when people appeal to group experience, such as "women's experience" or "workers' experience," to ground a presumed common interest or viewpoint. As critics of identity politics have argued, appeals to group experience tend to present certain kinds of experience as definitive of the group identity. As a result, they exclude some people and some kinds of experiences from recognition as part of the group while they elide differences within the group. For instance, appeals to "women's experience" have long focused on the experiences of white, middle-class, heterosexual women with the effect of obscuring hierarchical relations among women as well as the political and economic concerns of the majority of the world's women. Finally, when political movements and epistemologies are founded on group experience, they risk advancing the power and authority of (some) people in that group, yet without changing the structures of domination that have made knowledge and politics into exclusionary practices (Alarcón 1990; Bar On 1993; Butler 1990, 324–25, 336–39; Gilliam 1991; Grant 1987; Haraway 1990, 200–02; Lorde 1984, 116–19; Mohanty 1982; 1991b, 71–72; Moya 2000, 3–6).

Joan Scott's Strong Critique of Experience

Poststructuralist-oriented theorist Joan Scott presents the strongest critique of experience. While many feminists caution against appealing to ideologically formed experience and seek instead richer, more reflective dimensions of experience,[3] Scott identifies experience with ideological processes. In her words, experience is nothing other than a "linguistic event," an ideological phenomenon that is "discursively organized in particular contexts or configurations" (1991, 793; 1988, 5).[4] This strong poststructuralist position on experience highlights both the lessons and the limitations of an approach that reduces experience to an effect of discursive practices.[5]

Central to Scott's poststructuralist critique of experience is the claim that the subjective realm of visual and visceral experience is constituted as a meaningful, knowable realm only through discursive practices that delineate identities, naturalize desire, divide the personal from the political, and otherwise categorize subjectivity in terms of culturally specific discursive rules.[6] This claim draws on Derrida's analysis of discourse as a system of differences as well as Lacan's and Foucault's analyses of the discursive constitution of subjectivity. With Derrida, Scott emphasizes that words do not operate as isolated signs but rather generate meaning by virtue of their difference from, and association with, other words in historically specific, constantly renegotiated discursive systems. The word "woman," for instance, does not simply denote a distinct group of people but creates meaning by its opposition to "man" and by its association with other gender-inflected terms in our culture, such as "home" and "dependent," which are themselves understood, respectively, against "the public sphere" and the "independent" wage-earner (Scott 1988, 4–5, 41–48, 54–59, 66–67). Scott links discursive systems to subjective experience through the work of Lacan and Foucault. Lacan explains how gender identification is a symbolic process that occurs through language and that demands constant reconstruction in order to maintain the "fiction" of discrete male and female subjects (Scott 1988, 37–38). Foucault broadens this insight when he examines how subjectivity per se, that is, the awareness we have of ourselves as desiring, knowing, and moral subjects, is formed by discursive practices that measure, diagnose, and regulate individuals through multiple "normalizing" procedures (Foucault 1979 [1975]; 1984, 334–339).[7] Medical and psychoanalytic discourses, for instance, produce what we know as "our sexual experience" while they make possible sexuality's surveillance and disciplining. (Foucault [1976] 1990, 60–70).

Scott's Critique of Histories of Experience

Scott pursues the radical implications of poststructuralist analysis of discourse and subjectivity for historical narratives of experience. From her poststructuralist perspective, she finds a fundamental flaw in the attempt by social historians to critique dominant worldviews by narrating the experiences of marginalized groups. "[T]he most ardent defenders of experience," says Scott, are "'professed anti-empiricists'" who seek an alternative to the naive empiricism of mainstream historiography (Scott 1991, 781). They rightly criticize "fact"-centered historiography because such historiography forgets that its presumably objective and foundational facts are themselves produced by social factors and conceptualized in terms of tradition-given discursive categories. Ironically, however, these same critics of positivist historiography produce yet another unexamined foundation, for they treat discursively constituted experiences as previous historians have treated facts: as indubitable evidence of a prediscursive reality. As a result, says Scott, notwithstanding the information that marginal experience narratives present about the lives of people in oppressed and exploited groups, the project of documenting marginalized groups' experiences is inherently incapable of radical critique, for it "precludes critical examination" of the ideological systems that structure experiences and that define and hierarchize subjects in the first place (1991, 778).[8]

Scott illustrates the unwitting ideological character of narratives of experience with reference to Samuel Delany's memoir, *The Motion of Light in Water* (1993). Although this text is not technically historiography, Scott recognizes that such autobiographical uses of experience have historical significance insofar as they offer a perspective on the broader sociohistorical world. More importantly for Scott, such autobiographical texts succumb to the same positivism as do histories of experience. She finds this problem dramatized in a passage in Delany's memoir in which he describes his experiences at a gay bathhouse. Focusing on Delany's attempt to present a more "clear, accurate, and extensive picture" of existing homosexual institutions

(Delany cited in Scott 1991, 775), Scott claims that "a metaphor of visibility as literal transparency is crucial to his project" (1991, 775). He presumes that his vision of the bathhouse and other homosexual institutions constitutes "direct apprehension of a world of transparent objects" and that his writing merely reproduces his visual experience (Scott 1991, 775). Reinterpreting Delany's text from a poststructuralist standpoint, Scott determines that Delany's presumed visual experience is really an *interpretation* of shadowed images that is structured by available discourses on sexuality. Likewise, his presumed clear perception of his gay identity is really a "discursive event," that is, not the unveiling of his true self but "the substitution of one interpretation for another" (Scott 1991, 794). The memoirs are thus "discursive productions of knowledge of the self, not reflections either of external or internal truth" (Scott 1991, 795). When Delany presents this discursively constituted vision as truth, says Scott, he ends up naturalizing "homosexual identity" along with the phallocentric economy of desire in which both "homosexual" and "heterosexual" have been defined.[9]

Scott argues that historians seeking to document the experiences of people excluded from mainstream histories fall into a similar trap. Like Delany, these historians conceive of their contribution to historical knowledge as "a correction to oversights resulting from inaccurate or incomplete vision" (Scott 1991, 776). Because they view their project as one of presenting more accurate and complete representations of the social world by documenting missing, presumably self-evident experience, the historians who narrate "women's experience" or "workers' experience," like Delany in his narration of "homosexual experience," place those categories of identity and the logic underwriting them outside critical scrutiny. In the end, despite their radical intent, they "take as self-evident the identities of those whose experience is being documented" and thus cannot help but "reproduce rather than contest given ideological systems" (Scott 1991, 777 and 778).

Beyond the Critique of Experience

[W]hy deny the importance of writing and its possible revolutionary role in the exploration, revelation, and diffusion of our real and potential identity?

—Eduardo Galeano[10]

After recent critiques of experience, what can remain of the project of writing, reading, and teaching marginal experience narratives? Some theorists have responded to the critique by asserting that not all marginal experience narratives are naively empiricist. Social historian Eleni Varikas, for instance, argues that even the earliest women's histories both narrate women's experiences and "expose the mystifying character of the categories used for thinking about women in history" (1995, 93). Varikas speaks for many when she charges that Scott's bold criticism of histories of experience "risks throwing out the baby with the bathwater"(1995, 99).[11] Elizabeth Weed also expresses concern for salvaging certain narratives of experience. Although experience has long been associated with traditional notions of the subject, says Weed, feminists can also use experience "not to pin down the truth of the individual subject but as a critical effort to open up ideological contradictions" (1989, xxv). We might cite, for instance, Temma Kaplan's histories (1982, 1990), which recast the logic of natural, discrete, "private" identities not through discourse analysis but by narrating historical moments in which women began to realize new forms of identity and politics. Even while Kaplan begins with traditional notions of self-evident "women" and public sphere "politics," her stories of women's struggles adumbrate heterogeneous, context-dependent identities and politics that confound the logic of discrete identities and separate public and private spheres.[12] Such examples of more critical uses of experience indicate that Scott has cast her net too wide, failing to distinguish between the positivist narratives that she criticizes and the more nuanced experience-oriented writing.

Despite her oversights, however, Scott's generalizations about the naivete of "experience" still hold considerable influence in feminist and critical theory. The reason for this continued influence of poststructuralist critiques of experience, I would argue, lies in the absence of a theory of experience that adequately accounts for the critical work that is accomplished by the more subtle experience-oriented texts. In other words, poststructuralist claims about the empiricist nature of marginal experience narratives remain influential because, although we can point to counterexamples, we have no alternative interpretive framework with which to conceptualize the genre in a nonempiricist way. Without such a nonempiricist theory of marginal experience narratives, even those narratives that, like Kaplan's, complicate the status of experience are often read and evaluated in empiricist terms.[13] After recent critiques, then, proponents of experience-oriented writing must clarify how the more interesting marginal experience narratives treat experience, if not as evidence, and how we can read and defend such texts without invoking a naive "completing the picture" empiricist epistemology.

In the rest of this chapter, I examine some more subtle and subversive uses of experience in three representative marginal experience narratives. This text analysis does not yet constitute a theory of marginal experience narratives, but it prepares the way for the transnational feminist theory of marginal experience narratives that I develop in the next two chapters. I begin with Delany's memoir because the memoir highlights the critical potential of experience-oriented writing as well as the inability of poststructuralist theory to register this potential. I then turn to *A People's History of the United States,* by Howard Zinn, as this book is precisely the kind of social history that poststructuralists such as Scott target. I show how even this textbook example of a seemingly positivist narrative of experience contains elements that supercede the poststructuralist critique. Finally, I address Arundhati Roy's controversial essay about India's big dams, "The Greater Common Good." This essay belongs to a growing body of genre-defying texts that narrate historical experience in self-consciously creative ways, ways that painstakingly engage historical experience and yet flout the conventions of evidence-based "objective" historical writing. Even while each of these texts is anchored in historical experience, and even while the first two exemplify the kind of texts that poststructuralists criticize, they nevertheless each use experience to destabilize the discourses and institutions that have organized experience. Together, these texts indicate elements of experience and narration that make possible genuinely subversive uses of experience and that must be accounted for in any effective theory of marginal experience narratives.

Delany: Narrating the Tension Between Experience and Language

From well-read books we absorb the unquestioned laws of genre, the readerly familiarity with rhetorical figures, narrational tropes, conventional attitudes and expectations. From the others, however, we manufacture the dreams of possibility, of variation, of what might be done outside and beyond the genre that the others have already made a part of our readerly language.

—Samuel Delany[14]

Ironically, although Scott invokes Delany's memoir to illustrate the limits of marginal experience narratives and the insights of poststructuralist theory, closer attention to this memoir reveals elements of experience and narration that escape poststructuralist theory and that constitute a genuinely radical use of experience. These elements are, first, a subjective experience that is not a neat reflection of discursive categories but is instead ambiguous and resistant to clear articulation and, second, a narrative approach that does not naively report ideologically formed experience but instead responds creatively to tensions within experience. By artfully narrating tensions within his experience, Delany demonstrates the possibility of using experience to problematize precisely the identity categories that poststructuralists fear are naturalized with appeals to experience.

Delany draws on experience to problematize the identities that have been imposed on him, but not by appealing to experience as if it were clear evidence of an alternative truth. Despite occasional use of empiricist metaphors, Delany pursues a project much more creative and complex than an empiricist disclosure of a presumably self-evident and internal "identity." Throughout the memoir, he acknowledges that no single, authentic "self" can be distilled from the multiple elisions, displacements, and over-determined images in his memories because "these excesses are, after all, memory itself," that is, the multiple, conflicting, and overlapping elements that seem to cloud his memory are in fact the essence of his past experience (1993, 315). Likewise, he acknowledges that his memoir is only one way of ordering the multifaceted and conflicting memories and is "only one possible fiction among the myriad" that can be written about his life (1993, 14). Delany thus agrees with poststructuralists that experience-oriented writing does not represent but, in fact, produces what it calls "past experience" through creative discursive work; however, departing from poststructuralists, he also recognizes such writing to be rooted in lived experience—not because experience is self-evident but because the excesses and ambiguities of remembered experiences are indicative of existentially meaningful struggles, including conflicts between experience and discourse. Thus, while he is "not about to try here for the last word on event and evidential certainty," he does nevertheless work through the complex contours of his experiences in order to rewrite his life in a way that is meaningful to him (Delany 1993, 14).

When we attend to Delany's attempts to respond strategically to ambiguous experiences, we see that the memoir emerges from Delany's retrospective reckoning with his experience, even while it challenges and recasts the categories that have organized his experience. For instance, Delany does not simply affirm "gay," "black," or "artist" identity, but instead confronts his uneasy experience of those received identities: On the one had, received identity categories do not capture who he is; on the other hand, he cannot counterpose to those categories a presumably authentic "private self," for he cannot make sense of his life, even his "private" life, apart from those social labels and from social and cultural institutions that treat him accordingly. He responds to this double-edged experience of his identity by carefully interweaving stories of his independence from received identity categories with stories that relate his life as a gay man, a black man, and an artist who confronts specific obstacles on account of those roles. For instance, he recounts being a queer teenage boy who had just slept with his friend, Marilyn, and who asks himself, "Just who was I?," responding,

> I was a young black man, light-skinned enough so that four of five people who met me, of whatever race, assumed I was white. . . . I was a homosexual who now knew he could function heterosexually.
>
> . . . So, I thought, you are neither black nor white.
>
> You are neither male nor female.
>
> And you are that most ambiguous of citizens, the writer.
>
> . . . It seemed, in the park at dawn a kind of revelation—a kind of center, formed of a play of ambiguities, from which I might move in any direction (Delany 1993, 102).

If, however, the park at dawn allowed him to savor the freedom of uncategorizability, the following days brought identity-related constraints: Marilyn was pregnant by him, abortion was illegal, and the only way that Marilyn could leave her mother's abusive household was by getting married (in 1961, girls were legally under the custody of their parents or husband until age 21). After the marriage, he works at Barnes and Noble to support the two, both penniless writers, although his mother-in-law does not believe that this writer, this black man, has a real job. By thus maintaining a tension between, on the one hand, his irreducibility to received identity categories and, on the other, the formative influence on his life of those categories, Delany does more than counterpose "homosexual" to "heterosexual," "artist" to "worker," or "black" to "white." He challenges the logic that presents these categories as internal and discrete properties.

An incident in which Delany tells his story to a psychiatrist dramatizes the way that Delany draws on his experiences not to present indubitable evidence of an internal truth but to denaturalize and explore the limits of the discourses that have structured his experience. Upon recently having "confessed" his "homosexual identity" to fellow psychiatric patients, Delany realizes that the sexual discourses of medical and literary texts that he had drawn upon had betrayed him, forcing him to define his sexuality, to himself and others, as a deviancy, a "private" problem to be discussed only with shame. In defiance of those received languages, Delany decides to speak openly about his sexual life and to do so in his own voice. The available language for homosexuality, he says, "was tantamount to silence. I just had to find my own" (1993, 372). Here Delany may seem to embrace the illusion that Foucault warns against: that his sexuality, if only freed from censorship and repression, is a truth whose expression is inherently liberating (Foucault 1990 [1976], 6–7, 56–67). Despite this gesture toward a presumably authentic personal expression, however, Delany's subsequent narrative is no naive attempt to communicate a "private truth." He begins by identifying himself matter of factly as black, homosexual, married, 22, and a writer who has just published four science fiction novels. These are the same categories that society would use for him, but Delany changes their meaning when he publicly embraces the three "deviant" aspects of himself, black, homosexual, and writer, and when he presents them as no more "privy" than his marriage or age. He further defies the compartmentalizing of "public" and "private" life when he proceeds to relate his anxieties to the broader social context. He explains, for instance, that he had difficulties in bringing his homosexual relationships into standard social structures and trouble balancing those homosexual relationships with his marriage (itself a result of social pressures), and had to compromise in order to make a living doing what he liked, for he had to tailor his writing to a popular (white, heterosexist) audience. Thus Delany does not deny that "homosexual," "black," and "writer" are relevant to his experience, but he refuses to accept these properties as internal, "private" essences, for he relates their "abnormal" status to the social and cultural institutions that regulate our professional as well as personal lives.

The psychiatric interview demonstrates the critical approach to experience that Delany pursues throughout the memoir: By confronting tensions within his experience, he explores tensions between his experience and discursive categories and, ultimately, challenges the seemingly natural status of those categories. This approach does not presume a pristine space outside of discourse from which to criticize discourse. In fact, the memoir, like the psychiatric interview, had its origins within the pressures of discursive norms. In accord with genre norms, Delany had earlier set out to write a two-column journal, with one column devoted to the "private" inner realm of desire and the other to the "public" realm of professional activities. As he attempted to distinguish his presumably private from his presumably public material, however, he found that there was nothing "to maintain the split, the gap, the margin between columns" (1993, 208). After this problematic journal experience, his subsequent memoir boldly defies discursive norms. As in his second psychiatric interview, the memoir does not try to invent a new language but rather works self-consciously with his received language to explore his difficult experiences, including his frustration with discursive norms. In the memoir, he explores the source of his troubles by strategically splicing together, with disregard for smooth transitions and conventional logic, various memories of his sexual relationships, economic troubles, and artistic endeavors. He thereby allows connections to come to the foreground that the logic of separate "private" and "public" spheres suppresses. For instance, the strategically disjointed memoir indicates how Delany's "public" life as a writer is affected by the ups and downs of his personal relationships, while his "private" life is shaped by the laws that regulate marriage and ban homosexual activity as well as the economic institutions that condition how he and his partners survive daily life. Thus, as he attempts to make sense of daily struggles that defy conventional modes of representation, he not only takes ownership over the representation of his life but problematizes the logic of separate "public" and "private" lives.

When Delany uses his writing to come to terms with aspects of his life he had been taught to consider shameful, he also challenges the discourses of "normalcy" and "propriety." Significantly, he does not simply invert received hierarchies and valorize "improper" behavior but displaces the division between normal and aberrant activity. For instance, with disregard for the rules of proper public discussion, Delany candidly presents tales of his sexual life and his relationships with underworld characters that would ordinarily be hidden from public view. In one thread, he describes his ménage à trois with Marilyn and Bob, a young homeless man and the son of a prostitute. Certainly, the tales of their sexual life and household together do not constitute an analysis of phallocentrism; however, neither do they (as Scott charges) simply invert heterosexual institutions while leaving intact its phallocentric structure, for the tales of the three housemates' sharing of chores, finances, and multidirectional relationships of desire adumbrate the possibility of social relations that defy the traditional family structure and the oedipal triangle on which phallocentrism is based. In addition, Delany's tales of his interactions with Bob challenge the presumed division between "normal" and "deviant" existence that upholds the seeming respectability of "normal" life. When Delany invites into his household and then writes about a character whom "respectable" society and public discourse try to ignore, and when he gives Bob a personality, a face, and a history in his story, the lines that separate Bob from "normal" people become blurred, for we see that Bob has not only lived much of his life on the streets but that he is also a working man who sends part of his paycheck home to his mother. As Delany gives recognition to "unspeakable" lifestyles and puts faces on "deviant" characters, he makes it more difficult for us to peg the "normal" and "abnormal" subject.

In addition to challenging received discourses on the subject, Delany also offers "dreams of possibility" for other ways of conceptualizing and organizing our lives. In the context of his reflections on the artifice of writing codes and the uncertain and "fictional" character of his own memoir, his stories, including his fragmented tales of his life with Marilyn and Bob, remain incomplete and artful sketches, not indubitable evidence of an alternative reality. Nonetheless, while the stories could be ordered differently and while the specific dates and places are admittedly unreliable, the open-ended and sketchy status of his stories also has a virtue: It invites readers to reflect further on the stories' possible significances and more radical implications. As Delany suggests, stories that "we know only slightly and fleetingly . . . end up being even more 'influential' than the works we encounter full on" that conform to our discursive norms, for from the former stories "we manufacture the dreams of possibility, of variation, of what might be done outside and beyond" codified ways of narrating and governing our lives (1993, 176).

Even Delany's bathhouse scene, the center of Scott's empiricist reading, contains elements that subvert empiricist notions of representation and invite readers to participate in exploring the significance of obscure, seemingly uncategorizable experiences. Despite his occasional empiricist metaphors, Delany does not document the bathhouse scene reporter-like but instead offers what he calls "a fragment of an encounter," describing vaguely "an orgy of a hundred or more," and telling us that he "moved forward into it" (1993, 269, 271). This "fragment" clearly does not offer indubitable evidence of reality but it does achieve the effect that Delany attributes to fleeting stories. It prompts our imagination. It prompts us to imagine the bathhouse world as well as the kind of lifestyle and interpersonal relations that openly gay institutions make possible. It thus points our vision beyond the logic of current discourses on sexuality and encourages us to consider ways of life that defy simple opposition to a heterosexual norm or clear separation into "private" and "public" spheres.

Delany's memoir is thus not simply one discursive production among others but a discursive production that potentially empowers Delany and his readers. For Delany, the memoir constitutes a way to take control over his own representation and thereby participate actively in the discursive practices that construct his identity. The epistemic power he gains from telling his own story is manifest when he tells his story at the psychiatric hospital, for the interviewing doctor repeatedly slips, calling him "Doctor Delany." The memoir also enables Delany to rearrange, even if not escape, dominant discourses on the subject. Through telling his story, in his journal, to psychiatrists, and finally in his memoir, Delany discerns the social categories and customs that he has internalized and that have led him to adapt his behavior to social expectations. As he comes to identify these social pressures, he organizes his storytelling to resist these pressures. Thus the memoir resists, for instance, the sanctioned silence on any sexual or social experience different than "the norm," the division of our life into separate "public" and "private" spheres, and the acceptance of a presumably natural "identity." In defying these social and discursive conventions, Delany not only upsets the logic that structures received discourses on the subject but also challenges the power of so-called experts to label him and fit him neatly into social hierarchies.

For readers, the memoir offers much more than mere "evidence for the fact of difference" (Scott 1991, 777). Beyond this, the text helps us to examine critically the way that differences have been defined in our society and have structured our own lives. When, for instance, Delany reflects on his uneasy yet inescapable relation to the binary categories "heterosexual/homosexual," "white/black," and "worker/artist," he sensitizes us to both the artifice and the social force of binary defined identities. The memoir thus challenges us not simply to reject current ways of categorizing subjects but to investigate their historical effects, including their impact on our own "private" selves and our own conceptions of "natural" and "normal" lifestyles. In Foucault's terms, the memoir contributes to "practices of freedom," for it encourages us to expose and rearrange those pervasive but little-noticed institutions that regulate our everyday lives (Foucault 1984, 245–246).[15]

Zinn: Reconstructing a Heritage

*Remembrance of the past may give rise to
dangerous insights. . . .*

—Herbert Marcuse[16]

Not only autobiographical narratives but also histories of social experience can be reread for elements that supercede the poststructuralist
critique of experience. Zinn's classic social history, *A People's History
of the United States,* on the surface typifies Scott's description of texts
that "take as self-evident the identities of those whose experience is
being documented" and thereby "reproduce rather than contest given
ideological systems" (Scott 1991, 777 and 778). Many of the book's
chapters are organized according to predefined social groups, such as
"women," "Indians," "laborers," and "blacks," while the book presents these people's experiences as if they were "evidence" of social
contradictions. For instance, a chapter treating the antiracist revolts of
the 1950s and 1960s refers to "black people" as if this were a self-
evident category, while it presents poems and prose by African American artists as "signs of a people unbeaten, waiting, hot, coiled" (Zinn
1995, 438). Insofar as the quoted poems and speeches serve as evidence
of black people's pent-up anger, they help us to understand that anger,
but they also leave intact the category "black" as well as the logic of
separate "races."

Closer attention to the language and effects of the text, however,
reveals that even this classic, evidence-rich history of marginalized
groups contains elements that supercede positivist representation. As he
narrates specific historical experiences, Zinn confronts elements of
those experiences that defy the logic of ruling discourses on identity and
history. Moreover, by reclaiming these defiant experiences as part of
history, his narrative also helps us to *experience* our own identity and
history in ways that cannot be contained within ruling discourses.

The chapter on the black revolts, for instance, problematizes the
seemingly clear cut category "black" that Zinn himself employs, for the
quotations from black activists and intellectuals serve not only to
provide evidence of suppressed black anger but also to humanize and
complexify "black experience." The quoted passages complicate "black
identity" because they confront us with the multifaceted experiences of
unique, multiply aligned individuals. These include individuals who are
"black," happy eight year olds on vacation who are stung by the label
"nigger"; "black" men whose "deepest instincts had always made

[them] reject the 'place'" assigned to them; "black" elderly women who walk miles rather than ride boycotted segregated buses; and "black" socialist feminists who "don't want to compete on no damned exploitative level . . . don't want to exploit nobody . . . want the right to be black and me."[17] These words of anger, pain, resistance and vision ask readers to consider the experiences of "black people," even while they destabilize the homogeneity, objectification, and seemingly self-evident meaning of that term.

By presenting various, sometimes internally contrasting testimonies from marginalized standpoints and counterposing these testimonies to official reports, Zinn also problematizes the national-level generalizations and the stale, unexamined political categories that have organized "common sense" representations of American life. For instance, when he juxtaposes 1960s government proclamations on "equality," and "democracy" with critical comments from antiracist activists and figures on the number of African Americans who remained unemployed, impoverished, and subject to police violence during that same time period, he not only presents evidence of difference from the dominant culture, but he also indicates the partisan character of the rhetoric of "equality" and "democracy" when this rhetoric, used by both politicians and historians, glosses over differences and alleges to present one truth for the nation. By highlighting the experiences that commonly accepted generalizations occlude, Zinn thus encourages us to question whose interests are served, and whose neglected, by narratives that structure American history in terms of national advancement toward an abstract equality and democracy. In addition, because he counterposes ruling narratives to a plurality of explicitly subjective and particularized testimonies and letters, he does not replace official narratives with another authoritative story but instead indicates the dangers of any rhetoric that becomes unaccountable to historical experience. Ultimately, his collection of testimonial counterevidence to official narratives, far from perpetuating ruling discursive logics, provokes us to *think*, in Arendt's sense, that is, to not simply follow clichés and doctrines but to examine for ourselves the complex significances of specific historical phenomena (Arendt UP, 380–92; TH, 4–5, 176–78; 1971).

Finally, *A People's History* defies Scott's account of marginal experience histories as hopelessly complicit with ruling ideologies insofar as the book destabilizes the rhetoric of "progress." The discourse of progress is at least as trenchant and dangerous an element of modern ideology as are the identity categories of concern to poststructuralist theorists, for the idea of "progress" has organized our experience of history in a way that denies our responsibility for the course of events (Arendt LK, 4–5; Ricoeur TNiii, 210–15; White 1982, 134–35). As Ricoeur explains, the idea of progress presumes that "Time is no longer just a neutral form of history but its force as well" (TNiii, 210). This notion of time as the motor of history inhibits people from formulating their own strategies for change and leads ultimately to "despair of all action" (Ricoeur TNiii, 215). Martin Luther King attests to the wide influence as well as the dangers of this "myth of time" when he describes the white moderates who naively preached that civil rights for blacks would come with time. Ironically, such a faith in time produces a situation in which time, far from ushering in progress as supposed, becomes "an ally of the forces of social stagnation," as people become increasingly complacent (King 1963, 24). In a similar vein, Eduardo Galeano observes that the mystification of the march of history as a seemingly sanctified process encourages "the defeated people [to] accept their lot as destiny" (1989, 217).

Zinn disturbs our unquestioned faith in progress when he makes vivid the human costs of war, suppression of dissent, and other forms of violence that have been rationalized in the name of "progress" and associated values. He tells stories, for instance, of Native Americans massacred by early settlers in the name of God and progress, Mexicans whose communities were plundered for the sake of "civiliz[ing] that beautiful country," and striking coal miners and their families whose tent colonies were machine-gunned and set on fire by National Guardsmen on behalf of "individual liberty; private property; and inviolability of contract" (Zinn 1995, 12–16; the *American Review,* cited in Zinn, 152; National Civic Federation memorandum, cited in Zinn, 346). Stories of Pequot families set on fire in their wigwams by English settlers, of Mexican communities raped and robbed by drunken North American soldiers (many of whom would die from battle or disease themselves), and of miners' children found burned to death in their tents do not constitute a definitive judgment on history. They do, however, impress on us the human significance of losses that are irreducible to aggregate economic figures or national-level generalizations and they resonate in our minds as dissonant undertones to abstract proclamations of "victory" and "progress." Thus, even while they cannot claim complete or objective truth, such stories interrupt our complacency with a historical paradigm that justifies the prevailing institutions simply by the fact that they have prevailed while they challenge us to judge, for ourselves, the elements of our heritage that we want to herald, amend for, cultivate, or resist.

While Zinn's stories of the dark side of progress problematize the belief in history as an inherently rational and self-justifying force, his stories of resistance movements challenge the related assumption that human beings are simply along for the ride, without responsibility for the course of events. Against this assumption, Zinn tells the story of activists who catalyzed social and political reforms, such as the thousands of blacks and whites who demonstrated together for unemployment relief in the 1930s. He conveys a sense of the experiences that animated such activism by telling the story of specific individuals involved in the demonstration. One of these activists, for instance, is Angelo Herndon, a young African American Communist party organizer who worked in Kentucky coal mines as a boy and lost his father to miners' pneumonia. When on trial for "insurrection" and confronted with literature found in his room, Zinn tells us, Herndon was asked by state prosecutors: Do you believe "that the bosses and government ought to pay insurance to unemployed workers? That Negroes should have complete equality with white people? . . . that the working-class could run the mills and mines and government?" to which Herndon replied, "I believed all of that—and more . . . " (Herndon, cited in Zinn 1995, 439). Such stories indicate that social progress has arisen not from the mere flow of time but from people motivated by painful and powerful experiences to risk violent reprisal and imprisonment to fight for change. This casts a new light on the present as well, for it implies that our current world can become more advanced and enlightened not through time but only through active resistance to prejudices and social ills.

Zinn's stories of less successful struggles also challenge the neat closure and clarity of the progress paradigm. While the progress paradigm reduces vanquished struggles to casualties of history, Zinn keeps lost struggles alive in our minds by narrating the positive experiences within defeated activism and by ending chapters with questions and references to remaining contradictions. For instance, he forestalls closure at the end of his chapter on the black revolts when he asks (recalling Langston Hughes), "what happens to a dream deferred?" and leaves us to ponder the possibilities (459). He also renews the relevance of forgotten struggles, such as the struggles of Native Americans in the 1960s and 70s who staged "fish-ins" and occupied land in attempt to reclaim areas for Native communities. They were eventually defeated by arrests, bullets, and the U.S.

government's invoking of eminent domain, but, in the process, they renewed their sense of community and developed newsletters and other organizations to cultivate and disseminate Native American perspectives. Although conventional history books present Alcatraz and other Native American resistance movements (if they present them at all) as unwinnable battles with progress, Zinn's account of the experiential dimension of these struggles helps us to appreciate the ethics, such as concern for community, "thinking with the heart," and concern for the sacredness and interconnectedness of all life, that motivated these struggles and to see such ethics as enduring threads of North American history. Zinn thus uses historical experience not as mere empiricist evidence but as a window to the openness, the polysemy, and the unrealized possibilities of history. He thereby upsets the idea of history as a singular, inexorable process while he reminds us that what counts as progress is not determined by "History" but depends on how we remember the past and engage with possibilities in the present.

A social theory or philosophy might make similar points about the human role in history. Arendt and Ricoeur, for instance, explain that a properly historical notion of time recognizes both the groundedness of the future in the past and the openness of the past itself, such that the present is a space of judgment and ethical initiative (Arendt BPF, 13–15; Ricoeur TNiii, 215–16, 227–30). The intellectual value of their analyses notwithstanding, however, their theories do not affect our *experience* of our history and ourselves as do Zinn's stories of resistant experiences. When Zinn tells stories of specific people who suffered and resisted oppression, such as Angelo Herndon, imprisoned but determined in the fight for unemployment relief, and Oglala Sioux Indians and their white allies, who set up communal kitchens and healthcare to support one another while under siege, he not only sketches an alternative tradition of American heroes and values, but, in so doing, he contributes to our own sense of historical identity. His stories help us to affirm resistant communities as part of our heritage, to connect our own seemingly anomalous resistant impulses to a deeply rooted historical community, and to expand our sense of the kind of resistant activities of which we, too, might be capable. Insofar as Zinn's stories enrich our sense of historical identity and remind us of neglected potentials within ourselves, his text intervenes in discursive processes in a way that is perhaps more substantial than poststructuralist discourse analysis: It enables us to resist the force of ruling narratives on our own experience of who we are.[18]

Roy: Debunking "Expert" Knowledge

*It's very important to me to tell politics like a story,
to make it real, to draw a link between a man and
his child and what fruit he had in the village he
lived in before he was kicked out and how that
relates to Mr. Wolfensohn at the World Bank.*

—Arundhati Roy[19]

Although Arundhati Roy is not a professional historian, her study of the experiences surrounding India's big dams offers another important corrective to the poststructuralist critique of historical experience. Like Delany, Roy is openly literary, demonstrating the immense poetic freedom that is possible, even in detail-sensitive narration of experience. While Delany breaks the norms of realist autobiography, Roy subverts the conventions of evidence-centered, detached political analysis. Insofar as she rejects the norms of "objective" professional writing, Roy agrees with the poststructuralist critique of realist discourse; however, like Delany and Zinn before her, Roy challenges the norms of professional discourse not through analyzing discourse but through narrating specific people's experiences. Her engaged and artful story of the families displaced by dams does what Scott claims the narration of experience cannot do: It not only counters official reports with different evidence but also questions the norms that define "evidence" and the logic that underlies official explanations. In particular, her story challenges the logic of impersonal, aggregate, market-defined values that structures the official discourse of "national interest" and "the greater common good."

Roy challenges the logic of "the common good," in part, by debunking the seeming objectivity and precision with which the government presumably determines this common good. On one level, she discredits the authority of official reports by situating them within the story of their social production: a story of "experts" who are hired (or fired) by the dam industry, of estimates that shift with political winds, of pertinent information kept secret or never collected, and of preliminary reports produced *after* projects have been initiated and loans approved. Alongside this well-documented account of the social roots of "objective" data, another level of the story responds to the government's pretense of objectivity with sarcasm and humor. Her playful language does not contaminate but in fact complements her historical analysis, for it underscores the not-to-be-taken-seriously side of "serious knowledge." For instance, commenting on the government's fluctuating figures on the number of people who will receive water from the Sardar Sarovar canal—28 million according to the first report and 32.5 million a few years later—Roy muses, "nice touch, the decimal point!" (1999, 33). Mocking the serious and authoritative-sounding reports known as "Environment Impact Assessments," or "EIAs," Roy informs us that EIAs are produced by consultants who are paid by the dam builders and that a consultant who exposes a problem with the dams is an "OOWC," an "Out-of-Work consultant" (31). Such comments highlight the absurdity of rhetorical strategies that feign objectivity and precision, allowing us to laugh at, and thereby destabilize the hegemony of, representations that would normally command unquestioned authority.[20]

Roy further destabilizes the authority of "official knowledge" by telling the story of what is absent from this knowledge. The state, she says, has no post-project evaluation of any of its 3,600 dams nor a count of the number of people displaced by the dams. At a private lecture, the Planning Commission secretary estimated that big dams have displaced 40 million people, but the stated that figure cannot be repeated because it is not official. Or perhaps, Roy suggests, it is the other way around; "[w]e daren't say so, because it isn't official. It isn't official because we daren't say so" (Roy 1999, 17). While Roy's wry comment highlights the censorship that underlies "official knowledge," her figurative prose grapples with the meaning of the censored numbers. Reckoning with the staggering dimensions of the secretary's 40-million-people estimate, she says, "You have to murmur it, for fear of being accused of hyperbole. You have to whisper it to yourself, because it really does sound unbelievable. . . . I feel like someone who's just stumbled on a mass grave" (1999, 16 and 17). Thus Roy does not deny the relevance of quantitative data but shows us, rather, that the collection of such data depends on political choices while its ultimate import depends on a story that animates its existential significance.

Roy also challenges official reports on the dams by following stories across disciplinary and discursive boundaries. The resulting sketch of the dam's multiple repercussions does not present certain truth but it does highlight the compartmentalization and the arrogance of "expert" knowledge. For instance, when Roy pursues the experiential effects of dams beyond what can be easily categorized and measured, she reminds us of links between people, places, and rivers that "expert" knowledge overlooks: ancient ferry, fishing, and cultivating communities that are (or were) sustained by the river, forests that moderate(d) river siltation, and tens of thousands of indigenous people who find (or found) all they needed to survive from the forest.[21] Such links among life forms limit our knowledge of dams, for our knowledge can never be more accurate than our always-partial understanding of the role that a river plays in the interconnections of life. When planners are bent on rigid categories and mastery, they ignore even our partial understanding of ecological interconnections. "Have engineers made the connection between forest, rivers, and rain?," asks Roy of the professionals who designed the dams that would submerge 50,000 hectares of old-growth forest. "Unlikely. It isn't part of their brief" (Roy 1999, 64). Ignoring the complex links between people, trees, and rivers, our "experts" are not only unreliable but dangerously overconfident of their own creative powers. Thus government engineers could audaciously presume to compensate for the loss of the 50,000 hectares of forest—a forest that was sustained by a complex river ecosystem and in turn sustained 40,000 people and countless animals—with a wildlife sanctuary and a tribal museum.

In addition to exposing the holes and the politics in "expert knowledge," Roy challenges all of us to grapple with the human effects of the dams. Addressing her readers directly, she says, "Whether you love the dam or hate it, whether you want it or you don't, it is in the fitness of things that you understand the price that's being paid for it" (Roy 1999, 81). She addresses all of us because she believes that fault lies not only with a government that distorts and conceals information concerning the displacement of tens of millions of people but with all of us who look away, who pretend that "it can't be helped," who "believe what we're told . . . what it benefits us to believe" (1999, x, 21). "[W]e make it easy for them," she warns, "we, its beneficiaries. We take care not to dig too deep. We don't really *want* to know the grisly details" (1999, 23). In response to such widespread complacency with government deception, to which all of us are susceptible, Roy asks each of us to "have the courage to watch while the dues are cleared and the books are squared," to face honestly the human realities behind our seemingly neutral numbers and euphemisms (1999, 81).

To help us consider the human implications of the dams, Roy "tell[s] politics like a story," reconstructing empathetically the details of particular people's daily lives. Her engaged storytelling is not incompatible with material analysis. She makes clear that the experiences she narrates are a function of national and transnational political and economic systems, including a $20 billion dam industry. She also makes clear, however, that the meaning of these transnational institutions consists of immeasurable effects on people's lives. No economic charts can make palpable, for instance, what it means for farmers who have cultivated the same land for generations to watch their homes dismantled and their standing crops bulldozed; for families who had obtained all they needed from the forest, including 48 different kinds of fruit, to never again be able to afford to eat a piece of fruit; for displaced people to be "dumped in rows of corrugated tin sheds that are furnaces in summer and fridges in winter" and that seasonally flood, producing scenes of "[f]rightened, fevered eyes [of children who] watch pots and pans carried through the doorway by the current, floating out into the flooded fields, thin fathers swimming after them to retrieve what they can" (1999, 52); for people who were "self-sufficient and free" to be forced to sell themselves on the market as wage laborers "like goods for sale"; and for people whose homes are slated for submergence to wade in chest-deep water for hours, preferring to face arrest rather than be "resettled."

Roy's stories help us to confront the effects of the dams on people's lives, yet without presuming that such effects are self-evident, easily representable perceptual data. Along with descriptive tales of displacement and references to policy reports, Roy often presents the experiences of displacement in terms of people's indirect expressions. For instance, she asked the man who was displaced from the forest and who had commented on the fruit he would no longer enjoy about the sick baby he rocked in his arms: "He said it would be better for the baby to die than live like this. I asked what the baby's mother thought about that. She didn't reply. She just stared" (Roy 1999, 54). By presenting words that we cannot necessarily take literally, especially given their contrast with the father's nurturing behavior, and by recounting questions met with silence, Roy highlights the unspeakable, not easily representable human meaning of displacement. At the same time, her attention to select details in individuals' lives, such as the man's concern that he will never again be able to afford a piece of fruit and his despair for his baby's future, impresses on us the profound implications of displacement for people's everyday lives. Her story helps us to consider such implications as pertinent to "the price that's being paid" for the dam, even if we cannot easily articulate—let alone quantify—their significance.

Roy also uses poetic, provocative prose to make vivid for us the effects of the dams that confound objectifying analysis. She explores, for instance, what it means for someone whose life has revolved around a river to find the river suddenly inaccessible or flooding without warning. "It's like a loved one who has developed symptoms of psychosis. Anyone who has loved a river can tell you that the loss of a river is a terrible, aching thing" (1999, 50). With her poetic comparison of a river to a loved one, Roy helps city dwellers to begin to imagine the unspeakable loss that big dams bring upon river communities. Elsewhere, her hypothetical questions prompt us to consider what it would be like to fit our own lives into the common interest calculator: "From being self-sufficient and free, to being impoverished and yoked to the whims of a world you know nothing about, *nothing* about—what d'you suppose it must feel like? Would you like to trade your beach house in Goa for a hovel in Paharganj? No? Not even for the sake of the nation?" (1999, 55). Although clearly sarcastic and rhetorical, Roy's challenge to us that we consider relinquishing our own home for the sake of "national interest" suddenly gives palpable significance to the abstract idea of displacement.

Insofar as Roy helps us to consider the significance of displacement for people's everyday lives, she not only deepens our understanding of the dams but also challenges the discourse of the national interest and the greater common good that is fundamental to contemporary forms of power. Contemporary rulers, Roy observes, wield greater power to destroy and manipulate life than any past dictator; however, they do so in "democracies" with the consent of "free people," in part by couching their actions in lofty phrases like "the greater common good." The discourse of the greater common good gives a semblance of virtue and rationality to policies that displace hundreds of thousands of people. It performs this deception by pretending that social losses can be weighed against social gains like numbers on a balance sheet. When Roy animates the stories of displaced individuals and when she challenges us to put ourselves in their position, she reminds us that people cannot be reduced to fungible figures and that social value cannot be defined by market calculations. She thus compels us to confront the violence of any discourse that allows abstract, aggregate totals to replace reckoning with the human effects of policies on specific people's lives.

Finally, Roy's stories undermine the discourse of the greater common good by introducing us to worlds beyond the bounds of that discourse, worlds in which people and rivers have value irreducible to market utility. In helping us to imagine such worlds, Roy interrupts the discourse of the greater common good in a way perhaps more powerful than discourse analysis, for she heightens our sensitivity to value that confounds monetary measurement, identity that exceeds people's role in the market economy, and community that cannot be duplicated by socially engineered "rehabilitation." She thereby enables us not only to analyze but also to *experience* the perversity of an aggregate, market-defined common good.

Reclaiming Experience

Delany, Zinn, and Roy each narrate experience in ways that are more subversive than either empiricists or poststructuralists recognize: They each use experience to challenge and transform the discourses that have organized experience. Their texts suggest elements of experience and writing that make such transformation possible and that a more effective theory of marginal experience texts must address.

First, these authors indicate that experience is not only shaped by discourse but also reacts to and potentially disrupts discursive practices. Scott rightly points out that disruption is an inherent potential of discourse, for any discursive system is indeterminate and conflicts with other discursive systems (1991, 793). The impetus for such disruption, however, lies not in discourse itself but in people's everyday *experience* of discursive practices. In their everyday lives, people endure as well as react against discursive practices on multiple bodily, emotional, and intellectual levels. Such experienced reactions to discourse include, for instance, Delany's discomfort with the label "homosexual," Herndon's detest of a discourse that placed "Colored" beneath "Whites," Roy's frustration with the inability of government charts and speeches to empathize with uprooted lives, and the displaced man's refusal to accept his condition as a "resettled" way of life for either himself or his children. Such resistant experiences are not prediscursive or self-evident truths, for they are formed in relation to discursive logics. Nevertheless, such resistant experiences also include unofficial, uncodified reactions to ruling discourses and thus belie the violent effects of those discourses on our daily lives.[22]

Second, the above authors indicate that we can realize the power of experience to disrupt the hegemony of ruling discourses only if we confront experience as a multifaceted, internally contradictory phenomenon. The experiences that register the hidden costs of discursive practices on our everyday lives are often complex and contradictory because such experiences must compete with our ideologically formed consciousness. Delany's discomfort with his own apologetic confession of his homosexuality, for instance, represents levels of his awareness that conflicted with his ideologically formed acceptance of his "sexual deviancy." Other times, resistant experiences present themselves as confused and contradictory because someone lacks the power to act fully and publicly on his discontent, so that his discontent becomes expressed in multiple, sometimes contending reactions, none of which is fully adequate. For instance, when the displaced man is unable to resist government "resettlement" practices effectively, he waivers between unsatisfying responses, such as wanting to nurture his sick child but also not wanting to accept the resettlement camp as a way of life worth living for the child. Although such tensions manifest themselves as contradictions within experience, they point toward conflicts between resistant experience and the social and cultural regulation of experience and thus problematize the latter.

Delany, Zinn, and Roy also exceed the poststructuralist account of experience insofar as they present experience as an effect of both language practices and political and economic systems. Delany's inescapable "homosexual" experience, for instance, is a function of discourses on sexuality as well as the laws that regulate sexual relations and the publishing institutions that market his books. The marriage laws and marketing institutions that confronted Delany, like the segregation laws faced by Herndon and the $20 billion dam industry faced by the displaced man, operate jointly with discursive practices that categorize and hierarchize people. While these institutions are not outside of discourse, they exceed representational practices insofar as they affect people's lives in concrete ways, governing how they survive every day, where they live, and what they eat.

One consequence of the materially and institutionally organized dimension of experience is that marginalized experience consists not only of the identity-related experiences of concern to poststructuralists—for example, the experience of being a "woman," a "black," or a "homosexual"—but also of living and working within specific social, cultural, and political hierarchies. "Women's experience," for instance, is not only the experience of "being a woman" but also the experience of the social world from within historically specific gender positions. Thus Varikas finds that Saint-Simonian feminists "speak not only of what it was to be a woman, a female worker or citizen but of how *they themselves experienced and interpreted their lives as women, female workers and non-citizen*" (1995, 99, her emphasis). Similarly, Angelo Herndon and fellow activists studied by Zinn did not redefine "black," but they did rethink liberty and justice in a way that was unique to their position as working-class African Americans. In effect, because the experiences of people in marginalized positions consists not only of experience of identity per se but also experience of the world from specific positions within it, marginalized experience can offer radically new perspectives on basic historical categories and values, such as "work," "progress," and "justice." We can recognize this importance of marginalized experience, however, only if we situate experience in relation to both language practices and extradiscursive social institutions.[23]

Finally, Delany, Zinn, and Roy suggest that narratives that grapple with (even if they cannot directly represent) complex, contradictory, historically situated resistant experiences provide a source of meaning and motivation that the analysis of discourse cannot replace. Poststructuralist theorists might argue that alternative meanings and worldviews find expression in alternative political discourses, such as the discourses of queer culture and global justice, and that analyses of such discourses provide counterhegemonic perspectives without messy appeals to "experience." However, notwithstanding the political importance of alternative discourses and the insights of discourse analysis, such analysis is limited in its ability to animate resistant worldviews. Discourse analysis is limited because alternative political discourses often remain fragmented, still influenced by elements of the ruling discourse, and not fully coalesced into categories and narratives adequate to the full significance of resistant activities.[24] Moreover, alternative discourses are ultimately meaningful only with reference to the subjective experiences that motivate them. The experiences of anger, frustration, hope, and care that move people to pursue alternatives to the ruling discourses on "identity," "globalization," and "progress" point not merely to logical lapses in those discourses but to the latter's limits with respect to some meaning in our lives. Although we may not be able to register this meaning except through our received language, such experienced meaning exceeds language and makes us aware that the ruling language, for instance, our received concepts of "homosexuality," "development," or "resettlement," violate something valuable. Such an experienced sense of violation—which stories of experience can adumbrate even if not directly represent—guides our intervention in discursive practices and ultimately makes those interventions meaningful to us.

The poststructuralist account of experience as a discursive phenomenon cannot account for the elements of experience that motivate and inform discursive intervention. When Scott "refuse[s] a separation between 'experience' and language" (1991, 793), she reduces the complex, variously constituted, sometimes contradictory levels of our experience to that particular level of experience that is directly and entirely formed by discursive practices. Harding calls such one-dimensional experience "spontaneous consciousness," for it is our awareness of ourselves and our worlds prior to any reflection on that experience or the factors behind it (1991, 269, 287, 295). Empiricists naturalize this spontaneously conscious awareness. Poststructuralists such as Scott recognize it to be prefigured by discursive logics. Both, however, presume that such spontaneous awareness exhausts experience. As a result, despite Scott's interest in "seeing differently," she cannot explain the role of experience in driving alternative discourses. Neither can she explain the role of experience-oriented writing in helping us to confront experienced struggles. In the end, she reduces powerful narratives, such as Delany's memoir, to the mere "substitution of one interpretation for another" (Scott 1991, 794).[25]

The poststructuralist critique of experience cannot, therefore, be the last word on marginal experience narratives. While this critique exposes the discursive constitution of identity and experience, it cannot account for those elements of experience that exceed discursive determination, that inform alternative discourses, and that make those discourses meaningful to us. We can account for these crucial elements of resistant experience only if we confront marginal experience narratives as neither collections of indubitable evidence nor mere discursive constructions but as creative responses to socially situated, multilayered, only partly ideologically constituted experiences.

The next chapter draws on transnational feminist theory to develop such a broader account of marginal experience narratives and to investigate their role in global politics.

Chapter 5

Storytelling and Global Politics

*[W]e, the revolutionaries, should not be restrained
by borders, and wherever a revolutionary is, he or
she should communicate the experience of our
people to others. . . .*

—Domitila Barrios de Chungara[1]

I argued in the last chapter that poststructuralists have generated more
critical perspectives on marginal experience narratives, for they have
exposed the ideological mechanisms that underlie representations of
"experience" and "identity." I also argued, however, that this critique
of experience and identity remains a dangerously one-sided approach to
marginal experience narratives. It highlights the way that such narratives can naturalize ideologically constituted concepts of "women's
experience" or "homosexual experience," for instance, but it overlooks
the way that people excluded from public discourse can use experience-
oriented writing to develop discursive agency and, ultimately, to
rearticulate identity and history in ways more responsive to their
struggles.

Fortunately, the absence of an adequate theoretical account of
marginal experience narratives has not stopped many writers and
activists from powerfully narrating their own and others' lives. Nevertheless, this absence does forestall an effective reading and defense of
such narratives. Faced with a choice between either defending marginal
experience narratives as authentic truth or exposing the rhetorical
mechanisms behind such "truths," critics often overlook the full value
of many narratives that do not present certain truths nor analyze
discourse but that nonetheless contribute in their own ways to
emancipatory knowledge and politics.

We can effectively engage and defend marginal experience narratives
only with a more balanced account of such texts, one that addresses not
only their slips into positivism but also their radical potential. To do
this, we must surpass the poststructuralist account of marginal experience narratives in two key respects. First, we must examine not only

how narrative mechanisms "produce" experiencing subjects but also how subjects can be empowered as language users and knowledge producers. Second, we must analyze not only the logic of local signifying systems but also the way that different discursive logics help to sustain, or resist, far-reaching relations of domination.

Transnational feminist analysis, that is, analysis that addresses the multiple and interlocking kinds of power relations that affect women's lives within and across national boundaries, is particularly useful in both of these respects. Critics, including Gloria Anzaldúa, Chandra Mohanty, Uma Narayan, Kavita Panjabi, and Domitila Barrios de Chungara, are acutely aware of the repressive, ideological effects of discursive practices, many of which disempower women in Third World countries by representing them as mere victims or dependents.[2] At the same time, these theorists recognize that the objectification of Third World women is located within and supported by far-reaching economic and legal institutions, such that an effective feminist politics must confront relations of domination on multiple cultural, social, and political levels. Finally, these critics explore concrete ways that the most disempowered people can use resources in their daily lives to challenge the discourses and the institutions that keep them in subservient positions. They include among these resources the experiences of tension with, or resistance to, social and cultural norms; that is, they do not valorize the experience of oppression as the alleged ground of truth or politics, but they do investigate how we might transform lived experiences of discontent into critical knowledge and political consciousness. They recognize narration to be key in the transformation of experience into useful knowledge.[3]

This chapters draws on transnational feminist analysis, together with my Arendtian account of storytelling, to theorize the role of marginal experience narratives in oppositional knowledge and politics. Arendt helps me to explain the epistemic status of narratives that do not present certain evidence but that respond strategically to uncertain, contradictory experiences. Transnational feminist theorists help me to investigate how such narratives can intervene in ideological processes when those processes sustain and are sustained by transnational state, labor, and property relations. In view of this transnational feminist study of narratives, I present a case for stories that use language creatively to address the tensions and contradictions of people's daily lives and that situate these experiences in a broader social context. I argue that such texts not only destabilize received representations of experience but can also facilitate the political consciousness and the political communities that are necessary in order for us to resist varied and far-reaching forms of domination.

Storytelling and Transnational Feminism

I argued in part one that Arendt points toward an alternative to both empiricist and poststructuralist accounts of historical narration. "Storytelling," in Arendt's account, is a simultaneously creative and historically rooted practice in which a specifically located storyteller peruses the traces and remains of past phenomena and, by drawing on and revising received narrative resources, creates a story that helps her contemporaries to consider the significance of yet unspoken and untheorized aspects of those phenomena. Such storytelling counters reductive, prejudicial thinking not by presenting certain truths but by turning our attention to the difficult-to-understand, overlooked elements of our heritage, thus grounding political thinking in historical reality while highlighting the plurality, complexity, and unpredictability of that reality. Unlike claims to objective knowledge, such storytelling encourages a community's creative reckoning with its past and continual public exchange of stories.

Because Arendtian storytelling destabilizes ossified representations of the world and facilitates more critical-minded and inclusive public discussion, such storytelling is particularly suited to the struggles of socially and culturally marginalized groups. Arendt does not address this more specific political role of storytelling. We can elucidate the role of stories in oppositional politics, however, if we situate storytelling, as well as the experiences that storytelling narrates, in relation to broader social and political institutions.

Transnational Feminist Frameworks

Transnational feminist theory offers a particularly useful analytic framework with which to investigate the role of stories in struggles of resistance against exploitative and oppressive relations. Transnational feminism is particularly relevant here because it situates discursive practices in relation to extradiscursive political and economic institutions. In addition, transnational feminist theory allows us to identify experiencing subjects in terms of specific social, political, and cultural hierarchies, yet without naturalizing identities. Below, I briefly review the transnational feminist project. I then use this theoretical framework to examine the dangers and virtues of stories for a feminist and democratic politics.

By *transnational feminism* I refer to a theoretical and political project that confronts, with a view toward resisting, far-reaching political, economic, and cultural relations of domination and the specific dangers that these relations present to women. Such a project is *transnational* because the relations of domination that it confronts cross over national boundaries and produce historically specific cooperative as well as hierarchical relations among women of different nations, races, and classes. It is also *postcolonial* in the sense that it takes seriously the continuing social and psychological effects of colonialism and neocolonialism and seeks ways to move beyond such colonialist relations.[4]

Because it addresses far-reaching and interlocking forms of oppression and exploitation, transnational feminism foregrounds the concerns of people who have been the most marginalized in social and cultural life. At the same time, transnational feminism is defined more by its goals than by its tie to any specific identity. In effect, transnational feminism includes people of diverse cultures, nations, classes, and genders who share a common aim: to resist structural relations of domination in all of the varied and unsuspecting forms that they may appear. Put positively, the aim is to promote "feminist democratic politics," that is, to seek continuously to remake all spheres of life in a way that allows the conscious and collective participation of all people in governing the conditions of their lives (A and M 1997b, xxvii-xxx). This project serves the widely held values of democracy, liberation from oppression, and social justice while it responds in particular to women who have not benefited from what currently passes as "democracy," "feminism," and "progress."[5]

Transnational feminism differs significantly from European and American versions of "global sisterhood," from Third World nationalism, and from postmodern feminism. Eurocentric movements for global sisterhood position all women against a supposedly single, universal "patriarchy." From a transnational feminist perspective, this exclusive focus on an allegedly universal gender oppression is possible only for white, middle-class, and otherwise privileged women who can easily forget about issues of race, class, and sexual orientation. Many other less privileged women are daily reminded that their oppression as women is inseparable from their oppression as members of specific races, classes, nations, or other social groups and that their struggle cannot be reduced to a simple binary opposition to "man." Thus transnational feminists examine the distinct racially and culturally coded forms that gender oppression takes within historically and geographically specific communities (Alarcón 1990, 356–60, 364, 366;

Anzaldúa 1990a, xix-xxv; Gilliam 1991, 216–220; Mohanty 1991b, 64–66; Johnson-Odim 1991).

While transnational feminists take care to situate feminism within specific Third World contexts, they also expressly distinguish themselves from Third World nationalist movements. Such nationalist movements, even when they espouse freedom and democracy for a formerly colonized Third World nation, frequently leave intact sexist laws and customs. Transnational feminists criticize the sexist elements in Third World cultures and emphasize that democracy and freedom must be sought in domestic and cultural spheres as well as formal political arenas, or in Panjabi's terms, on "microsocial" as well as "macrosocial levels."[6] At the same time, even while they criticize dominant forms of Third World culture, they also seek to retain a Third World standpoint with respect to colonialism and neocolonialism. In effect, they walk a fine line between, on the one hand, too easily accepting the dominant sexist versions of Third World culture when they advocate a Third World standpoint, and, on the other hand, sliding too close to Western imperialism when they criticize ruling Third World cultures. In the attempt to chart an alternative to both sexist Third World cultures and imperialist Eurocentric cultures, transnational feminists emphasize the heterogeneous, contested, evolving character of culture itself, while they attempt to cultivate the more feminist and democratic elements within the Third World (A and M 1997b, xxv-xxxv; Gilliam 1991; Narayan 1997, 3–39; 1998, 91; Panjabi 1997; Shohat 1997, 184).

Finally, transnational feminists share with poststructuralists a concern to address the ways that discursive practices categorize and hierarchize subjects. Going beyond poststructuralism, however, transnational feminists situate language practices within far-reaching political and economic systems. Transnational feminists remain concerned with systemic relations of domination because they recognize that the current global economy, with its transnational corporations, capital mobility, and international division of labor, has exacerbated (even while it has complicated) race, class, sex, and gender hierarchies. Although these social and political hierarchies are mediated by language practices and although they do not define our inner nature, they do profoundly affect our daily choices and concerns. Thus transnational feminists direct our attention to the specific cross-culture, cross-border processes and institutions, such as the World Bank, transnational corporations, sex tourism, and transnational trade agreements, that generate a complex of hierarchical relations among and within historically specific communities (A and M 1997b, xii-xx, xxix; Gilliam 1991;

Hennessy 1993a, 30–32, 122–24, 134–35; Mohanty 1991a, 1–31; Moya 1997, 136–49; Narayan 1997, 35–39).

In order to describe how representational practices and far-reaching political and economic institutions jointly govern our everyday lives, transnational feminists find useful Dorothy Smith's concept, *relations of ruling*.[7] "Relations of ruling" refers to the ensemble of bureaucratic, legal, and business institutions that, together with language practices, such as those of legal documents, the media, and academic social sciences, order our lives according to standard procedures and categories. Although this modern form of rule seems neutral insofar as it operates in an impersonal and detached manner, its abstract categories and impersonal governing mode actually represent the perspective of professionals who are detached from the interpersonal, bodily, and subjective details of everyday life while the same mode facilitates the peremptory categorization and regulation of people's lives (Smith 1987). The concept *relations of ruling* thus recognizes the systemic as well as the pervasive, anonymous, and textually mediated character of modern power relations.

Transnational Feminist Goals

When we view feminism from this global-minded and multileveled perspective, the goal of feminism is no longer simply to empower women or to analyze gender ideology. By itself, the empowerment of women does not change entrenched structures of domination, especially when we consider that women themselves are a diverse group, no more essentially wise or moral than any other group (Mohanty 1991b, 71; Gilliam 1991, 216–217). Neither is feminism's goal adequately captured by the aim to analyze "knowledge about sexual difference" (Scott 1988, 10), for analysis of gender ideology is not adequate to address the imbrication of gender with other social hierarchies or the material dimensions of oppression (Hennessy 1993a, 16–21, 34–36, 123; A and M 1997b, xvii–xviii).

When we address women's struggles from the perspective of transnational feminism, both the empowerment of women and the analysis of gender ideology become subsumed within a broader goal: the development of democratic practices that continually resist relations of domination in all spheres of life. Such a feminism is inseparable from other social struggles because, as Barrios explains, "for us [Latin American popular class women] the primary and principal task is not to fight against our compañeros but with them, to change the system we live in for another in which men and women have the right to live, to work, to organize" ([1977] 1986, 221). In essence, a feminism that is responsive to Third World women's concerns will intersect with other social struggles because women who seek to challenge the power of transnational corporations, the World Bank, and repressive Third World states share projects with labor, environmentalist, and indigenous rights organizations and other social justice groups. Indeed, like Barrios, many Third World women themselves belong to such groups.

Transnational feminists thus join an increasing number of scholars and activists who argue that single-issue and single-identity politics are unresponsive to the complexity of many people's struggles. Moreover, such narrowly conceived politics are too weak to counter the powerful neocolonialist institutions that popular movements must confront. This is true now even more so than when Barrios wrote that revolutionaries "should not be restrained by borders." In the last two decades, neoliberal economic and political institutions have mushroomed that cross national borders and that often have more power than national governments. For instance, the North American Free Trade Agreement (NAFTA) encourages international trade by allowing transnational companies to sue host states if any state regulations interfere with their profits. The treaty thus dismantles the power of governments to regulate industry while it prevents Mexican workers from exercising their Mexican labor rights when they work in factories of U.S. origin. At the same time, NAFTA undermines the bargaining power of unions and environmental groups in the United States, for these groups now face companies that can escape regulation by moving across the border (A and M 1997, xxiv; Anderson et al. 1996; Economic Policy Institute 1997; Galeano 1973, 225–308; Instituto del Tercer Mundo 1999, 62–71, 394; Kamel 1990). In this context, activists and critics have emphasized the need for oppositional political movements to organize across class, race, gender, nation, and traditional issue boundaries so that labor, small farmers, and women's, environmental, and human rights groups can coordinate their strikes, media campaigns, and political agendas (A and M 1997b, xvii-xx, xl-xli; Anderson et al. 1998; Anderson et al. 1999; Greider 2000; Kamel 1990, 66–67; Moberg 2000; Mohanty 1991a, 2–4, 22–29; Nichols 1999; U.S./Cuba Labor Exchange 1997).

The overriding aim of such multi-issue, cross-border coalitions, like the aim of transnational feminism, is to advance democratic participation in official government forums as well as in all of the social and cultural practices that determine the conditions of people's lives. The specific steps implied by such a broadly envisioned democracy vary in specific contexts but have included calls for land rights, food security, laws against spouse abuse, public support for educational and artistic collectives, and a rethinking of "equal protection under the law" in a manner that does not limit this to a specific nationality or sexuality. Transnational feminists and their allies likewise seek democratic openness and public accountability, not only on the national level but also on the part of the transnational organizations, for instance, the World Trade Organization, the International Monetary Fund, and the regulatory bodies of multilateral trade agreements, which are currently beyond popular control but whose decisions affect all of our lives (A and M 1997b, xxvii-xlii; Anderson et al. 1998; Anderson et al. 1999; Borosage 1999; Coalition for Justice in the Maquiladoras 1999; Economic Policy Institute 1997; Greider 2000; Kamel and Hoffman 1999, 111–15; Nichols 1999; U.S./Cuba Labor Exchange 1997, 19–27).[8]

Situating Storytelling

Transnational feminism's broad-minded analytic framework, with its attention to the interrelations among local cultural practices and far-reaching political and economic institutions, is particularly useful for studying the social role of storytelling. Stories, from this standpoint, are meaning-making practices with their own logic and cultural specificity. At the same time, stories are also social practices that are regulated by the institutions that produce, legitimate, and distribute knowledge. Viewed in this light, the stories that are available for interpreting our worlds are not determined entirely by social institutions, but they are inevitably influenced by (and can potentially influence) those institutions.

From the standpoint of transnational feminism, stories are bound up with social institutions and related social hierarchies, first, because stories do not circulate directly from storyteller to readers. They reach a wide audience only with the assistance of publishers, educators, and various news media, as well as academic and research institutions that legitimize certain stories as valid knowledge. Given the economically and politically influenced as well as the increasingly centralized character of these knowledge-producing institutions, stories from the perspective of the more powerful social groups gain a much greater public visibility than stories from less powerful groups (Hebert 1993; Jaquet 1998; McChesney 1999; Mines 1998; Manning 1999; Polter 1995; Shenk 1999; Smith 1987, 2–8, 17–36).

On a more subtle level, social hierarchies also affect stories because the socially dominant stories provide the shared "common sense" interpretive frameworks on which all stories depend in order to be communicable. Arendt described the way that highly publicized stories influence the basic conceptual paradigms that make up a community's "common sense" and thereby structure communication in that community. Each storyteller, she observed, cannot simply invent her own language but depends on received narrative resources that are familiar to her community. Specifically, she depends on the narrative constructs that I have called (in chapters one and two) narrative matrices and story images. Such narrative resources serve to organize phenomena into identifiable units of actors, actions, and events and to instantiate abstract political concepts through their vivid, metaphorical descriptions of specific historical incidents. Arendt emphasizes the social value of such tradition-given narrative resources: They provide a shared sense of how to organize information and interpret the meaning of political concepts and thereby enable a community to remember and meaningfully discuss historical phenomena.

When we situate Arendt's account of storytelling in the context of the social production and distribution of knowledge, then we see that tradition-given narrative resources not only enable a community's storytelling but tend to do so in an ideological manner. The social processes that produce shared narrative resources tend to produce these as ideology because, when certain narrative paradigms become widely known by virtue of being endorsed and repeated by powerful research institutions, publishers, and the media, such narrative paradigms appear to us as if they were timeless representations of the historical world. As a result, the structure of these widely distributed narrative paradigms, including the way they delineate characters and actions, the way they distinguish the historically significant "event" from the insignificant, and the way they illustrate and interpret moral and political concepts, come to be accepted as natural and necessary ways of ordering the world.

The narrative paradigms that are common in a particular cultural community are themselves informed by the more basic discursive logics that prevail in that community. In modern Western cultures, dominant narrative paradigms are structured, in particular, by Enlightenment discourses on the subject. Thus dominant narrative paradigms present "actors" as discrete and innately autonomous units, "actions" as direct public expressions of an actor's will, and "events" as phenomena of the so-called public sphere that are separate from interpersonal and bodily life. As a result, when history books or news reports organize events in terms of ruling narrative paradigms, they inscribe this Enlightenment logic into our understanding of particular historical phenomena. Historiographical and political narratives are thus informed by our

tradition's dominant discursive logic while such narratives also constitute a central medium through which this logic is instantiated and made
meaningful to us.

Finally, stories are also bound up with social hierarchies because the
dominant, "common-sense" narrative paradigms not only regulate
subsequent narration but, in so doing, exercise a strong social and
psychological impact. This impact is akin to the power that Foucault
ascribes to scientific discourses. Foucault explains that scientific discourses do not merely describe but *constitute* their objects of study
(Foucault [1969] 1972, 49). Similarly, dominant narrative paradigms
define what counts as the historical field, historical problems, and
,historical objects, while they generate technologies practiced on these
"objects." In Foucault's terms, ruling narrative paradigms "function as
true," informing social and legal responses to certain groups of people
as well as individuals' own experiences of themselves (1980, 131).
Susan Griffin (1992) describes these sort of interrelations among
narrative, experience, and social practices. Griffin describes how traditional war narratives and the images of masculinity they articulate have
led soldiers to experience their own aversion to war as deviant and
effeminate, while they have enabled governments to address such
responses with shock therapy or other "treatments" for supposed
psychological deviancies. Narratives of the global economy also inform
socioeconomic practices. For instance, neoliberal narratives of "globalization" present the current set of transnational political and economic institutions as if they were the result of an inexorable process in
which capital and companies flow naturally toward places that can use
them best.[9] In the words of two popular authors, politicians need only
"step out of [globalization's] way" so that the "waves" of global trade-
activity can allow "people to specialize in what they do best" and
resources to be allocated "to the country that can use them best, even if
that activity is linking Chinese hands with American consumers"
(Micklethwait and Wooldridge 2000, xviii, 29, 111).[10] Such narratives
obscure the political and military institutions that maintain this seemingly "natural" system, while they foster perceptions of certain people
as inherently "cheap" and inherently suited to manual labor, thereby
helping to rationalize exploitative practices that deprive people of labor
rights and pay them substandard wages.

When stories perpetuate dominant conceptual paradigms and rationalize social practices, they participate in the relations of ruling that
govern our everyday lives. Like many cultural forms of rule, however,
their influence on how we interpret and organize the world is rarely
noticed. In the following section, I use transnational feminist analysis to

elucidate the specific ways that current stories rationalize and reinforce social hierarchies.

Narration and Colonization

In order to maintain the status quo in these lands,
where every minute a child dies of disease or
hunger, we must look at ourselves through the eyes
of those who oppress us.

—Eduardo Galeano[11]

[T]he silence and silencing of people begins
with the dominating enforcement of linguistic
conventions. . . .

—Norma Alarcón[12]

Both Arendt and Scott begin to address the politics of narrative discourse. Arendt emphasizes the positive role of the more historically sensitive stories in enabling us to understand historical phenomena, but she also warns that ideological narratives can impose on historical phenomena a totalizing and deterministic logic that fosters complacent and prejudicial forms of thinking. In a different vein, Scott explains how, independent of any conscious intent by authors, historical narratives perpetuate the ideological mechanisms that categorize and position subjects.

Transnational feminist analysis takes these insights a step further. From a transnational feminist standpoint, ruling narrative paradigms are dangerous not only because they tend to reduce phenomena to predetermined categories, or because they reinscribe modern discourses on the subject, but because, when they do so, they reinforce social hierarchies. In light of transnational feminist theory, I examine how dominant narrative paradigms, including dominant ways of categorizing "actors," "actions," and "events," tend to efface, misconstrue, and ultimately thwart the struggles of people who are already the most marginalized in social and cultural life.

Narrative "Actors"

Ruling narrative logics reinforce the marginalization of people who are. already disempowered, first, because they obscure the struggles and the subjectivity of people who face multiple oppressions. Like poststructuralists, transnational feminists criticize the Enlightenment logic that defines "actors" in terms of discrete, unified, and binary-structured identities. Going beyond poststructuralist discourse analysis, transnational feminists argue that this limited notion of identity leads us to view power relations strictly in terms of binary oppositions, such as the opposition between men and women. Consequently, this logic obscures the historically specific, complex, and overlapping oppressions that burden many women of color (Alarcón 1990, 357–62; Anzaldúa 1990b, 378–84; Collins 1986, 519–20; Mohanty 1982, 33–38; 1991b, 56–64, 71).

From a transnational feminist perspective, the logic of discrete and unified "actors" also rules out the possibility of multiply aligned historical subjects. When historical narratives construe "actors" as fixed and homogeneous units, they restrict actors to a stable set of discrete units, such as a set of different nations, different classes, different races, or different political parties. Such a focus on discrete and single-dimension actors is incapable of recognizing Third World women as historical actors on their own terms, for Third World women are neither strictly class, strictly nationalist, or strictly gender identified and therefore do not fit conventional notions of "workers," "feminists," or "Third World nationalists"—even when they may be all of these. We can recognize Third World women as multiply aligned historical subjects only if we redescribe "historical actors" in such a way that acknowledges the many social relations in which selfhood is constituted, the consequent heterogeneity within identity groups, and the possibility for strategic alignment with varying social groups (Alarcón 1990; Anzaldúa 1990a; Mohanty 1982, 38–42 and 1991b).

For transnational feminists, the logic of naturally existing, discrete, and stable actor-units is also dangerous because it leads theorists who do study "Third World women" to treat such women as a homogeneous and naturally existing group. Such a reductive and reified notion of "Third World women" leads to the problem that Mohanty calls "discursive colonization" (1991b). Scholars, the news media, and policy makers tend to treat "Third World women" as an easily knowable object of their discourse, with the result that they reduce such women to passive victims or dependents, creating an "average Third World woman." Writers and policy makers, including Western feminists, participate in such discursive colonization (even if unwittingly) when they claim authority to speak for women in other countries, when they suppress those women's heterogeneity in order to fit them neatly into analytic categories, or when they neglect the history and politics behind their definitions of group identity (Gilliam 1991, 218–19; Mohanty 1991b, 52–54). Liberals also perform discursive colonization when, in attempt to recognize cultural differences between "the West" and the "the Third World," they presuppose a unified "Third World" that is defined in opposition to "Western" culture and values. Recent media representations of Afghani women illustrate how even well-intentioned Westerners often project "average Third World women" and treat the women they seek to aid as mere helpless victims (Flanders 2001).[13]

Whether or not intended, such reductive representations of "the Third World" or "Third World women" abet the social and cultural repression of women in Third World countries. When people affirm "Third World culture" as if this were a homogeneous entity, they overlook the tensions within that culture, notably tensions between sexists and feminists, and end up identifying "Third World culture" with its dominant (hence patriarchal) elements. Such oversimplified representations of "the Third World" allows men in Third World countries to accuse women in their countries who oppose sexist practices of being traitors to the country's supposedly "true" culture (Chow 1991, 90–95; Narayan 1998, 91–99; Shohat 1997, 184). Likewise, when Westerners paint "culture" in crude analytic strokes, "respect for cultural differences" turns into cultural caricaturing that reifies dominant conceptions of culture and provides a convenient excuse for people to ignore abuses against Third World women and other culturally marginalized groups (Chow 1991, 85–90; Narayan 1998, 87–91; Okin 1998, 36–37, Said 2001).[14]

In addition, when writers use the category "Third World women" as if this were a homogeneous and naturally existing unit, they obscure the range of activities that have been pursued by many Third World women, including feminist, environmental, and global justice activism.[15] In obscuring the self-conscious resistant activities of many women, the reductive use of "Third World women" prevents Western European and North American men and women, as well as Third World men and even many Third World women themselves, from recognizing the agency of women in Third World countries (A and M 1997b, xxviii; Gilliam 1991, 218–219; Jehl 1999; Mohanty 1991b, 56–61; Narayan 1998, 91). The discursive colonization of "Third World women" thus reinforces the idea that such women are mere objects of, rather than participants in, the organization of social life. From here it is a short step toward public policies such as certain local and internationally sponsored population policies that, instead of educating and empowering women, attempt to exercise control over women's bodies and sexualities, often doing so in the name of "progress" or "morality" (A and M 1997b, xxiii-xxiv; Bauza 1994; Barroso and Bruschini 1991; Correa and Petchesky 1994).

Narrative "Action"

Prevailing narrative paradigms further reinforce the marginalization of people who are already disempowered because these paradigms presuppose an Enlightenment notion of "action" in which action stems from the innate agency of a "private" individual who expresses himself in "public" deeds. Feminists have long argued that this notion of action tends to obscure the activities of women who, historically, have been excluded from public affairs (Scott 1988, 17, 24; Rowbotham 1974). From a transnational feminist standpoint, the Enlightenment construction of action is not simply gender biased but, more specifically, is biased against people who lack prominent public positions and representation by organized movements. Thus, as white, middle-class women have entered high-status professions and have formed organizations with national stature, the media and history books have recognized many such women among the makers of history. At the same time, however, the status of "agent" continues to be refused to poor and racially oppressed women, many of whom neither hold public offices nor are represented by formal political organizations. While many such women have in fact galvanized projects from work strikes to environmental justice campaigns, their activities generally lie outside of the public spotlight and are relayed in testimonies or smaller journals that are overlooked by the more established scholarly institutions and news media (Collins 1986, 523–24; Di Chiro 1996; Mohanty 1991a, 33–35; 1991b, 56–71; Kaplan 1990; Nazma, n.d.; Panjabi 1997).

When narratives construe action in the conventional terms, as the public-sphere expression of individual will, they not only limit the status of "actor" to those who wield public power but also remove from critical scrutiny the social background conditions that enable some people to express their will, in both the home and the public arenas, and that place severe constraints on others (Lugones 1997). Historical narratives obfuscate this social underpinning of agency when they report the actions of people who dominate political and economic life and leave unexamined the social and cultural institutions that made their dominance possible. In addition, when historical narratives represent agency as an individual achievement, they obscure the need for many people to engage in collective struggle in order to realize effective agency.

Some feminist theorists have exposed the social preconditions of agency by investigating the mutually reinforcing relations between "public" sphere and "private" sphere power hierarchies. According to these theorists, social and legal institutions back up men's power in the home, while many "private" family and cultural practices reinforce patriarchal states (de Beauvoir [1949] 1989, xxviii-xxx, 110–37; Okin 1998, 34–37; Mackinnon 1989; Scott 1988, 6, 20, 24–26; Smith 1987, 54–77). A transnational feminist perspective reveals how colonialist and neocolonialist processes exacerbate these relations of complicity among microsocial and macrosocial power hierarchies (Alexander 1997; A and M 1997b, xxi-xxviii; Mohanty 1991a, 15–20; Narayan 1997, 15–21, 45–80; 1998, 90–91; Okin 1998, 34–37). In particular, transnational feminists describe how many patriarchal practices have passed as "private-sphere," "traditional" customs but are actually the result of collusion between a colonialist or neocolonialist government and local male elites who have selectively supported the cultural practices that serve both of their interests. For instance, the British colonial state in India gave legal sanctification to a practice, highly questionable under Muslim law, in which Indian widows were forced by their in-laws to remarry within the same family. (The intention was to stabilize land ownership, a goal of both landholding elites and the colonial state.) When widows challenged the legality of this practice, British rulers defended the always-questionable practice by appealing to "tribal custom" (Mohanty 1991a, 19).

When historical narratives treat action as a self-evident individual achievement, people such as the Indian widows who were unable to exercise their options in their personal lives or to pursue their interests effectively in public affairs appear as if they were a naturally passive group. In other words, thwarted agency is simply not recognized as agency. This compounds the social effects of discursive colonization, for it helps dominant groups to treat people who are socially marginalized as if these people really had no independent will or projects. Perhaps most dangerously, narratives that presuppose conventional notions of agency abet the efforts by transnational businesses to pretend that the women who they hire are "naturally" inclined to tedious labor and thus inherently deserving of pay even more meager than the substandard wages of Third World men. Representations of Southeast Asian women are infamous, or "famous" as one Malaysian promotional brochure puts it: "The manual dexterity of the oriental female is famous the world over. . . . Who, therefore, could be better qualified by nature and inheritance to contribute to the efficiency of a bench-assembly production line than the oriental girl?" (cited in Kamel 1990, 83).[16] The representation of "actors" as if they were naturally given units and "action" as if this were an expression of individual will in the public arena does not in itself determine this stereotype of "the oriental girl." Nonetheless, these ways of construing actors and actions facilitate such stereotypes, for they foster worldviews that regard people who have been excluded from public affairs as mere passive recipients of history and as naturally destined for a single role.

Narrative "Events"

Conventions of narrative discourse also obscure the struggles of the most marginalized social groups by the way that they define historical "events." These conventions locate events in a public realm that is presumably separate from family, interpersonal, and "private" life. They also presuppose that events are clearly visible and effective developments that occur within a specific time frame. Thus standard event-units, such as "war," "election," or "revolution," have specifiable outcomes and definite beginnings and endings that are marked by clear-cut boundaries, such as a change in leadership, a military attack, or an international treaty.

This notion of "historical event" as a clearly delineated public phenomena with a definite outcome effectively excludes from history the resistant activities of the most marginalized groups. This is so, first, because many such activities occur during times that seem uneventful by standard criteria. For instance, the Indian widows' legal battle with the British state in colonial India, the refusal by contemporary Adivasi Indians to move when waters from the dams submerged their homes, the street demonstrations by Guatemalan and Argentinean women whose children had "disappeared," the hunger strikes by Bolivian housewives' committees, Jamaican women's political theater, and petitions for land rights presented by transnational indigenous groups all have taken place in "peace time," that is, in the time in between seemingly important events.[17] These activities also fail to qualify as "events" because most yielded no immediate or self-evident "products."[18] Many also fall outside standard definitions of "historical events" because they seem to be motivated by "personal" concerns, such as concern for one's home, children, or marriage choice. Finally, many of these activities also confound customary narrative paradigms because the participants resist conventionally defined actor-units. The women who protested as "widows," "mothers," and "housewives," for instance, defy the standard division between public and private characters, while the transnational indigenous movements resist lexicons that divide the globe into separate nations. As a result, mainstream political narratives tend to overlook or oversimplify these struggles while narratives that pursue innovative styles to address such obscure, seemingly uncategorizable activities are generally considered too creative, too particularized, or too subjective to count as knowledge (Mohanty 1991a, 36; Roy 2001, 11–13, 25–29; Smith 1987, 60).

Standard criteria for "events" also overlook the struggles of the most marginalized people because such struggles lack clear public definition. Excluded from public life and lacking the resources to realize goals effectively and completely, many of us can indicate our resistance to social institutions and public policies only in indirect, seemingly nonsensical gestures, such as disrupting public meetings, sabotaging equipment, going on hunger strikes, wading in the chest-deep water of submerged homes, subtly protesting against daily routines, or even committing suicide or infanticide. Since such activities do not fully achieve their intention, they do not present observers with a self-evident meaning and, consequently, leave behind few public records sensitive to their project (Borosage 1999; Collins 1986, 523–34; Lugones 1997; Mohanty 1997, 24–27; S. Mohanty 1997, 220–29; Nichols 1999; Roy 1999; 2001, 28; Spivak 1988, 307–08).[19]

Lack of meaningful public reception not only prevents an action from being recognized as part of history but, in so doing, thwarts an action's impact in the present. As Arendt explains, when an action is not meaningfully interpreted by the surrounding community, it lacks the "completion . . . accomplished by remembrance," that is, it is never crystallized in narrative form and consequently escapes what people recognize and respond to as their history (BPF, 6). In effect, an action has full historical force only when an audience (or, perhaps, a powerful audience) narrates and remembers it, for only such a reception "makes opinions significant and actions effective" (Arendt OT, 296). Those of us whose actions are misunderstood by the dominant culture or who, like refugees or noncitizens, are judged by our classification rather than by our individual deeds, "are deprived not of the right to freedom, but of the right to action; not of the right to think whatever they please, but of the right to opinion" (Arendt OT, 296).

Because an action's historical impact depends on an audience who narrates and remembers it, those of us who act outside recognized public forums or whose projects challenge received worldviews face particular obstacles in contributing our words and deeds to history. We will be obstructed not only by social institutions that disempower us but also by interpretive practices that overlook or misunderstand us. This helps to explain why "the subaltern," according to Gayatri Spivak, cannot speak (1988). The subaltern does not lack thoughts or voice but rather social institutions and cultural communities, including tradition-given narrative paradigms, that will support her projects and make sense of her aims.

Toni Morrison in *Beloved* (1987) offers a vivid fictional illustration of such social and cultural obstacles to historical action. When Sethe, who escaped slavery while pregnant, is hunted down by her former master, she considers that her best option, given the current slavery laws, is to kill the baby she loves rather than relinquish her to slavery. The dilemma is underscored later in the novel when we learn that Sethe's mother and other women who were raped by slave traders threw their infants into the sea. Given their circumstances, such acts of infanticide may have been the only way for enslaved African women to defy an institution that claimed them and their children as property and that deprived them of family relations. Nevertheless Sethe's act is interpreted by both the white and the black community as a case of individual insanity, for tradition-given conceptions of "morality" and "motherhood" place both of these phenomena in an ahistorical "private" realm and thereby deny any historical meaning to the act of killing one's infant.

Reclaiming Narration:
Anzaldúa and Barrios de Chungara

Encrucijadas, haunted by voices and images that violated us, bearing the pains of the past, we are slowly acquiring the tools to change the disabling images and memories, to replace them with self-affirming ones. . . .

—Gloria Anzaldúa[20]

A simple solution may seem to provide a corrective to the current under-representation of marginalized people's resistant activities: Narrate more of these activities! Effective narration of such activities is difficult, however, given that most leave few clear marks in public records. Moreover, the dominant ways of conceptualizing "identity," "action," and "historical events" that I have described influence all of our thinking and writing, so that even marginal experience narratives risk repeating the biases and exclusions of received narrative logics. For instance, a narrative may address some women actors but fail to challenge the categories that deny recognition to multiply aligned subjects and to less successful resistant activities. In addition, the conventions of genre divide the "experience" of autobiography from the "public events" of history, so that even histories of marginalized groups often overlook activities outside the formal political arena. At the same time, historiographical norms dictate a realist style that demands the use of conventional categories and narrative structures (Barthes 1989, 133–34; White 1975, 58–63). Autobiographical conventions, for their part, dictate a single-voiced and autonomous-speaking subject, in effect presupposing that the subject is a discrete and self-made individual (Alarcón 1990, 365).

Thus, on the one hand, transnational feminists have an urgent need to narrate little-known struggles of resistance. On the other hand, however, we cannot simply call for increasing the quantity of marginal experience narratives, for unless we alter the basic norms and categories of narrative discourse, the activities of the most marginalized people remain obscure. The challenge, then, is to avoid problematic categories of "identity," "agency," and "public event" and yet still to use marginal experience narratives to empower feminist democratic struggles.

Anzaldúa and Barrios demonstrate possible ways that the narration of marginalized experiences can contribute to a genuinely broad-based feminist and democratic politics. In her groundbreaking essay, "La conciencia de la mestiza: Towards a New Consciousness," Anzaldúa self-consciously turns to "new theorizing methods" that "maneuver between our particular experiences and the necessity of forming our own categories" (1990b, xxv). In order to form categories more responsive to Third World women's lives, she strategically mixes poetry, autobiography, and history, using the tensions in her own experience as a springboard to "change the disabling images and memories" of women of color (Anzaldúa 1990b, xxvii). Unlike Anzaldúa, Barrios is not a professional writer but the wife of a Bolivian mineworker. Her testimony, *"Si me permiten hablar . . .": testimonio de Domitila una mujer de las minas de Bolivia* ([1977] 1986), is pieced together from speeches and interviews with the help of her editor, Moema Viezzar. Despite her minimal formal education, however, Barrios is equally effective at using experience-oriented writing to challenge ruling discourses and to present not a blueprint for revolution but "a little grain of sand" that others might use to orient themselves in their struggles (Barrios [1977] 1986, 13). In their own ways, both women use experience not simply to confirm their oppression but to affirm historical "actors" that encompass heterogeneous and strategically chosen allegiances, historical "actions" that are performed by people with limited public power, and "historical events," the impetus and significance of which are inseparable from so-called private lives. In so doing, they not only recast basic narrative categories but also help to build a resistant politics that is anchored in the realities of people's everyday lives.

Renarrating "Identity"

Both Anzaldúa and Barrios ground their narratives in socially and geographically specific experiences, yet without naturalizing identity and without reverting to what Anzaldúa calls a mere "counterstance," that is, a mere affirmation of a formerly devalued group (1990b, 378). Instead of simply asserting the value of a pregiven identity, they each use their writing to explore the forces that condition their experience and to renarrate their identities in ways that help them to confront those forces more effectively. In the process, they also recast "identity" as a historically rooted yet also strategic category.

Through her personal writing, for instance, Anzaldúa rethinks what it means to be Mexican American. Ruling representations of "Mexican American" construct this identity as an ahistorical category whose difference from "American" is defined in terms of a pluralistic notion of difference. In this view, "Mexican American" is structurally equivalent to other minorities. The poverty and cultural alienation endured by many Mexican Americans can only be interpreted as a personal failing (Moya 1997, 139–40). Anzaldúa challenges this naturalized and ahistorical construction of her identity. Her challenge (like that pursued by Delany) begins not on an abstract theoretical level but with her own experiences, in particular, her "internal strife" (1990b, 377). Although she initially interprets her strife as a personal problem, she reinterprets her "personal" anguish as she traces its sources. Tracing the sources of her pain and confusion, she relates that she is American, yet her art and language are derided as "unAmerican"; she is a lesbian, yet she lives among a people who equate "woman" with defect; and, moreover, she watched her father die from overwork as a farm laborer on originally Indian land, debilitated from doing the work that enriched others (1990b, 384–388). As Anzaldúa articulates images and draws connections that help her to make sense of these lived contradictions, she foregrounds social phenomena that are formative of her identity but that ruling narratives of "Mexican American" efface. Such phenomena include her ancestors having become part of the United States through United States appropriation of Mexican land, Mexican American labor and resources having sustained North America's wealth, "Mexican machismo" having been formed in reaction to North American exploitation and degradation of Mexican men, and cultural ideologies that have tried unsuccessfully to fit her into a single culture. By highlighting phenomena that condition her borderlands existence but that are omitted from ruling narratives of "Mexican American," Anzaldúa shows how her poverty and mental anguish are not as "natural" as they may seem but are, rather, an effect of the social and cultural hierarchies that position Mexican women in North American society.

Anzaldúa also uses her writing to explore alternative ways of interpreting her cultural confusion. She finds that when she embraces the contradictions of being at once American and Mexican, at once a cultural outcast and a lesbian with ties to all races and cultures, her seemingly schizophrenic existence has potential value. As she puts it, the coexistence of opposites in the person of mixed heritage "makes us crazy constantly, but if the center holds, we've made some kind of evolutionary step forward" (1990b, 380). She creates new metaphors to highlight this positive potential of the mestizaje. For instance, the spiritual growth that someone can achieve when she reclaims her mixed heritage is a spiritual "morphogenesis" akin to the physical process of morphogenesis discovered by the chemist Ilya Prigogine in which two substances interact in new, unpredictable ways. She also likens the mestiza to the crossbred indigenous corn, which, clinging to both the cob and the earth, is particularly resilient. Anzaldúa's organic metaphors reclaim biology from the racial "purists." While they remain metaphors, they remind us that the biological world equally lends itself to being described in ways that value miscegenation. In terms of the Arendtian schema of storytelling, we could say that her metaphors help us to appreciate qualities of her borderlands existence that were always real but that were not consciously noticed or publicly acknowledged due to the limitations of tradition-given narrative frameworks. Significantly, while Anzaldúa's lived experiences of strife motivate her to renarrate her borderlands identity, her narrative presumes neither complete self-knowledge nor a comprehensive social analysis. It presumes only her courage to confront the various "forces weighing on her daily choices and concerns" and her initiative to contribute to the terms in which those forces are represented.[21]

Like Anzaldúa, Barrios does not need "expert" social theory but only the initiative to confront the contradictions in her own experience in order to challenge popular discourses on her identity. Against the popular idea that "women don't work," for instance, Barrios counters her daily schedule of waking at four in the morning and working until eleven at night making meals for her family in their one-room apartment, standing in line at company stores, making clothes and washing them in troughs, and making and selling *salteñas* to supplement her husband's meager income. This experience is worth more than a degree in economics in enabling her to recognize the economic importance of women's work. "One day," she says, "it occurred to me to make a chart. We put as an example the price of washing clothes per dozen pieces and we figured out how many dozens of items we washed a month. Then the cooks wage, the babysitter's, the servant's. . . . So that way we made our men understand that we really work. . . . Even though . . . for all this work we don't receive a single penny" (Barrios [1977] 1986, 35–36). Her daily experiences as a member of the mining community likewise lead her to appreciate the social value of mineworkers' labor and the lie of popular representations of mineworkers. "Many people don't understand us because they don't know us. There are many Bolivians who say, 'don't you know that they [the mineworkers] chew coca, that they're drug addicts?' . . . But for us, the mineworkers are not *khoya locos,* they're not ignorant, they're men who are supporting the country's economy" ([1977] 1986, 210–11).

In addition to affirming the social value of the labor performed by housewives and mineworkers, she reclaims these supposedly subordinate and outcast roles as important standpoints from which to struggle for a more just world. This insight resonant of Marxist and feminist standpoint theory is, again, based on her everyday experience. Her daily life tells her not only that women and mineworkers are integral to the economy but that the hardships and the meager (or nonexistent) wages that mineworkers and women endure indicate the contradictions of that economy. After describing her onerous daily chores as a mineworker's wife, for instance, she concludes, "I think all this shows very clearly how the mineworker is doubly exploited, no? Because, with such a small [mineworker's] wage, the woman has to do much more in the home. And that's ultimately unpaid work that we're doing for the boss, isn't it?" ([1977] 1986, 34–35). Since women's (and children's) unpaid domestic labor sustains the system of exploitation, she reasons, we must "let the woman, the man, the children participate in the struggle of the working class" and must "throw out forever that bourgeois idea that the woman should stay in the home and not get involved in other things, in union or political matters," for the exclusion of women from politics only upholds the system of exploitation by keeping women undervalued while the inclusion of women in politics is necessary in order to expose fully the system's injustices and to build a system that is genuinely just ([1977] 1986, 36).

When she narrates her everyday struggles, Barrios not only affirms women's crucial role in politics but also recasts "woman" as a heterogeneous group whose interests overlap with others, including men. For instance, Barrios tells the story of the Housewives Committee that she and other women formed in order to address their common problems as miners' wives. She describes how the women first forged solidarity as housewives and then, in their attempts to secure basic necessities for their families, were led to align with mineworkers, other Bolivian laborers, peasants, the conservative Christian Family Movement, and even the young soldiers from the countryside who were sent to terrorize the miners. When she recounts her own experiences with necessarily fluid coalitions, Barrios makes compelling her rejection of any "feminism" that cannot appreciate her need to form alliances with men. She likewise gives historical substance to the reconstruction of "identity" as an amorphous, unstable phenomenon.

Through her testimony, Barrios also cultivates a shared identity with her readers. She enjoins her readers to identify with her by tracing conditions that she shares with other women of Bolivian mining towns, by speaking in the first person plural, "we," and by ending her claims with questions, asking readers to consider for themselves if what she says rings true to their own experience. On one level, this story creates community among Bolivian miners' wives, for it describes a history and a social location, "woman of the Bolivian mines," that similarly located woman can recognize as their own and can use to develop their own sense of historical identity. Insofar as she helps women in mining towns to identify with one another based on the shared character of their everyday hardships, her testimony has a consciousness-raising effect for "women of the Bolivian mines" similar to the effect of North American feminist consciousness-raising in helping North American women to appreciate their shared struggles as women.[22] Unlike the latter, however, Barrios (like many Latin American testimonials[23]) speaks not only to her gender and geographically specific identity group but also to a broader public. For, on a second level, she includes a broad range of readers within her potential community. She speaks to "workers, peasants, housewives, everyone, even the young people and the intellectuals who want to be with us" (Barrios [1977] 1986, 10). In projecting a community that encompasses herself and her readers in a common project, she promotes a fluid, value-based, and heterogeneous conception of identity.

The experience-driven revisions of identity that Barrios and Anzaldúa narrate are not mere imaginative exercises. They facilitate precisely the kind of multi-issue, cross-cultural, and cross-border coalitions that many activists argue are necessary if popular movements are to confront effectively the transnational institutions that increasingly govern our lives. Experience-based narratives contribute to such cross-border coalition building in ways that cannot be replaced by mere abstract assertions of "fractured identities." For instance, Barrios's broad-based "we" is convincing precisely because she traces her own experiences of building ties with union men, foreign prisoners, university students, and conscripted soldiers. The cross-border community she projects is also meaningful for readers because the personal details of her testimony humanize her struggle, making Bolivian working-class politics vivid and significant to people even when they are far removed from Bolivian life. Anzaldúa's narrative of the "mestizaje" similarly makes coalition building concrete and historically resonant because it begins with Anzaldúa's own everyday experiences as a lesbian, multilingual Chicana and because it relates her daily experiences of struggle to a specific history: a history of successive colonizations, miscegenation, prejudices within communities that are victims of prejudice, and overlapping aims among Chicanos and other formerly colonized peoples. Precisely because she rethinks her identity in light of the complexities of specific life experiences and historical struggles, Anzaldúa herself is moved "to use some of [her] energy to serve as a mediator" to Native Americans, Afro-Americans, as well as males and whites who can "follow our lead" (1990b, 384). Thus, "mestizaje," as Anzaldúa renarrates it, both resonates with Anzaldúa's very particular, geographically specific experiences and encourages her to build coalitions across borders and bloodlines.[24]

Identities as "Character-Units"

I have argued that Anzaldúa and Barrios not only redescribe their own identities but also the status of "identity": When they narrate their "mestizaje" and "woman-of-the-Bolivian-mines" identities, "identity" is no longer a fixed internal substance but a strategic response to their specific historical conditions. One consequence of their historically situated and strategic approach to conceptualizing their identities is that they do not present a universal category but rather an identity that is narrative dependent. Isolated from their articulation in these women's narratives, the terms "mestizaje" and "woman of the Bolivian mines" (and likewise "Third World women") can be naturalized and objectified. The susceptibility of these terms to being coopted by the dominant culture does not negate the radical import of their use by Anzaldúa and Barrios (or by Mohanty and other global feminists). It does mean, however, that global feminists can use and defend these identity categories effectively only if we acknowledge their context dependence.

The Arendtian theory of storytelling offers one way to conceptualize the simultaneously strategic, historically rooted, and narrative-dependent status of identities. In the Arendtian theory, identities are essentially character-units that are given definition through a story-teller's work of making sense of past phenomena in the light of her concerns for the future. As such, identities name a possible standpoint from which people can reflect on their history, draw connections between their experiences and the broader forces affecting those experiences, and thus determine the historical actors, actions, prob-lems, and projects to foreground when they narrate their world. This notion of identity as a character-unit accords with Satya Mohanty's description of identities as possible "ways of making sense of our experiences" (1997, 216).[25] Like Mohanty's "post-positivist" con-ception of identity, the notion of identity as a character-unit recog-nizes that an identity emerges from our reckoning with specific historical experiences, while it also serves as conceptual guide with which to organize subsequent experiences. In Arendtian terms, the identity qua character-unit is "between past and future": It is rooted in the stories we tell of our past, yet insofar as it foregrounds particular aspects of a multifaceted past, it also orients our approach to the future. Thus any preferred way of construing character-units offers not so much greater empirical accuracy as much as a preferred vantage point from which people can collectively interpret their past and confront their future.

This conception of identity as a character-unit that is located "between past and future" offers one way to affirm the value of narrating history from the standpoint of particular identities, such as "Chicana" or "Third World women," yet without naturalizing identi-ties. "Third World Women," in this view, remains only one way to categorize people. Nonetheless, it is a way that enables many women to highlight shared political concerns and to address the future with their common concerns as "Third World women" at the center. Thus, for instance, when Mohanty focuses strategically on the continuities among the struggles of Third World women workers, she can chart a notion of "development" that better responds to the needs of women in Third World countries who have suffered under current forms of technology-intensive, export-driven "development" (Mohanty 1997, 7–8, 24–29). Likewise, when Anzaldúa narrates her cultural confusion from the standpoint of her reclaimed mestizaje identity, she can tell a new story of progress. Although an admittedly partial and perspective-dependent story, it nonetheless elucidates an alternative possible future: "Progress," from her mestiza perspective, is defined not in terms of racial purity but rather of "cross-pollinization" and inclusivity (1990b, 377).

Renarrating "Agency"

Narration that serves a feminist and democratic politics must also redescribe "agency." Going beyond poststructuralism, it must not only debunk Enlightenment notions of "individual agency" but must reclaim the agencies of people who have been excluded from cultural and political power centers and for whom epistemic and political agency remains a struggle. Narration plays an important role here, first, because the act of telling one's own story is empowering for the storyteller, especially for people who have been excluded from official knowledge-producing institutions. Telling their own stories enables them to claim epistemic authority as well as to counter the objectified, dehumanized representations of them circulated by others. Storytelling thereby enables people to begin to overcome what Jacqui Alexander and Chandra Mohanty call "the psychic and pedagogical aspects" of colonization, that is, the internalized prejudices that make it difficult for many people, even when they are successful academics, to recognize themselves as producers of knowledge and history (1997b, xxviii).[26] Second, when a story shows the struggle and the preconditions of its own process of creation, it can do more than empower an individual writer. It can also challenge the notion of agency as an innate property and can recast agency as an achievement that is developed only with constant and collective work.

Anzaldúa highlights both the empowering effects and the struggle of experience-driven writing. In so doing, she affirms an agency that is neither inborn nor mere rhetorical illusion. Instead, her agency is one that she struggles for and develops as she writes about her life. Through her writing, for instance, she resists succumbing to other people's representations of her as naturally passive and naturally ill-suited to intellectual work. As she puts it, "the writing saves me from this complacency I fear. . . . I must keep the spirit of my revolt and myself alive. . . . I write to record what others erase when I speak, to rewrite the stories others have miswritten about me, about you. . . . To discover myself, to preserve myself, to make myself, to achieve self-autonomy. . . . I write because I'm scared of writing but I'm more scared of not writing" (1983, 168). Against an academic and a popular culture that construes her as ignorant and passive and whose constructs become true insofar as she believes them, Anzaldúa uses her writing to demonstrate, to both herself and her community, her epistemic agency.

At the same time that Anzaldúa stresses the empowering effect of her writing, she does not gloss over the difficulties of grappling with painful experiences nor hide her fears about failing in a writing process that is bound up with her own ego. As a result, her work also highlights the emotional work that burdens experience-oriented writing. "To write," she admits, "is to confront one's demons, look them in the face and live to write about them" (1983, 171). To write about her borderlands existence requires that she "stretch the psyche" in order to hold seemingly conflicting points of view and that she come to terms with a mestiza consciousness that is both a "source of intense pain" and creative energy (1990b, 378, 379). Such emotionally risky and taxing work demands a supportive community in whose company "the loneliness of writing and the sense of powerlessness can be dispelled" (1983, 172). Agency is thus gained through her storytelling, but only with arduous and community-situated work.[27]

Through her testimony, Barrios similarly affirms her agency as well as recasts her agency as a hard-won and collective achievement. For instance, when she narrates her struggles as a child to earn a grade-school education, even when this meant listening to lessons from outside the school window after having been expelled for arriving without supplies, or her struggles as an adult to speak up for miner families, even when this meant contradicting the claims of state "experts" and armed soldiers, she shows that even an Indian child and a mineworker's wife can play an active historical role. At the same time, she shows that the expression of agency from such positions is fraught with difficulties and not possible alone. Barrios herself can confront the obstacles only with various forms of community support, ranging from a sympathetic teacher to a politically minded father, from miners who risked their lives to harbor her when soldiers sought her arrest to coprisoners who shared food with her.

Significantly, Barrios is able to highlight effectively the collective character of her agency only because she writes in an unconventional testimonial genre. This genre was revived by the Cuban revolution for the express purpose of breaking historiographical norms and making the common people and their communities the subject of history (Sommer 1988). Autobiography would not allow Barrios's unusual beginning, but, through testimony, Barrios can elide the division between autobiography and history and open her book by announcing that her story is *not* "only personal" because "my life is related to my people. What happened to me could have happened to hundreds of people in my country" ([1977] 1986, 15). Accordingly, she proceeds to identify herself as a "woman of the Bolivian mines." In a chapter entitled, "Her People," she recounts struggles she shares with fellow miner families. In a strategy impossible in autobiography but encouraged in testimony, she segues from "I" to "we" as she describes the struggles and dreams that she shares with her community. She again transgresses autobiographical norms but follows the spirit of testimony when she de-emphasizes her own heroism and foregrounds instead the broader community and anonymous heroes that made her own activities possible. "There have been many people who have done much more than I for the people," she says, "but who have died or who have not had the opportunity to be known" ([1977] 1986, 15). Locating her testimony in terms of the conditions that made it possible, she also identifies the book as a development of her work with the International Women's Year Tribunal, a United Nations–sponsored conference that was itself enabled by the increasing prominence of feminism worldwide. Although Barrios found much of the conference to be irrelevant to working-class women, she acknowledges that her appearance at the conference created the opportunity for her to meet Viezzar, who subsequently pursued the book project in order to give Barrios a more adequate forum for her story.

Barrios and Anzaldúa thus demonstrate that, while narration can be empowering, it is also a necessarily collective, and politically and emotionally risky practice. As Arendt suggests, narration is a kind of *work*: It involves drawing on given "material," often suppressed memories, and "processing" this material so as to make it more useful. In the case of narration that seeks to reclaim and revalue a subjugated community, this narrative processing involves "drawing the *connections* between the experiences of [people] and the powers exerted upon them" (Panjabi 1997, 155). In other words, the work of narration must bring into focus tensions within experience and must trace the social sources of those tensions. For Barrios, identifying the social sources of her domestic burdens and voicing these publicly makes her susceptible to death threats and imprisonment. For Anzaldúa, narrating and situating historically her personal strife is psychologically taxing, requiring that she sift through internalized demeaning conceptions of herself and through painful memories of her past to recover resistant modes of being. For both, such narrative work is empowering as well as treacherous and is possible only with a supportive community.

Renarrating "Action"

Strategically written marginal experience narratives must also recast "action" so that this category does not exclude people who lack the means to execute their will but instead affirms the most marginalized people's resistant activities. I have argued that such resistant activities are difficult to narrate, for such activities are often overlooked by public records and fail to yield complete products. When, however, writers stretch the conventions of historical narration in order to trace activities on which we have little historical data and no standard "action-units," they can help us to understand the political importance of more diffuse, more subtle kinds of historical activities.

For instance, when Barrios uses her personal experience as a fulcrum for narrating Bolivian history, she brings into focus activities of the Bolivian Housewives Committee that are absent from most historical records. These activities include women helping each other with daily domestic difficulties and women supporting work strikes with the few weapons that they possess, such as a radio transmitter, hunger strikes, and threats to use dynamite that would kill them and their children along with their enemies. Such activities have none of the clear results or individual aggrandizement that we usually associate with political action. Moreover, even on an occasion when the women's activities had momentous results—when their hunger strike initiated worker and student support strikes throughout the country, forcing the government to accept the women's demands to free and pay their imprisoned husbands—the women's achievements were quickly forgotten by people who thought that women have no role in politics.

When, however, Barrios addresses politics from the perspective of her own life, the little-known Housewives Committee becomes a main character in her story. In addition to highlighting the political activities of this committee, Barrios's testimony also shows, more generally, how little-known acts of resistance can play an important historical role, both as sources of inspiration and as small steps in a long-term battle. For instance, when Barrios recounts her struggle to continue in oppositional politics, despite her fatigue and fear for her family's safety, she indicates that she has been inspired to continue by men and women who have risked their lives to support work strikes or who have shared their scarce resources and moral support for each other even when beaten and imprisoned. These people's everyday acts of courage and commitment and the comradery of the Housewives Committee impress on Barrios that more ethical social relations are possible and are worth struggling for, even if (as an anonymous coprisoner once reminded her) their individual struggles bear fruit only as part of a broader, long-term struggle.

At the same time that Barrios redescribes "action" as a collective and long-term phenomenon, she does not fall into the trap of subordinating individuals to an abstract whole and imposing on them a predefined goal. She avoids both the Enlightenment privileging of the autonomous individual and its inverse, the subordination of individuals to an abstract collective, by carefully balancing her collective focus with experience-oriented stories. For instance, even while she emphasizes the collective and long-term character of her struggle, the personal and engaged elements of her testimony anchor her political commitment in specific life relationships, such as her relationship with her father, who (although abusive at times) first inspired her interest in politics, with miner families who share the little they have and demonstrate the power of solidarity, and with her children. She underscores this dialectic between broader political goals and individual life experiences that is implicit throughout her testimony when she tells us that Bolivia's socialist struggle cannot be defined by any formula for socialism but must be continually redefined by each generation with attention to the details of their historical world ([1977] 1986, 256).

Dominant notions of "action" cannot do justice to the simultaneously individual and collective character of Barrios's political activities. Arendt, however, provides an apt metaphor: Political phenomena are "constellations" of actions that are made up of individual deeds and sufferings but are irreducible to the plans of any individual. In this view, even the most powerful person acts in a context that exceeds her control, while even "the smallest act in the most limited circumstances bears the seed of [boundless reactions], because one deed, and sometimes one word, suffices to change every constellation" (Arendt HC, 190). When Barrios narrates her political growth and its dependence on the many people "who have died or who have not had the opportunity to be known," she illustrates the historical importance of diffuse, little-known, "small" activities, especially in long-term struggles of resistance against coercive powers. Barrios also makes concrete the rethinking of "action" that Arendt's metaphor implies insofar as her work with the Housewives Committee is goal-oriented but unpredictable and risky, productive but barely visible to the outside world, and dependent upon the continual collective action of a broad range of people.

Thus, although Barrios does not theorize "historical action," her narrative of her own activities stretches our sense of the meaning of that term. When she narrates everyday experiences of resistance that are too obscure or short-lived to qualify as "action" in the traditional sense, such as hunger-strikes or the harboring of evicted mineworkers, she helps all of us to recognize the historical significance of resistant activities that are not visible in our mass media or history books. For fellow women of the Bolivian mines, her story claims little-known resistant activities as part of their heritage and thus helps them to experience their own everyday resistant gestures as part of a broader and potentially powerful resistant community.

Renarrating "Events"

Finally, when marginal experience narratives attend to the daily life of people who are excluded from public affairs, they must do so without simply replacing political analysis with personal stories. To substitute personal stories for political analysis, as various critics have warned, only reverses the hierarchy between public and private spheres without addressing the interrelations between the two (hooks 1989, 105–07; Mohanty 1991a, 34, 36). Through their innovative narrative approaches, Barrios and Anzaldúa show what it can mean to rethink "historical event" in light of the mutual imbrication of public and private life.

For instance, through her skillful use of testimony, Barrios relates public events to motherhood. She presents the historical achievements of the Housewives Committee, for instance, in a chapter that begins with tales of her childhood and the growth of her own family. This unconventional format brings into relief how her personal travails with poverty and her intimate concern for her children fuel her sensitivity to social outcasts and her passion to create a more just world. Furthermore, through her personalized account of political events, we see that she remains a mother even while she is an activist. For instance, her torture when she imprisoned is directed to the child in her womb, she stands up to her torturers with rare courage as a mother trying to protect her unborn child, and, upon the death of her newborn, she finally finds the strength to continue fighting when she thinks of her remaining children. On the one hand, this mix of history and autobiography shows how Barrios's political work often competes with her motherhood, leading not only to the death of her newborn son but on another occasion to her whole family's eviction from their home and on another to her young daughter's confinement with her in prison. On the other hand, however, the testimony also suggests how Barrios's political activism enables her to teach her children the value of sacrifice and self-respect and to show them, even when they are evicted, that they are "people who have their dignity" ([1977] 1986, 138). Thus, through her testimony, Barrios demonstrates that political commitment does not demand a simple triumph of the "public" over the "private" self but can affirm the interconnections between these two realms, which sometimes compete but can also draw energy from one another.

At the same time that Barrios anchors her politics in her personal life, she also politicizes the latter. Specifically, she shows how her everyday experience registers the effects of, as well as alternatives to, broader relations of ruling. For instance, when she traces her onerous schedule to the unlivable wages of miners, she shows how her daily hardships reveal the exploitative nature of the larger economy. Likewise, when she narrates the obstacles she confronts in her struggle to achieve basic rights and livable conditions for her family, she makes visible the many state practices—from the intimidation of community leaders to the cultivation of mistrust between workers and peasants and between husbands and wives—that regulate people's everyday lives and that serve to keep both women and mineworkers in subordinate positions.

In a typical autobiography, the details of Barrios's poverty and oppression would merely authenticate her individual suffering, cultivating pity from North American readers and renewing conceptions of Latin American women as helpless victims waiting to be saved by Northerners (Mohanty 1991a, 34; Gilliam 1991, 218–19). However, because Barrios uses testimony to situate her daily hardships in relation to broader historical struggles, her personal suffering appears as an effect of long-standing systems of exploitation and political repression in Bolivia that have spurred various social movements that seek not pity but political alliance. Moreover, by combining her personal story with a broader historical focus, Barrios also highlights the way that conditions for miners have remained the same for decades, notwithstanding the U.S.–supported "democracy." She thereby implicates both the Bolivian and the U.S. government in her oppression. The testimony thus underscores the political character of Barrios's personal story and demands from a North American audience not mere pity but a political response that addresses the systemic relations of domination in which both North American readers and Barrios are situated.

Anzaldúa similarly uses an unconventional style to relate minute details of her personal life to far-reaching relations of domination. In her case, her everyday life registers the compound effects of social institutions that exploit Mexican labor and cultural ideologies that rationalize such exploitation by presenting Mexicans as uncivilized and incapable of their own productive activity. This ensemble of economic exploitation and cultural devaluation of everything Mexican was blatant during the Mexican American war. North American politicians and pundits rationalized the invasion of Mexico by describing Mexicans as a people about to yield to "a superior population" who would "exterminat[e] her weaker blood," or a people waiting for the United States to "regenerate and disenthrall" them and "civilize that beautiful country" (the *American Review* and the New York *Herald,* cited in Zinn 1995, 152). More recently, neoliberal narratives of U.S.-Mexican relations are more subtle but equally racist. These narratives justify NAFTA by presenting it as a means to facilitate the flow of North American industry and capital to a Mexico that is hopelessly underdeveloped and unable to provide employment for its own people.[28] Such narratives overlook the ways that NAFTA itself undermines Mexico's own businesses and agriculture and thereby helps to create the pool of unemployed "cheap labor" to which it supposedly responds. (Many argue that these effects arise because NAFTA releases North American companies from Mexican environmental and labor regulations and opens Mexican borders to government-subsidized U.S. grain [Anderson et al. 1996; Anderson et al. 1999; Economic Policy Institute 1997; Instituto del Tercer Mundo 1999, 62–76, 170, 394]).

While North American economic institutions appropriate Mexican resources and cultural practices concurrently devalue Mexican people and culture, these phenomena recede from view when narratives focus only on official public events and when they present Mexican Americans as simple minorities defined within an abstract pluralist notion of difference. If, however, the social institutions that regulate the lives of Mexican Americans are invisible in ruling narratives, they nonetheless leave their marks on Anzaldúa's everyday life. They underlie, for instance, the poverty that plagues her hard-working family and the psychological strife that she endures from being American yet excluded from "American" culture. Thus, when Anzaldúa narrates her childhood experiences of poverty despite her whole family's hard work, when she relates being punished in school for speaking her family's language, and when she situates these experiences historically, her story points toward structural relations of domination that position Americans of Mexican descent.

Finally, Barrios and Anzaldúa also tie historical events to everyday life insofar as they show how everyday life not only registers the contradictions of ruling institutions but can also demonstrate alternative modes of social relations. When, for instance, Anzaldúa refuses to choose between Mexican and American cultures, when the Bolivian mineworkers share their homes and food with evicted families, and when Barrios and her companions defy the docile role of "housewife," they enact alternative kinds of communities and projects: heterogeneous communities that resist binary conceptions of identity, nurturing relations that counter detached and hierarchical modes of rule, and gestures of defiance in everyday life on the part of people who refuse confinement to passive, "private-sphere" roles. Such everyday resistant activities demonstrate the possibility of organizing our lives differently.[29] Nevertheless, as I have explained above, such phenomena are easily forgotten and have limited historical impact if they are not narrated into the public record. Anzaldúa and Barrios demonstrate one way out of the mutually reinforcing political and narrative marginalization of their communities. When they break narrative norms to trace interrelations between personal and public life, they confirm the historical significance of obscure, seemingly uncategorizable resistant activities and thereby help to transform what Arendt calls "shadowy phenomena" into publicly acknowledged alternatives to ruling ways of life.

Conclusions: Narration and Feminist Democratic Politics

Marginal experience narratives play a role in oppositional politics that discourse analysis, social theory, and factual data cannot replace. When storytellers use writing creatively to grapple with obscure or contradictory experiences and when they situate these experiences historically, they bring into public view the social pressures and social alternatives that have shaped many people's daily lives but that have been systematically omitted from ruling narratives. Moreover, when marginal experience narratives bring into our language and historical memory the muted tensions and ambiguities of daily experience, they initiate new ways of constructing the categories by which we interpret historical life. They sketch, for instance, "actors" that cross cultural and national boundaries, "action" that is enacted in diffuse gestures by people who are excluded from public life, and "historical events" that develop outside the parameters of official events and government arenas. Narration of historical experience is, in fact, crucial to a meaningful rethinking of these categories, for only close attention to the nuances and contradictions of historical life can recast such categories in a way that resonates in our daily lives, moves us to engage in political projects, and enables us to do so with attention to the complex contours of our world. While a theory of language or society may contribute to ideology critique or to the development of counterhegemonic discourses, only the continual reckoning with historically specific experiences ensures that those alternative discourses do not themselves become dogmatic but are responsive to evolving, multifaceted historical struggles.

Finally, when writers use narration strategically to publicize obscured experiences, they enrich not only language practices but experience itself, for they provide a new lens through which we can organize our everyday experience and historical world. Neither empirical reporting nor discourse analysis has this effect on our experience of our identity and history. Certainly the reporting of empirical data can add crucial, missing information to historical documents. And the rhetorical analysis of such documents can elucidate the ideological mechanisms that structure our interpretation of our world. Beyond this, however, narratives that probe ways to articulate and situate unspoken tensions in everyday life can transform experience, helping those of us who have been reduced to "victim" or "cheap labor" to claim agency and helping all of us to identify with cross-border, cross-culture democratic struggles.

Chapter 6

Stories and Standpoint Theory: Toward a More Responsible and Defensible Thinking from Others' Lives

What kinds of knowledge . . . do we need in order to live at all, and to live more reasonably with one another on this planet, from this moment on?

—Sandra Harding[1]

Some classrooms have broadened their horizons since my classmates and I learned about "primitive" African cultures, presented reports glorifying "the great European explorers," and studied the history of states. In recent years, more teachers and scholars have brought under discussion perspectives excluded from dominant cultural texts. Publications and films have likewise multiplied that narrate the world from the standpoint of people who have struggled against oppression and exploitation. Feminist standpoint theorists, including Sandra Harding, Nancy Hartsock, Dorothy Smith, and Patricia Hill Collins, lend philosophical support to such efforts to integrate marginalized perspectives into the curriculum, for they argue that knowledge that serves the interests of all people, and not just an elite few, must begin by thinking from the standpoint of members of oppressed and exploited groups.

Nevertheless, despite the growing concern among progressive scholars to engage accounts of the world written from the standpoint of socially and culturally marginalized positions, we have few guidelines for how to read effectively the texts—often stories—that present others' views. Some critics have begun a discussion of how to investigate "difference" in a responsible manner[2]; however, the problem of how to engage and defend the storylike medium in which many alternative viewpoints are presented remains largely unexplored. As a result, the stories that present perspectives from marginalized lives are often seen as "mere stories" and command little authority in broader academic and political debates. Moreover, even well-intentioned readers often fail to realize the more subversive implications of marginal experience narratives, sometimes appropriating others' tales without confronting the challenges those stories pose to their own assumptions and authority.[3]

Using the theory of storytelling developed in this book, this chapter contributes to discussions of how people in more privileged positions can engage, in an effective and responsible way, stories that describe the world from more marginalized positions. I first examine the reading practices that make possible a responsible engagement with others' stories. I then address the sense in which "thinking from the standpoint of others' stories" serves broad ethical and epistemological values not reducible merely to taking the side of the victim. Such a broad-minded defense of thinking that begins from marginalized standpoints can help to promote thinking from others' lives more widely in schools, policy institutions, and amongst a broader public, even when such thinking relies on seemingly subjective and unconventional "stories."

Story Reading and Standpoint Theory

Feminist standpoint theorists have presented powerful arguments to the effect that knowledge that begins from the lives of people who have struggled against oppression or exploitation can offer critical insight into existing beliefs and institutions and can help us to transform those beliefs and institutions toward the end of a more just, democratic world. Harding (1991) presents a particularly comprehensive account of standpoint theory, for she draws together the analyses of leading standpoint theorists as well as clarifies ambiguities in early versions of this theory. Perhaps most importantly, Harding presents "women's standpoint" without naturalizing the identity, "woman," for she explains how gender (and other social positions) affects our experiences and views of the world in a way that is epistemologically significant, even while such social positions do not determine our inner nature. She also takes care to distinguish the critical *standpoint,* which is the insight that one gains upon reflecting on one's own (or another's) struggles and upon resisting relations of domination, from the mere unexamined beliefs that a particular person who is oppressed or exploited happens to hold. When Harding calls on those of us in more privileged positions to "think from others' lives," she is essentially asking us to view the world in light of the experiences and insights of people who have struggled against oppression in order thereby to develop a more critical standpoint on our own lives and world.[4]

Despite her careful elaboration of feminist standpoint theory, however, Harding leaves unanswered some crucial questions concerning what it can mean to "look at the world from the perspective of . . . [others'] lives" (Harding 1991, 124). First, this proposal raises the question, which Harding only begins to address, of how one person can view the world from the perspective of someone else. In the section below, I use the theory of storytelling to elucidate the intellectual and imaginative practices that enable someone to transform, in a respectful and responsible manner, someone else's experiences of struggle into a resource for her own critical knowledge.[5]

Thinking from Others' Lives: The Need for Stories

Harding begins to address the issue of how a thinker in a more privileged position might view the world from the standpoint of someone in a more marginalized location. She explains that this person should apply to her own life theories that have been "originally generated" by others (1991, 283). For instance, a white North American should not repeat mechanically the theories produced by African Americans but should "learn how to see the world differently for [herself] in an active and creative way through the theoretical and political lenses that African American thinkers originally constructed" (1991, 291). Ultimately, this project should lead the white person to view her own life from an African American perspective and to examine critically her own social situation and prejudices.

Harding rightly emphasizes the need for all people to study and actively apply the theories that have been produced by people in more marginalized positions. Often, however, the viewpoints of people who have been the most socially and culturally marginalized are not presented in "theories," in the standard sense of the term, but in engaged, creative, community-situated "stories." Especially when people are excluded from official knowledge-producing institutions or when they attempt to articulate experiences that have been systematically suppressed in ruling discourses and ignored by official research institutions, academic theorizing and professional norms tend to obscure and distort their experiences.[6] In such circumstances, people often turn to passion-driven, community-rooted, exploratory writing to reflect on their common experiences and forge an account of the world from their particular social standpoint. Both Harding and Smith implicitly recognize the need for artful, community-situated storytelling when they describe the kind of experiences that make possible a critical standpoint on ruling beliefs and institutions. Such experiences, they tell us, are "a struggle to articulate," "forbidden," and "incoherent" (Harding 1991,

282) and are seemingly "personal, idiosyncratic, and inchoate" (Smith 1987, 58). If the experiences that make possible a critical standpoint are obscure and inchoate, then they can be confirmed and rendered intelligible only with a community exchange of stories, that is, an exchange of views in which people share their tales with one another in a tentative, creative, open-minded and soul-searching manner.

Furthermore, even when marginalized standpoints are presented in more theoretical forms, a reader gains a sense of what it means to experience the world from the standpoint of another only with imagination. Stories facilitate such imaginative work. Thus, stories are an invaluable resource in the process of learning to see the world through others' eyes. A complete account of standpoint thinking must therefore include an account of how one can effectively read and learn from others' stories.

A Hermeneutics for Thinking from Others' Lives

It is not easy to learn from another's story in the critical, responsible manner that Harding advocates. If, as Harding stresses, the point is not to mimic others' views but to "see the world for [ourselves] in an active and creative way through the theoretical and political lenses" developed by others, then we must somehow learn from others' stories, yet without passively repeating those stories as given. We must, in other words, be open to what the other's story has to tell us and, at the same time, be careful to think for ourselves. In addition, we must use the other's story to examine critically "common sense" beliefs and our own lives, yet without approaching the story as an absolute truth.

Some narratives, such as those by Griffin, Roy, Anzaldúa, and Delany, are constructed strategically so as to acknowledge their own partiality and to encourage readers to use them as prompts for their own imaginative and critical work. Nevertheless, if Gadamer and Ricoeur are correct that a text's meaning is actualized only upon its interpretation by a reader, then even the most skillfully written marginal experience narrative has little impact without a sensitive reader who is able to realize the text's full value. In earlier chapters, I tried to read the aforementioned texts in a manner responsive to each text's subtle twists of language, imaginative prompts, and conceptual challenges. These individual readings, however, did not yet constitute a hermeneutic theory with general guidelines for reading others' stories.

The account of storytelling developed in this book points toward a way of reading that makes possible "thinking from others' lives" in the manner that Harding seeks. This account of storytelling tells us that any meaningful representation of a historical event is not only an empirical document but also a *story*: a tradition-informed and creative attempt, by a historically situated writer, to transpose a plurality of ambiguous, boundless, existentially rich experiences into a coherent pattern of beginnings and endings and actors and actions that are intelligible to her readers. Insofar as a text is a story, it does not represent objective reality; however, it does present a way of organizing and describing phenomena that can sensitize readers to qualities and relationships that are relevant to the phenomenon's meaning as part of their world.

This notion of the historical text as a story throws light on what it can mean to pursue the simultaneously receptive, critical, and active engagement with others' views that standpoint thinking demands. When a reader approaches a text *as a story,* that is, a creative recon-struction of subjective, not easily representable phenomena, then what comes to her attention are the text's tentative, provocative, and poetic elements. Likewise, viewed as a story, the text reveals gaps, contradic-tions, and abrupt transitions, incoherences that reflect the writer's never-complete attempt to come to terms with multiple, often contend-ing memories. Read as a story, the text also appears open-ended, as one attempt to render coherent a complex of boundless, continually evolv-ing phenomena. Insofar as a reader attends to such tentative, poetic, and open-ended elements of a text, she cannot find certain truths to repeat robot-like. She can, however, find poetic insight into aspects of the world that are historically meaningful but not easy to see or theorize. In terms of the vocabulary I presented in chapter one, the reader who approaches the historical text as a story finds *narrative matrices* (patterns of actor-and action-units related together within beginnings and endings) and *story images* (poetic renderings of existen-tial qualities) that help her to imagine distant and obscure phenomena in terms meaningful to her. When such narrative resources help a reader to make sense of seemingly alien phenomena, they often throw a new light on her own world as well, for the narrative patterns can indicate historical connections between strange and familiar events while the story images can help her to discern kinds of experiences in her midst that she had not previously noticed or thought possible.

Insofar as a reader attends not only to empirical information but also to narrative generated ways of organizing and imagining historical life, she can begin to "see the world through others' lenses" in the sense Harding advocates. Like the "lenses" sought by Harding, narrative matrices and story images are not absolute truths. Instead, they are conceptual tools that thinkers can employ in their own attempts to make sense of historical phenomena, aids in the endless and ultimately personal task of understanding a strange world. Significantly, narrative matrices and story images emerge from a writer's reckoning with historically and geographically specific experiences; however, at the same time, they constitute narrative patterns to which other incidents can be related and metaphors that can be applied to phenomena found in other contexts. Narrative resources are therefore anchored in historically specific circumstances while they also constitute conceptual "lenses" that can help readers view their own world in light of the concerns and insights of another.

We can illustrate how the hermeneutics of story reading facilitates "thinking from others' lives" by applying this story-sensitive way of reading to the texts addressed in previous chapters by Howard Zinn and Gloria Anzaldúa. Like most history books, Zinn's book *A People's History of the United States* is not explicitly poetic. Nonetheless, a story-sensitive reader can find in this text not only empirical data but also story images and narrative matrices that can guide her in exploring new ways of narrating historical phenomena. The section that I analyzed in chapter four on the black revolts of the sixties and seventies, for instance, presents an image of suppressed anger as percolating energy that can "explode" if not otherwise released. It also presents a narrative pattern that traces the highly publicized race riots of the seventies to decades of less visible institutionalized racism, unenforced civil rights legislation, and racially stratified power hierarchies. A reader who confronts these metaphors and patterns as narrative resources can acknowledge that they are discursive constructions, not objective truths, yet she can still avail herself of these resources to make some historical sense of the seemingly sudden eruptions of urban violence in the 1970s. In addition, the image of anger as compressed energy and the tracing of violent outbursts to a pattern of institutionalized abuses provides a conceptual lens for exploring the sense of race-based politics and seemingly inexplicable acts of violence in the present.

More self-consciously poetic texts, such as Anzaldúa's essay "La concienca de la mestiza," are especially fertile grounds for a reading that is attentive to narrative resources. When a reader approaches this text as a story, she finds a vivid simile in Anzaldúa's comparison of the Chicana to the crossbred corn. While the description of the resilient and unpredictable crossbred corn is motivated by Anzaldúa's deeply personal experience of being torn between cultures and of discovering a creative potential amidst the confusion, the simile can also help a reader to imagine what it might be like if she herself were to embrace multiple identities. A white North American reader who studies this essay for narrative resources can also find a narrative matrix that draws connections between Mexican history and everyday life in the United States. If the reader ventures to weave her own life into this narrative web, she can begin to view her own material wealth and privileged "American" identity in relation to some of the labor, resources, and cultural biases that subtend her own privileges.

A hermeneutics of story reading not only encourages the creative use of narrative "lenses" but also the kind of critical examination of dominant beliefs that is central to standpoint thinking. As standpoint theorists have emphasized, the most trenchant ruling beliefs are rarely explicitly articulated but rather constitute assumptions that structure a community's "common sense" beliefs and conceptual frameworks (Harding 1991, 116–17, 287; Smith 1987, 55–69) . Such assumptions include, for instance, the belief that historical actors have discrete identities, that historical action constitutes the clear expression of an actor's will in the public sphere, that good and evil oppose each other in a Manichean conflict, and that "history" is independent from emotional and "private" life. Some writers, such as Anzaldúa and Susan Griffin, have transgressed discursive norms and challenged these basic cultural assumptions; however, the critical force of their texts depends on how they are read. When readers approach marginal experience narratives in the customary empiricist fashion, they tend to collect information that fits within their preconceived narrative frameworks and to overlook elements incongruent with those frameworks. For instance, Norma Alarcón describes how the groundbreaking book *This Bridge Called my Back: Writings by Radical Women of Color* traces overlapping gender, racial, and cultural divisions that defy conventional discourses on "woman"; and yet "Anglo feminist readers of *Bridge* tend to appropriate it, cite it as an instance of difference between women, and proceed to negate that difference by subsuming women of color into the unitary category of woman/women" (1990, 358).

A reader who approaches a text as a story cannot so easily ignore the text's narrative innovations or the broader implications of those narrative strategies. A story-sensitive reader attends to the rhetorical strategies by which the text identifies actors and actions and organizes these units into a coherent whole. She focuses on rhetorical mechanisms and narrative form not in order to peg the text to a particular genre but to understand how that particular text creates meaning through narration. A reader mindful of the narrative construction of *Bridge,* for instance, finds that the text identifies the "woman of color" character by presenting a plurality of unique and internally heterogeneous characters, while it forms a whole precisely by challenging our conception of "wholes," allowing for a plurality of styles, voices, and genres within one cover. When a reader takes seriously the unique narrative construction of this text, she confronts a radical challenge to the norms of autobiographical discourse as well as to the unitary "identities" that those norms presuppose. Such a reader cannot so easily revert back to presupposed unitary identities without recognizing the latter to be only one contested way of identifying historical characters.

A reader who confronts a text as a story is also more likely to address challenges that the text presents to received cultural frameworks because such a reader understands that the text is not a representation of a self-evident whole but an incomplete attempt to construct a narrative whole from multiple memories. The story reader is thus cognizant of gaps and tensions within the text. Such internal textual tensions can point the story reader to limitations in received narrative discourses, for they are often symptoms of the author's simultaneous use of received discourses, on the one the hand, and his attempt to reckon with memories that exceed the logic of those discourses, on the other. In Samuel Delany's memoir, for instance, the memoir, on the one hand, identifies Delany as "homosexual" and, on the other hand, relates tales of unique relationships and lifestyles that resist the label "homosexual." When the reader approaches this memoir as a story, that is, not a straightforward report of events but an attempt to bring together multifaceted, ambiguous memories, she sees that Delany's waivering between affirming and refusing his "homosexuality" is not a mere logical inconsistency; more importantly, it is an attempt to communicate a subjectivity that is irreducible to received sexual discourses and that conflicts with his own socially formed consciousness of himself. When the reader recognizes the memoir's tensions to be symptoms of Delany's conflicting memories, some of which have been formed by ruling discourses on sexuality and some of which resist that discursive logic, then the text raises questions for her about that formerly taken-for-granted logic. For instance, why is sexual identity assumed to be fixed and singular, in the first place? Why are certain lifestyles considered "normal"? If sexuality is "private," then why do social institutions regulate Delany's sexual relations? Such a reading may leave the reader with more questions than answers, but fresh questions are central to what Harding hopes thinking from others' lives will achieve.

Harding and others who advocate thinking from others' lives also present warnings. As we attempt to view the world from another's perspective, we must not romanticize "the exotic" nor abstract people's differences from the historical institutions that produced those differences, for such approaches ignore how we ourselves are related to "others" through historically specific, often hierarchical social relations while they overlook the claims that "different" people make on us as members of our shared world. Furthermore, we must not reduce the people whose different perspectives we investigate to "victims" or easily known objects of our analysis, for such approaches only expand our authority while failing to engage the others' perspectives in their depth and complexity. A responsible standpoint thinker must therefore confront the other people whose perspectives she seeks as complex and active historical subjects. She must do so even if, as is often the case, these people do not qualify as "subjects" in the modern Western sense of agents who command history and language. A responsible standpoint thinker must also situate others' perspectives in a broad social context and allow those perspectives to cast a critical light on her own world. Finally, a responsible standpoint thinker must not remain a mere recipient of others' views but must take responsibility to participate in the creation of oppositional knowledge by theorizing her own life and world in light of the power relations that others can help bring to light (Harding 1991, 246–47; Kadi 1996, 52–56; Lorde 1984, 117–23; Mohanty 1990; 1991a, 34; 1991b; Narayan 1997, 43–117; Taylor 1993).

The hermeneutics of story reading cultivates the kind of receptive and self-transforming engagement with another's perspective that feminist theorists demand. When we read a text as a "story," we cannot analyze it from a detached viewpoint nor can we authoritatively impose on it our presupposed categories, but we must respond with emotional sensitivity and intellectual openness to its unique and subjective content. For instance, when North American readers approach Roy's tour of World Bank politics, Indian government deceptions, and submerged homes as a story, we confront the characters as specific individuals who are part of our moral universe and we thus allow ourselves to be moved by the narrative's human details. At the same time, we recognize that this story presents humanly possible ways of thinking and organizing social life that transcend its particular context and that challenge us to view our own world in terms of its conceptual framework. If we pursue the ways that our own lives tie into Roy's story, we may find that we wear clothes produced by displaced Indian farmers, that we, like the Indian elite, ignore the human and environmental costs of our material comforts, or perhaps that we benefit from investment portfolios whose holdings include corporations that displace people for the sake of "development."[7] Insofar as we approach Roy's text as a story, the text also suggests possibilities for resisting the kind of "development" it describes. For when we view the events that Roy narrates as part of a story, we see that the dominant forces of "progress" that drive the dam industry coexist with multiple and undecidable historical elements, including elements that resist the dam industry and that present alternative views of development and the common good. When we read the text as a story of experiences belonging to our world, such elements of resistance also suggest possibilities for our own lives and lay claim on our own commitments.

Finally, a hermeneutics of story reading promotes the responsible kind of standpoint thinking sought by Harding and her colleagues insofar as this kind of reading implies reader responsibility for if and how to continue the narrative. When we confront a text as a story, we are receptive to the particular worldview that the text opens up, while we also recognize that the story offers one possible interpretive framework with specific epistemic and political implications, not an absolute truth. Thus, as story readers, we must examine critically the implications of that text's particular way of telling the story and we must take responsibility for the extent to which we appropriate, revise, or reject that narrative paradigm in our own subsequent storytelling.

The hermeneutics of story reading thus points the way toward the mature kind of "thinking from others' lives" envisioned by Harding. This hermeneutics tells us that we can venture beyond our own conceptual framework if we read another's story with sensitivity to its subtleties, ambiguities, and narrative innovations. At the same time that this hermeneutics demands receptivity to the unique perspective presented in the text, it also calls for active and critical engagement with that perspective, for it directs us to explore the world for ourselves, with the narrative resources that we glean from the text, and to own up to the ways that we subsequently choose to employ those narrative frameworks. Insofar as the hermeneutics of story reading asks us to view our own communities in light of the text's narrative resources, this hermeneutics confirms the emotionally and intellectually challenging, unsettling nature of thinking from others' lives. But this hermeneutics also confirms that, through the medium of stories, responsible thinking from others' lives, while difficult, is not impossible.

"Thinking from Others' Stories": The Problem of Justification

Even while stories are the medium through which many of us forge critical standpoints on the world and many of us "think from others' lives," stories fall outside the bounds of knowledge proper, for the still-influential Enlightenment theories of knowledge deny the status of knowledge to anything but detached, seemingly objective texts. The exclusion of stories from publicly recognized knowledge has multiple repercussions for everyday knowledge practices. Smith, for instance, describes how the norms of sociological, psychiatric, and other professional discourses "require the suppression of the personal" with the effect that women are inhibited from developing knowledges rooted in their own experiences while scholars who do try to address women's experiences are dismissed as not properly professional (1987, 60). In a similar critique of institutionalized discursive norms, bell hooks describes how "[w]ork by women of color and marginalized groups . . . especially if written in a manner that renders it accessible to a broad reading public, is often delegitimized in academic settings" due to elitist conceptions of what counts as theory (1994, 63). Roy describes how the keepers of "expert" knowledge denigrate her essay on India's dams, charging it with being too emotional and too partisan (2001, 28–30, 97) In my own experience, a group of professionals studying the global economy rejected for inclusion in our common reading prominent Third World and labor perspectives, seemingly because these perspectives were presented in literary essays, personal testimony, and by politically identified research groups. For the sake of rigor and objectivity, they passed over the storylike texts for a single book that seemed to them more "balanced" and "neutral," a book whose authors claim in their preface that "[t]he subject, the arguments, and many of the characters are substantial enough by themselves" so that authors will henceforth "disappear" from the text (Micklethwait and Wooldridge 2000, viii).

Standpoint theorists need a way to justify those texts that do not allege objectivity, those texts that are explicitly engaged, literary, historically situated stories. Current justifications for standpoint thinking are not adequate here. Harding tries to defend standpoint thinking as a means to "less false" and "less partial" knowledge, but this defense cannot explain the value of stories from marginalized standpoints that are openly creative, tentative, and partial. Others try to defend the inclusion of marginalized perspectives on the basis of explicitly political criterion such as justice or democracy; however, these critics fail to address standpoint thinking as a means to better knowledge. In the meantime, the practice of "thinking from others' lives," along with the stories that make such thinking possible, remain open to charges that they are too partisan, too subjective, and too particularized to count as serious components of intellectual inquiry.

Below, I critically examine current defenses of standpoint thinking. Drawing on my Arendt-inspired theory of storytelling, I then present an alternative justification that responds better to the storylike format and the distinct epistemic value of many texts from marginalized perspectives. This alternative evaluative framework gives expression to the achievements that Harding and others attribute to standpoint thinking but that Harding's own evaluative standards overlook

"Less False" as the Goal of Knowledge

Woven throughout Harding's work is a subtle defense of knowledge that begins from the standpoint of oppressed and exploited lives. She suggests that the value of "thinking from others' lives" is not precisely a matter of truth but rather of developing knowledges that are more useful in enabling all people to participate democratically in shaping the conditions of our world. When, however, she summarizes the virtues of standpoint thinking, she appeals to conventional, correspondence-based standards: Standpoint thinking, she says, yields "less false" and "less partial" knowledge, "clearer and more nearly complete visions of social reality," and a less distorted "picture of nature and social relations" than that which emerges from conventional research (1987, 182; 1991, 121, 126). Likewise, when she reclaims "objectivity" from its historical association with masculinist and Eurocentric beliefs, she (at least sometimes) describes objectivity in terms of accurate representation: Objectivity, she claims, promotes "distinguishing between how I want the world to be and how, in empirical fact, it is" (1991, 160).

Harding's defense of standpoint thinking in terms of "less false" and "less partial" knowledge is motivated by a legitimate concern for accuracy and thoroughness. Her attention to accuracy and thoroughness not only engages scholars who work in more traditional empiricist frameworks but also reminds poststructuralists and feminists that, although "facts" may not be fashionable, we should remain insistent upon factual accuracy. Harding is persuasive that holding knowledge claims accountable to "how, in empirical fact, [the world] is" remains urgent in a world in which "there are powerful interests ranged against attempts to find out the regularities and underlying causal tendencies in the natural and social worlds" (1991, 160). Given the suppressed, deceptive, and outright false information that has circulated concerning everything from the environmental effects of pesticides to the efficiency of dams, from the perpetrators of human rights abuses to the causes of breast cancer, the standard of accurate and thorough information is not a standard that feminists and other advocates of social justice can afford to dismiss.

Beyond "Less False"

Harding's call for "less false" and "less partial" knowledge reflects legitimate epistemological concerns, but it is not adequate as a defense of standpoint thinking. It fails to do justice to her own subtle description of the connection between standpoint thinking and democracy while it misrepresents the issues at stake in the project of thinking from others' lives.

While accuracy and thoroughness remain important minimal criteria for knowledge, these standards do not suffice for expressing the value of standpoint thinking. The problem is not with the standards of accuracy and thoroughness per se. The problem is that, when Harding presents these standards as definitive epistemological criteria, she invokes an empiricist framework that obscures the interrelations between knowledge and power. Harding herself recognizes the dangers of taking empiricism too far: "while everyone thinks empirical research is important for finding out how nature and social life are organized, one can nevertheless criticize empiricism (and feminist empiricism) as a *theory* about how to do research and to justify its results" (1991, 112). Despite her own warnings, however, Harding remains squarely within the empiricist framework when she appeals to "less false" and "less partial" knowledge.[8] To be sure, this modified version of empiricist truth refrains from positing a final, complete "truth." The aim, "less false, less partial," refers rather to a provisional achievement, a truth that holds only until a more adequate knowledge claim is available. Nevertheless, Harding's standard of less false, less partial knowledge retains key assumptions of Enlightenment epistemology, namely that the function of knowledge is to represent, as closely as possible, an independently existing reality, that the value of knowledge is a matter of how well its representation corresponds with that external reality (even if this will always be only an approximate correspondence), and that "truth," or the way the world is, is separate from politics, or the way one wants the world to be.

Philosophers from Marx to Foucault, from Haraway to Harding herself, have criticized these Enlightenment assumptions. Critiques of Enlightenment epistemology are now well known (and I have addressed some of these in chapters one and four), but Marx's critique deserves brief review here, as Marx links knowledge to power in a way that is central to feminist standpoint theory. Marx explains that our beliefs about ourselves, others, and the social world are rooted in our everyday material activities and our position in social hierarchies. Thus people who experience the contradictions of social institutions in their everyday lives are better positioned to see the "truth" of those institutions, that is, their incomplete, historically contingent, and contradictory character (Marx 1997, 289–300, 414–15, 436, 458–60). The beliefs that prevail in any society, however, reflect the vision and serve the interests of the more socially powerful classes, for these classes control the institutions that produce and distribute ideas (Marx 1997, 438–40). What passes as knowledge in any society is also a function of social institutions insofar as the "facts" and "laws" that are the objects of our knowledge are actually social phenomena that are contingent on historically specific social arrangements (Marx 1997, 287–89, 442–60). Nancy Hartsock gleans from Marx's analysis a fundamental insight concerning the connection between knowledge and power: Claims to knowledge are political insofar as they validate and help to perpetuate certain ways of life; in turn, political movements are also epistemological claims insofar as they imply beliefs about what can be *made true* through social praxis (1997, 370–73). Given such connections between truth and power, standpoint theorists from Marx to Hartsock have been less concerned with finding "the truth" than with understanding and changing power relations.

In her critique of "physics," that is, the idealized myth of physics, Harding herself addresses the impossibility of a neutral truth claim. "Physics" posits that when rational minds follow the scientific method they produce neutral truths about an independently existing, fixed reality. Citing Marx, Thomas Kuhn, Hartsock, and other philosophers and scientists, Harding debunks this naive conception of truth. She argues that all of our society's beliefs, including our "best beliefs," are socially situated. A scientist's questions, ontological assumptions, and technological tools are given by the surrounding social world, yet these givens remain unthematized by the scientific method. In turn, knowledge claims affect the surrounding world, promoting certain technologies, lifestyles, and interests over others. Even seemingly "abstract" inquiries implicitly advance the interests of the status quo, for they direct intellectual and material resources away from pressing social problems (Harding 1991, 58–60, 77–102, 120).

Despite her criticism of the belief in a presumably fixed and neutral "truth," however, Harding's own standard of "less false, less partial" knowledge remains premised on this traditional belief. Most likely, Harding fell back upon an empiricist terminology (of which "less false, less partial" is only a slight modification) because it was the language available to her, a language that most readers understand. Critiques of Enlightenment epistemology notwithstanding, the language of "truth," in which "truth" means accurate representation of a fixed world of objects, persists in our culture. In fact, Harding acknowledges that "older modernist discourses" provided the initial framework for standpoint theory, even though those discourses and the feminist standpoint theory "turned out to be in a collision course" (1997, 383).

Because her standard "less false, less partial" partakes in the modernist epistemology that is at odds with feminist standpoint theory, Harding confuses the issues at stake when she attempts to defend standpoint thinking in these terms. When she calls for "less false" knowledge, for instance, she obscures the fact that outright falsehoods do not constitute the only or the most pernicious problem with dominant knowledges. Many knowledge claims from dominant perspectives, such as Gerhard Weinberg's catalogue of geographic and strategic details related to the bombing of Hiroshima (which I analyze in chapter one), suppress the perspective of marginalized groups, even when they contain no falsehoods. Likewise, as in Susan Griffin's alternative narrative of Hiroshima, which focuses on its human dimensions, the advantage of thinking from marginalized lives does not necessarily lie in greater factual accuracy. Harding recognizes as much when she compares two perspectives on Western science, the traditional Western perspective and her own Third World–centered account. The latter story has no apparent advantage in accuracy or reliability, for it is admittedly "pieced together from sources that feel lighter in weight, more fragile, in their evidential underpinnings" (Harding 1991, 220–22). "Less false" cannot explain why Harding ultimately gives preferences to the more tenuously grounded story.

"Less partial" is also problematic. "Less partial" reflects the legitimate concern that a knowledge claim should strive to be thorough and that our evaluation of a knowledge claim should identify the claim's lapses and limitations. If, however, all knowledge claims are partial, then, as one sympathetic critic puts it, "the pressing epistemological issue" is not a knowledge claim's "degree of partiality" but rather its social effects (Hennessy 1995, 142). Put another way, the question we must ask when faced with multiple, partial truth claims is not *Which claim is less partial?* but rather *What are the political implications of each claim's specific partialities?*

Feminists who remain committed to the empiricist model might respond that, even if an account of historical events from the standpoint of, for instance, women, is itself a partial account, nonetheless this account *contributes* to less partial, more nearly complete knowledge, for it adds a view that has been missing from dominant narratives. Thinking from the standpoint of marginalized lives certainly serves this additive function. If, however, this were the sole contribution of standpoint thinking, then the standpoint from marginalized lives would have no greater epistemic value than that of any other missing miscellaneous item. Yet Harding and fellow standpoint theorists all claim that the standpoint from marginalized lives offers something more than simply another piece of the picture.

Certainly we should demand that knowledge claims be thorough and that they be consistent with existing causal relationships and historical facts, at least insofar as we can provide evidence for such empirical realities. Once this general commitment to thoroughness and this minimal condition for accuracy is satisfied, however, much more needs to be said about how to evaluate the many aspects of knowledge claims that exceed questions of empirical accuracy. The standard "less false, less partial" cannot substitute for broad inquiry about the kind of knowledge a community should seek. It cannot answer the question that Harding poses at the end of her discussion of "Physics": What kinds of knowledge do we need in order to live more reasonably with one another?

"Justice" as the Goal of Knowledge

In response to the limitations in Harding's empiricist standards, some feminist critics have proposed more explicitly political theories of knowledge. Emphasizing the politics implicit in all knowledge claims, these critics argue that feminists should "cease to argue that social marginalization confers epistemic privilege" (Janack 1997, 136). Instead, we should defend certain knowledge claims, or the inclusion of certain people in knowledge making, on the grounds of democracy and justice. Like Harding, these feminist critics identify some important concerns for a feminist theory of knowledge; however, they ultimately cannot account for the full value of thinking from marginalized lives.

Harding's critics rightly identify several dangers with the appeal to epistemic privilege. When feminists appeal to epistemic privilege for marginalized groups, they argue, these theorists repeat the same kind of exclusionary and prejudice-informed operations by which the dominant culture has decided whose opinions should count in knowledge and policymaking (Janack 1997; Bar On 1993).[9] In a just world, no one should need special authorization in order to have their voice heard. Thus, rather than claim epistemic authority for marginalized groups, Bat-Ami Bar On proposes that feminists should justify the inclusion of marginalized voices in knowledge production on the grounds of justice: Justice demands that those who have been silenced "be given the same respectful attention given to the voices of socioculturally hegemonic experts" (1993, 95).[10] Along a similar line of thought, Marianne Janack would like to retain the concept of "epistemic authority" but with the understanding that such authority is a function of explicitly political and ethical choices: We should grant authority to those who bear the consequences of knowledge making and those whom we can trust to be accountable for the knowledge they produce. Based on this sort of ethical choice, says Janack, we should include marginalized peoples in knowledge and policymaking "because it is *right*" (1997, 137).[11]

Other feminist critics of standpoint theory address the problem of evaluating knowledge. The standard "less partial," says Rosemary Hennessy, obscures the pressing issue for feminists, which is not a knowledge claim's "approximation of the 'whole truth' but the implicit effects of the truths it claims—for/against the oppression and exploitation of all people . . ." (1995, 142). Thus she proposes that feminists should focus less on who is speaking, or from whose perspective they speak, and more on the kind of vision that the knowledge speaks *for*, that is, the kind of world it promotes.

Harding herself, alongside her appeals to more conventional epistemological standards, also defends standpoint thinking in ethical-political terms. Unless we develop knowledge from the standpoint of oppressed and exploited lives, she warns, "the majority of the world's people remain deprived of knowledge that could enable them to gain democratic control over the conditions of their lives" (1991, 312). Likewise, when she addresses the choice between the traditional Western narrative of science and her Third World story, she presents this as a moral issue. "It is not just the facts that are at issue," she explains, for when we accept one narrative or the other as our history, we make a moral choice about which past actions to glorify, which elements of our tradition to embrace, and how to focus our present struggles (Harding 1991, 237). Although the Third World story of Western science may have no more facts than the other story, it "opens up useful ways to problematize our identities as North Atlantic feminists—to be 'disloyal to civilization'—in one more illuminating and politically useful way" (Harding 1991, 248).

In the above account of standpoint thinking, Harding veers from her own notion of "less false" and "less partial" knowledge. When she calls for knowledge that criticizes colonialist social relations and that advances democracy, she is calling for something more than simply knowledge that "match[es] the world in better ways" (1991, 83). Certainly, lies and deceptions thwart democracy; however, knowledge that "matches the world" does not necessarily serve democracy. We need only consider, for instance, factually correct histories that obfuscate the human costs of war, economic theories that naturalize exploitative social arrangements, or physics that (to paraphrase Roy 1999, 126) grant the power to destroy the earth in an afternoon.

Beyond "Justice"

Advocates of justice- or democracy-oriented knowledge highlight the political character of any knowledge project. They likewise remind us that no theory of knowledge can avoid making ethical and political choices. Nevertheless, insofar as the above theorists present political goals as a *substitute* for claims regarding the epistemic privilege of marginalized standpoints, they abandon too much that is valuable about feminist standpoint theory as a theory of *knowledge*. When, for instance, Bar On and Janack call on us to include marginalized voices on the basis of justice, they underscore the injustices and exclusions that have characterized current knowledge practices; however, they also reduce feminist standpoint theory to a correction of such wrongs, to a pluralist model of knowledge that calls for everyone's voices to be heard. Such a pluralist model leaves behind the valuable kernel of standpoint theory, namely that our experiences and our views of the world are shaped by our locations in social hierarchies (even if these hierarchies overlap in complex ways and are discursively mediated) and that certain social locations—socially and culturally marginalized locations—are more conducive to critical insight.

Neither does Hennessy (1995) resolve the problem of more liberatory approaches to knowledge when she identifies social justice and democracy as the goals of knowledge. The advancement of democracy and justice may well be the highest goal that our knowledge can serve. Hennessy's litmus test, "is it for or against oppression," may well be the ultimate standard for evaluating the worth of any belief. In itself, however, the claim that the value of knowledge is a matter of its political effects ultimately raises more questions. For instance: What *kind* of knowledge practices contribute to democracy and social justice? And by what intellectual process do we define those political values? For instance, how do we know what constitutes "overcoming oppression" or constitutes "democracy"? Hennessy rightly emphasizes that we cannot evaluate knowledge claims without making political choices; however, neither can we meaningfully appeal to political goals to evaluate knowledge claims unless we reflect critically on the way we have defined our political goals. To do otherwise is to reduce feminist knowledge to knowledge that serves a predefined "right side" without attending to the processes by which we define our values and "sides."[12]

Harding indicates the need to exceed both strictly political and strictly epistemological standards when she ponders the value of her Third World perspective on Western science. Traditional measures of truth do not allow her to give preference to her story, but neither does she want to privilege the story simply because it serves her politics. She concludes we need "standards competent to distinguish between those claims . . . that benefit Western elites and 'less false claims.' At present, it is difficult to locate such standards" (1991, 239).

Standards Adequate to the Value of Stories

Harding never locates epistemological standards adequate to register the value of stories that present a standpoint from marginalized lives. Nevertheless, if we read beyond her modernist language and return to her various descriptions of "thinking from others' lives," we find considerable insight into the interrelated political and epistemological value of the marginalized standpoint. Below, I summarize the insights into the value of the marginalized standpoint that are woven through the work of Harding and fellow standpoint theorists. I then suggest a standard that helps to crystallize the insights implicit in Harding's analysis and that also gives due to the "story" form in which many marginalized perspectives are presented.

The Value of the Marginalized Standpoint

Throughout their writings, Harding and fellow standpoint theorists describe thinking that begins from socially and culturally marginalized standpoints as a way of knowing that facilitates critical social praxis. Contrary to the claims of their critics, they do not argue that standpoint thinking has this value because people who are oppressed have inherently superior cognitive capabilities or because such people engage in practices of resistance that are untainted by the dominant culture.[13] They argue, rather, that people in socially and culturally marginalized positions daily endure the uneven, contradictory effects of a society's accepted beliefs and institutions. Thus their everyday lives register the biases—that is, not simply partialities but politically significant partialities—in beliefs that have been so widely disseminated that they seem "normal" and institutions so entrenched that they seem "natural."[14]

Standpoint theorists identify specific respects in which people who are socially and culturally marginalized confront, in their everyday lives, the biases of a society's ruling beliefs and institutions. First, expanding upon Marx's theory of "ruling ideas," they explain that the beliefs that have been widely distributed in a society reflect the perspective of the socially dominant groups and consequently paint rosy pictures of the existing social order. At the same time that dominant groups determine the ruling beliefs, people in more socially and culturally marginalized positions tend to experience the social ills that people in privileged groups do not directly encounter, have an interest in ignoring, and systematically efface in their euphemistic representations of the world. For instance, people who are socially disempowered tend to take the most dangerous jobs, live by the pollution, clean up the messes, and fill up the jails that dominant representations of the social world gloss over. They often remain in poverty during "economic prosperity," subject to violence in "peace time," debilitated by "development," and with little legal or political representation under "democracy." Their daily experiences thus indicate the contradictions of the given social order, while the perspective from their lives reveals the partisan character of any representations that rationalize that order (Collins 1997, 377–79; Harding 1991, 126, 202–07, 219; Hartsock 1983, 288–303; Smith 1987, 19–25, 54–57; Roy 2001, 1–3, 13–18).

The everyday lives of people in socially marginalized positions also belie the biases of ruling beliefs, because such people tend to do the work that ruling representations overlook and undervalue. They care for dependents; grow, kill, and prepare food; and build, clean, maintain, and guard our physical infrastructure. People in more powerful positions depend on such work, but they rarely do such work themselves. Thus, when people in more privileged positions produce representations of the world, they generally overlook the importance and difficulty of many people's labors. This oversight has political effects. It makes it easier, for instance, for state institutions such as welfare and social security to deny women any credit for housework or caretaking. It also enables employers and the general public to overlook the hardships, and in some cases the violence, that accompanies the most marginalized people's labor and that makes possible many of our lifestyles (Adams 1995, 81–83; Hartsock 1983, 291–92; Harding 1991, 128, 131; Kadi 1996; Smith 1987, 81–88, 161–75; Schlosser 2001).

The perspective from marginalized lives also reveals a dehumanizing and coercive element implicit in the seemingly neutral categories of academic and professional discourses. Categories such as "casualty," "noncitizen," "industrial unit," and "project-affected person" (PAP) seem neutral. Their semblance of neutrality derives, in large part, from their abstraction from the details of individual lives. From the standpoint of academics and bureaucrats, such abstraction from the vagaries of particular lives allows for even-handed application of the categories to the objective conditions of people's lives and is the mark of "objective" knowledge. In addition, professionals and bureaucrats have no reason to doubt the objectivity of such categories, for, thanks to the help of secretaries, technicians, nurses, research assistants, and security officers who reckon with the nitty gritty details of people's lives, professionals can study and govern people without ever knowing or interacting with those people, except as category types. However, whereas white-collar workers can easily mistake their categories for reality and their abstraction for objectivity, those who are categorized confront the way that abstract categories distort and devalue their existence: "Casualties" reduces killed family members to accidents, "noncitizens" treats certain people as outsiders who have no legitimate role in the political community, and "industrial units" and "PAPs" define people who live on the margins of modern society as dehumanized statistics.(Adams 1995, 42–43; Collins 1986, 528; Mohanty 1997, 8–18; Smith 1987, 26–36, 56–85). From the standpoint of people on the receiving end of such categories, such categories attain "neutrality" only by negating people's subjective reality, in effect, "mutat[ing] muscle and blood into cold statistics" (Roy 1999, 32).[15]

From the standpoint of marginalized lives, abstract categories not only devalue many people's subjective and emotional life, but, in so doing, they facilitate the manipulation, and sometimes violent abuse, of those people by public institutions. The problem is not with general categories per se, which are indispensable to theorizing and policymaking, but with the unquestioned authority that categories gain when they are institutionalized. When abstract categories are institutionalized in academic and bureaucratic discourses, they gain the status of truths that override the existential realities of our lives and of norms to which "the actualities of our experience are to be brutally tailored" (Smith 1987, 223). Such reified categories then censor any attempt to address the uncategorizable human implications of social policies while they give a sense of normalcy and legitimacy to policies that disrupt people's lives. As Marx put it, our dehumanized, market-based language has so influenced our way of speaking and relating to one another "that the direct language of [human] nature [has become] an *injury to human dignity* for us, while the alienated language of objective values appears as justified, self confident" (1997, 280). Thus the seemingly objective category, PAP, for instance, allows policymakers to sport an air of disinterested professionalism as they engineer the displacement of hundreds of thousands of people. The same objective discourse of dam building allows the Supreme Court to accuse Roy, when she attempts to narrate the human impact of the dams, of "vicious stultification and vulgar debunking" that "pollute[s] the stream of justice" (Supreme Court of India, cited in Roy 2001, 79). From the standpoint of people whose lives have been reduced to PAP figures on a balance sheet, it is not Roy but the "objective" discourse of the Indian government that obstructs fair discussion of the justice of the dams.

The perspective from marginalized lives also throws a critical light on the binaries of professional discourse. When academic and professional discourses become institutionalized, the binary categories in those discourses, such as "work" and "home," "mind" and "body," "culture" and "nature," and "man" and "woman," appear to correspond to opposing realms of reality. The daily life of people in marginalized social positions problematizes such seeming oppositions, for such people are often charged with either mediating or upholding the boundaries between the realms of life that ruling categories oppose. For instance, women tend to be the caretakers who mediate between the "natural" needs of the people they care for and the demands of "cultural" life while they keep "private" bodily and emotional issues out of the "public" realm (Hartsock 1983, 292–99; Smith 1987, 81–85). When we view the world from the perspective of people who do such mediation and boundary maintenance, we see that current discourses oversimplify the human condition, which does not divide up into discrete spheres except through some people's labor. Moreover, such discursive divisions between supposedly separate realms of life inhibit people who are oppressed in their "private" lives from publicizing their discontent. For instance, dominant discourses present the "housewife" as a happy, private-sphere, nonworker, and thereby inhibit women who are frustrated in their domestic roles from registering their frustration as a social problem (Harding 1991, 130–31; Hartsock 1983, 302–03; Mackinnon 1989, 87–91; Smith 1987, 49–52, 108–110). At the same time, binary-structured identity categories, such as "black and white" and "man and woman," make it difficult for people who suffer from multiple interlocking oppressions to organize around their multidimensional, seemingly uncategorizable struggles (Collins 1986, 519–21). The perspective from marginalized lives thus reveals not mere limitations in dominant categories but limitations that naturalize and impede protest against status quo social arrangements.

The perspective from marginalized lives also exposes politically significant distortions in ruling beliefs because those who are culturally marginalized tend to be "outsiders within" the dominant culture (Collins 1986). They participate in the dominant culture as, for instance, workers or students, but they remain strangers who return home to other cultures. While members of the dominant culture can presume that their beliefs are universal and that their identities are defined absolutely by their roles in the dominant culture, those who are "outsiders within" inevitably confront different, contending belief systems and varying roles as they shift in and out of cultural worlds. Within these different worlds, they experience even their own memories, aims, and "identities" differently, as did Delany, for instance, when he experienced his identity as alternatedly deviant and liberating at the psychiatric hospital and at the bathhouse. Such "world-travelling" (to use Maria Lugones's phrase, 1987) produces what Smith calls a "bifurcated consciousness": an awareness of multiple cultural worlds that belies the gendered, class-centered, or otherwise biased character of the seemingly "normal" dominant culture. Travel between dominant and marginalized cultures also makes visible hierarchical relations between dominant and marginalized groups that are invisible to those who remain within the dominant culture (Collins 1986, 514–15, 525–30; Harding 1991, 130–31; Lugones 1987; Smith 1987, 6–7, 49–51).

Finally, the experiences of people who resist oppression or exploitation bring to the fore the many levels on which power relations operate. As Smith explains, modern forms of rule operate indirectly through "a complex of organized practices, including governments, law, business and financial management, professional organization, and educational institutions as well as the discourses in texts that interpenetrate the multiple sites of power," all of which serve to bring the particulars of daily life under the control of standardized rules and regulations (1987, 3). When people resist social hierarchies or their assigned social roles, even in small everyday gestures, they run up against those otherwise invisible "relations of rule" that regulate our everyday lives. They thereby expose the social and cultural institutions that enforce seemingly "natural" ways of life (Collins 1986, 523–24; Harding 1991, 127, 129–30; Mackinnon 1989, 91–100; Smith 1987, 78–97).

Resistance also affords critical insight into prevailing beliefs when people in marginalized positions resist their exclusion from knowledge production. Since people who are socially or culturally marginalized do not fit Western epistemology's model of the (white, male, upper-class) "universal subject," they can assert themselves as epistemological agents only by identifying themselves as knowing subjects *and* socially situated beings. When they do so, they defy the concept of the "universal knower." In addition, when they are refused recognition on the grounds that their social position taints their objectivity, they reveal how our concepts of "objectivity" and "the universal knower" effectively deny epistemic authority to people who in any way differ from "the norm," while those same concepts conceal the social situatedness of those people who have posed as universal (Collins 1986, 526–30; Kadi 1996, 52–53; Harding 1987, 180; 1991, 275–76).

In this account, the standpoint from marginalized lives does more than add facts or include hitherto excluded voices. Even more importantly, the standpoint from marginalized lives confronts the ideological character—that is, the concealed social origins and political effects—of our culture's taken-for-granted, seemingly neutral beliefs. In exposing the politics of our "common sense" beliefs, standpoint thinking contributes in a crucial way to the active and self-conscious participation of all people in social life: It allows us to examine critically the beliefs that have organized our perceptions and institutions, it holds professional knowledge accountable to people outside official knowledge production, and it opens an imaginative space for us to consider alternative ways of knowing and organizing our world.

Enlarged Thought as a Measure of Standpoint Thinking's Value

The theory of storytelling suggests one way to translate the virtues of standpoint thinking that I have described above into a broad-based "standard" for knowledge. This standard—"enlarged thought"—does not automatically valorize every narrative from the standpoint of the oppressed. It does, however, value precisely those narratives that grapple with those aspects of oppressed and exploited lives that standpoint theorists find powerful.

Significantly, the elements of life under conditions of oppression or exploitation that standpoint theorists identify as epistemologically valuable are also elements that make it difficult to represent events in a clear and straightforward manner. As I have noted above, the epistemological virtues of living in a socially or culturally marginalized position include, for instance: a daily experience with the obscured costs of social contradictions, a shifting in and out of cultural worlds, an engagement in activities that defy the dualisms and exclusions of received analytic categories, and a resistance to the social relations that ruling beliefs present as "natural." Insofar as a writer reckons with these aspects of marginalized lives, she cannot present a straightforward account of even one person's or one group's experiences. On the contrary, she will struggle with language and discursive norms in the attempt to express activities that confound our basic analytic categories. She may, like Anzaldúa and Griffin, experiment with new narrative forms to express the coexistence of multiple worlds and worldviews. She will likely, as Harding, Roy, Griffin, and Zinn do, draw on lesser-known books, journals, and interviews in order to document phenomena for which little official data or even official recognition exists. Or the author may, as is the case with Roy, Anzaldúa, Griffin, and Delany, turn to personal, passion-driven reflections to explore the lived significance of phenomena that are alien to accustomed interpretive frameworks. As a result, a text that reckons with the complex, contradictory aspects of marginalized lives that standpoint theorists value will exhibit neither the objectivity nor the resoluteness that our tradition has associated with rational thought. One would probably have a difficult time arguing (as Harding had with respect to her Third World story of science) that such texts are "less false" and "less partial" than texts that are written in more standard realist styles with extensive official data.

If a text that attends to the inchoate, ambiguous elements of marginalized experience fails to meet traditional scholarly standards, such a text will nonetheless promote what I have called "enlarged thought" in our storytelling. Enlarged thought, as I have revised this Kantian concept in the context of storytelling (in chapter three), refers to the extent to which a narrative helps readers to test and revise their community's taken-for-granted narrative paradigms and to anticipate communication with differently situated others. A text does so, I explained, when it both engages and problematizes ruling narrative paradigms, when it uses language creatively to help readers explore the significance of strange or uncodified phenomena and to test their familiar categories and norms, and when it denaturalizes its own narrative construction, thereby assuming responsibility for the way it identifies actors, actions, and events, and encouraging readers, likewise, to assume such responsibility and to remain open to unanticipated ways of telling the story. These guidelines for representing world events, encapsulated in the standard, "enlarged thought," recognize the particular value of texts that reckon with those aspects of marginalized lives that Harding emphasizes but that her own standard, "less false," overlooks.

Enlarged Thought and Harding's Third World Story of Science

We can appreciate the usefulness of "enlarged thought" for registering the distinct value of marginal experience narratives if we apply this standard to Harding's own Third World story of science. "Enlarged thought" brings into focus powerful elements of Harding's story that standard epistemological criteria elide. In particular, an evaluation of Harding's story in terms of enlarged thought reveals that Harding does not simply invert standard narratives of science, embracing the side of science's "victim," but challenges basic assumptions of the standard narrative.

For instance, enlarged thought directs us to examine the extent to which Harding's alternative narrative of modern science thematizes received narrative paradigms and explores phenomena beyond the bounds of those paradigms. From this vantage point, it is significant that Harding's story draws connections between spheres of life and parts of the globe that ruling discourses on science and history isolate. In particular, she traces connections between science and politics and between European and African history. For instance, from her African standpoint, Harding foregrounds ways that European developments in science and technology were part of a larger effort on the part of some Europeans to accumulate wealth and power. She also shows how the enrichment of European elites depended on the exploitation of African raw materials and labor, while such exploitation was rationalized by the idea that Europeans were a more "civilized" and scientifically advanced people. In turn, she shows how European colonization of African communities and enslavement of African people disrupted sophisticated cultures and sciences within African societies (1991, 223–33).

From the perspective of "enlarged thought," the connections that Harding draws between European and African history and between technological and political developments constitute not simply a "different" story of science but one that confronts, indeed jolts into relief, assumptions central to ruling narratives. Ruling narratives assume science to be an apolitical and unequivocally positive development. They create this ideal by separating Western science from other spheres of life and by mapping the history of Western science onto the modern narrative of "progress." In this scheme, history follows a singular path of advancement while science represents the overcoming of myth and the key to a "developed," "advanced" world. When Harding relates European scientific developments to the destruction of African societies, she problematizes the presumed neutral character of science as well as the categories "developed" and "undeveloped," which have been used to register an individual nation's social and technological maturity. In light of her narrative, she suggests alternative terms, "*over*development" and "*de*-development," for these terms emphasize the interdependent character of each communities' gains and losses (1991, 239). From the perspective of enlarged thought, Harding's terms are strategic narrative innovations that problematize the wealth of developed nations, not neutral descriptors. Nevertheless, they are epistemologically valuable insofar as they help those of us who have identified with the "developed" world to rethink our place in history in light of our connections and obligations to others across the globe.

When we apply "enlarged thought" to Harding's narrative, this standard also directs us to examine the style of the narrative and the extent to which it encourages more responsible narration. Such an examination reveals that Harding does not synthesize her sources into a seamless, conclusive report on modern science but instead narrates science from various African, Indian, and feminist perspectives, which she identifies as partial, politically interested perspectives. A reader who sought definitive historical truths may not even attend to Harding's fragmented and perspective-laden style, but if she did, she would consider these elements to be detrimental to the text's knowledge value. However, a reader who sought enlarged thought would value such explicitly partial elements, for such elements highlight the choices and responsibilities that accompany our storytelling. Such a reader would also appreciate that, although Harding's unresolved collage of perspectives does not present a definitive picture of science, it does raise vexing questions. For instance: How do we understand the value of scientific rationality when this rationality produces useful technology but also justifies the colonization of "lower" peoples? Or for feminists: Given the various connections between de-developed and overdeveloped countries, what kind of hierarchical relations and what potential common interests might lie between women in the First and Third Worlds? In addition to these questions about science and feminism, Harding questions the politics of historiography when she thematizes her historical terms. She asks, for instance, why we call the European expansion into other continents the "Age of Discovery"? Why not name it the "Age of Imperialism"? Questions without answers are not normally deemed knowledge; however, from the perspective of enlarged thought, such questions have epistemic value, for they encourage us to scrutinize taken-for-granted beliefs and to own up to the implications of how we choose to represent our heritage.

Finally, the standard of enlarged thought allows us to appreciate the unconventional, seemingly less-than-rigorous imaginative exercises that Harding includes within her history. Citing Walter Rodney (1982) and Ivan Van Sertima (1986), she asks European and American readers to consider how their own societies might fare if millions of its most productive members were enslaved in and outside of their country. How might history have been different, she asks (inspired by Rodney), "if millions of Britons had been put to work as slaves outside their homeland over a period of four centuries" (Harding 1991, 230). As a hypothetical question, this narrative ploy has little factual value. It does, however, promote enlarged thought, for it helps us to imagine how Africans have experienced European history while it provides a starting point for considering how Africans might view contemporary Europe.

Thus, viewed in terms of "enlarged thought," Harding's African perspective on Western science is not simply another "piece of the picture." More importantly, it is a historical account that promotes more self-critical and more broadly accountable (even if tentative) interpretations of Western science and Western identity. Ironically, her story has this value largely by virtue of its deviations from the norms of "knowledge," including its explicitly strategic tracing of narrative connections, its use of lesser-known sources to pursue these connections, its questioning of basic analytic categories, its imaginative exercises, and its admittedly "pieced together," unresolved construction. These elements make it obvious that the representation is a *story,* not a certain truth. In terms of enlarged thought, this is a good thing.

Standpoint Theory and Enlarged Thought

The concept of "enlarged thought" not only helps to articulate the value of stories from marginalized lives but also registers implicit Kantian motifs that resonate throughout Harding's analysis. Although she never makes explicit her kinship with Kant, Harding evokes Kantian themes when she emphasizes the need for self-reflexivity, which we best achieve by viewing our world from the standpoint of others. While Kant instructs us to "put ourselves in thought in the place of everyone else" in order to put aside "the limitations which contingently attach to our own judgment" (1951, 136, and 137), Harding similarly asks us to "pass over in thought" into the situation of the other, "not in order to stay there . . . but in order to look back at [ourselves] . . . from a more distant, critical, objectifying location" (1991, 151). Also in a Kantian vein, Harding emphasizes that we must take responsibility for the beliefs that we develop upon considering the perspective of others. For instance, in a variation on Kant's dictum to think *for oneself* from the standpoint of others (1951, 136), Harding stresses, "I cannot just repeat, robot-like, what African American thinkers say and never take responsibility for my own analyses of the world that I, a European American, can see through the lens of their insights. . . . [I] must be an actively thinking antiracist, not just a white robot 'programmed' to repeat what blacks say" (1991, 290–91). Harding calls this kind of self-critical and responsible mode of thought "strong objectivity" (1991, 142–52). While Harding's term affirms the progressive impulses of "objectivity" as well as the need for an even stronger commitment to objectivity than traditional methods allow, the Kantian term "enlarged thought" is perhaps more precise. Enlarged thought directs us to test our biases by actively considering the standpoint of others. Enlarged thought thus stresses precisely the kind of community accountability, ownership of one's beliefs, and self-reflexivity that Harding seeks to achieve with standpoint thinking.

Going beyond Kant, Harding, who works within an explicitly Marxist tradition, situates standpoints and prejudices in the context of unequal social relations. She recognizes that our standpoints are a function of our location in social hierarchies, which (however complex and discursively mediated) shape the conditions of our lives and influence our experiences and visions of the world. Thus Harding emphasizes that self-reflexivity must involve an awareness of how we are situated in hierarchical social relations and how our social position affects our beliefs. She likewise emphasizes that those prejudices within all of us that are most in need of testing are not individual idiosyncrasies but *ideology*: beliefs that are distributed by powerful social institutions and that have come to be accepted as common sense, but that actually serve the interests of dominant social groups.

When Harding and fellow standpoint theorists address the social-situatedness of standpoints and the social construction of prejudices, they challenge us to deepen and revise our concept of enlarged thought. In particular, they challenge us to investigate the kind of intellectual and practical work that is necessary in order to test prejudices when our prejudices sustain and are sustained by powerful social institutions. They also challenge us to account for the political interests at stake in pursuing enlarged thought when genuine enlarged thought demands that we engage specifically with marginalized standpoints and when it destabilizes ruling beliefs. When I developed my concept of "enlarged-thought storytelling" in chapter three, I used feminist standpoint theory and other post-Enlightenment theories to begin to extend "enlarged thought" in these directions.

Certainly, much room remains for further revising "enlarged thought" in light of the challenges posed by socially produced prejudices and the political stakes of confronting those prejudices. Nonetheless, with the appropriate revisions, the concept of enlarged thought offers one way to relate "thinking from others' lives"—in all of its engaged, storylike, and politically subversive dimensions—to long-standing epistemological values. "Enlarged thought" allows us to relate standpoint thinking to the widely held epistemological values of self-reflexivity, open-mindedness, and prejudice testing. Significantly, these deeply rooted epistemological values were never strictly epistemological but always

implied an ethical character and political responsibility.[16] The standard
of enlarged thought affirms the connection, implicit in our tradition,
between epistemological and ethical values, such that knowledge seeking also entails ethical commitments to self-examination, responsible
participation in public life, and accountability to others. When, through
the concept of enlarged thought, we relate standpoint thinking to the
jointly epistemic and ethical values of self-reflexivity, public accountability, and open-mindedness, then we can present standpoint thinking
as a practice that has deep roots in our tradition and that transcends
particular political agendas. At the same time, however, enlarged
thought does not commit us to political neutrality. Insofar as this
standard directs us to test prejudices and to anticipate communication
with differently situated others, it supports a politics that seeks forums
for marginalized views and that resists elitist and exclusionary knowledge practices. Insofar as "enlarged thought" directs us to engage the
perspectives of people in the most marginalized positions, this standard
also complements a politics that aims to transform relations of domination in all of their guises, for it contributes to exposing and publicizing
the most obscured forms of domination.

When we understand "thinking from others' lives" to be a practice
that promotes enlarged thought in our social narratives and that is
made possible by engaging others' stories, then we need not apologize
for the "lighter," more literary, subjective texts that thinking from
others' lives often demands. As in Barrios's testimony, Delany's memoir, Harding's Third World story of science, Griffin's "private" history
of war, Anzaldúa's tale of mestiza consciousness, and Roy's account of
families displaced by dams, those texts that present a perspective from
marginalized lives often lack the appearance of objectivity, the prepon-
derance of scientific data, and the stamp of approval from elite institutions that mark professional knowledge. From the perspective of the
theory of storytelling, however, these conventional standards of rigorous knowledge are themselves limited, for they provide no way to
examine critically the narrative paradigms and discursive norms that
structure "objective" knowledge and are presupposed by established
cultural institutions. From the perspective of the theory of storytelling,
only those stories that risk creative, engaged, tentative writing and
informal sources in order to reckon with aspects of historical experience
that resist "common sense" narrative frameworks can test the prejudices that underlie narrative norms, prejudices that are perpetuated by
powerful knowledge-producing institutions. Ultimately, ongoing and
serious engagement with such stories is the only way to keep knowledge
production accountable to those outside ruling institutions and to

sustain democratic communities in which all of us actively participate in narrating, criticizing, and renarrating our identity and projects.

Notes

Introduction

1. See, for instance, Butler (1990, 324–35, 336–39; 1992, 13–16), Butler and Scott (1992b, xiv), Foucault ([1975] 1979; [1976] 1990, 60–70; 1984, 334–39), Grant (1987), Haraway (1988, 581–89), Harding (1991, 123–24, 167, 184–87, 269–70), Hennessy (1993a, 68–74), Chandra Mohanty [hereafter Mohanty] (1982; 1991a, 33–34), Satya Mohanty [hereafter S. Mohanty] (1997, 202–04), Moya (2000, 3–6), Ruiz and Dubois (1994a, xv), Scott (1988, 2–6, 56–60; 1991), and Spivak (1988, 274–77).

2. To give just a few examples: The National Labor Committee uses worker testimony to develop public and Congressional opposition to the expansion of the North American Free Trade Agreement and to build the Students against Sweatshops movement (Kernaghan 1999; National Labor Committee 1999; Pleites 1998); the "Welfare Made a Difference" campaign and local chapters of Jobs with Justice intervene in the discourse of "welfare-reform" by providing public forums in which people affected by such "reform" tell their stories (Hanney and Crouse 1999); and community groups use individual stories to expose industry and government cover-ups of the dangerous effects of pollution and toxic wastes (Di Choro 1996; Lyderson 1998).

3. On the importance of experience-based writing in Third World feminisms, see, for instance, Anzaldúa (1983, 167–73; 1990a, xxii-xxv), Lorde (1984, 36–39); Mohanty (1991a, 32–38), and Moya (1997, 127, 135–37, 145–50).

   Following Mohanty, I use the term "Third World women" as a self-consciously strategic term that brings together a diverse group of people in order to emphasize their similar interests with respect to contemporary social institutions and their potential political alliance (Mohanty 1991a, 2–5; 1997 6–7, 28–29). I use the term "we" in connection with "academics" because I mean to include all of those people who are concerned with studying experience. The categories "Third World women" and "academics" are, of course, heterogeneous and overlapping categories.

4. Recently, various theorists have recognized the dangers that accompany the strong version of the critique of experience. See, for instance, Alexander and Mohanty (1997b, xviii), Canning (1994), Griffin (1997), Hennessy (1993a, 71–74), Haraway (1988), Harding (1991, 172–87), S. Mohanty (1997, 202–34), and Moya (1997).

5. *Discourse* here refers to socially reproduced signifying systems that yield meaning through rules for identifying and opposing terms and for conceptualizing basic aspects of existence such as subjectivity, agency, and historical change. See, for instance, Foucault ([1969] 1972, 48–55, 117; 1980, 96–98, 131–33; 1984, 334–35) and Scott (1987a, 40–41; 1987b 1–7; 1988, 7–9, 53–67; 1991, 778–79).

   Marginalized experiences here refers to experiences that are systematically obscured or omitted in culturally dominant representations of the world. I use this term, rather than "marginalized people's experience," because I understand marginality to be a property pertaining to certain kinds of experiences, not to people per se. I recognize that marginalized experiences are closely related to culturally, politically, and economically marginalized subject-positions insofar as people in these positions endure the hidden costs and contradictions of social policies and insofar as the subjectivity of people in these positions is denied in the dominant culture. Nevertheless, marginalized experiences are not restricted to predefined positions, for any person may endure a kind of experience that is systematically obscured in her culture.

I hereafter abbreviate the phrase "narratives of marginalized experience" to "marginal experience narratives."

6. Hennessy (1993b, 27–31), Mohanty (1991a, 32–38), S. Mohanty (1997, 206–08), Smith (1987, 59–60), Taylor (1993), and Zake (2001) begin, but only begin, to address this problem.

7. See, for instance, Bar On (1993), Hennessy (1995), and Janack (1997).

8. This definition of narrative discourse is based on Barthes (1989, 133–36), Mink (1987, 45–59, 200–01), and Ricoeur (TNi, ix-xi, 44, 54–57).

9. For instance, one narrative that gave me particular insight on the September 11 attacks was a short article by George Caffentzis (2001) that focuses on internal tensions within oil-producing countries. Although this article is a mere two pages, it is particularly effective because it presents not only crucial historical information, such as the ratification in 2000 of a Saudi Arabian foreign-investment law that gives substantial concessions to foreign-owned businesses, but also new ways of identifying characters; for instance, where the popular presses see "Muslims," Caffentzis identifies U.S.-backed ruling elites, dissident fundamentalist elites, and extremely poor sectors of the population, each with contending interests within the Middle East and different relationships to the United States. While his essay does not constitute a comprehensive analysis, it does indicate new ways of examining the conflicts and relationships between social groups, including new ways for North Americans to relate our own lives, as consumers of Saudi Arabian oil, to the growth of Islamic fundamentalism.

Various writers have also described how they have gained new insight into a situation not simply by virtue of new information but through a new way of organizing information into a narrative. To cite just a few examples: Delany sees his own social alienation in a new light when he tells a story that situates his sexual and artistic life in relation to the legal and cultural institutions that structure his "personal" life (1993); Mura reinterprets his own anger after viewing it in terms of Fanon's narrative of cultural colonization (1988, 142–43); Griffin sees new meanings in her own family's secrets when she creates a narrative that interweaves her own memories with historical phenomena characterized by denial and alienation (1992); and Mackinnon describes how women in feminist consciousness-raising groups reinterpret their "personal failings" as symptoms of patriarchal social institutions when they share stories and create new stories that make sense of their common experiences (1989, 83–101). In their ethical theories, philosophers Nelson (1995, 31–35) and Lauritzen (1997, 97–103) also describe how the articulation of a new narrative can help us to discern different moral significances in a familiar situation.

10. In my research in the late 1980s for Service Employees International Union, I discovered that Workers Compensation Boards collected few statistics on stress-related or repetitive-stress injuries, for these did not fit their categories for work-

related injuries. See *The Health Problems of Video Display Terminal Workers* (Service Employees International Union 1987).

11. See also Arendt (BPF, 261–62; HC, 182, 184), Benhabib (1992, 126–29), Carr (1984, 365–70; 1986; [1986] 1991, 18–52, 72), Ricoeur (TNi, 54–64, 78–81), Nelson (1995, 27–35), and Mink (1987, 59–60). The term "narrativity" is from Benhabib.

12. On the denigration of story in the historical and social sciences see, for instance, Smith (1987, 57–60), Stewart (1991), and Trinh (1989, 119–21).

13. Narration, says Spivak, is a human need "rather than the way to truth"; however, "we cannot but narrate," so that no truth is ever possible, because any knowledge claim will be "undermined by the way one says it" (1990, 19–20). See also Hayden White's critical remarks on narrative (1975, 58–59; 1980, 6–27; 1982, 136–37).

14. Following standard usage, I use the term "narrative" to refer to the written or spoken text insofar as it is an object of literary analysis; I use the term "story" to refer more broadly to the text as meaningful for a specific historical community.

15. On these assumptions of Enlightenment epistemology, see for instance Benhabib (1992, 206) and Gadamer ([1960] 1991, 552–68). The formation of historiography as a professional discipline at the turn of the century presupposed this epistemology, defining history proper by opposing history to the more literary, subjective storytelling. See, for instance, Higham (1963), Holt (1940), Novick (1988), Stone-Mediatore (2000, 92), and Trinh (1989).

16. I refer here to the strong version of the poststructuralist argument presented by Joan Scott (1991). Some poststructuralist theorists qualify their criticisms of experience. For instance, Haraway criticizes positivist appeals to experience, but she also reclaims visual experience as an embodied, critically positioned, multidimensional phenomenon (1988, 582–87). Spivak argues that "experience" and "desire" are manipulated by ideology and that intellectuals who "represent" the allegedly "concrete experience of the oppressed" conceal their own interests and political effects (1988, 275); however, she also indicates the need for self-consciously engaged intellectuals who can contribute to the reinterpretation of muted experiences (1988, 306–08). See also Linda Alcoff's discussion of Spivak (Alcoff 1995, 110, 115–16).

17. Feminist epistemologists, often drawing on Marx's theory of ideology (1997, 414–42) or Gramsci's theory of hegemony (1995, 12–13, 57–60, 210–12, 333–35, 365–66, 416), have investigated the way that dominant beliefs come to comprise a community's "common sense." See, for instance, Harding (1991, 218–221), Hartsock (1983, 162, 169–70), Hennessy (1993a, 118, 125, 137), Mackinnon (1989, 87–92, 99–100, 237–40), and Smith (1987, 19–22, 49–60).

In claiming that the experiences of socially dominant groups come to make up our "common-sense truths," I do not deny that perspectives from dominant social groups are also sometimes presented explicitly as stories. Such stories, however, tend to be presented as if they were *general truths*, applicable to any person. (Consider, for instance, Clinton's oft-repeated anecdote about the woman who, upon losing her welfare payments, became successfully integrated into the labor force.) Such seemingly generalizable stories can be presented as impartial, general truths only because they presuppose the same premises that underlie dominant cultural worldviews and social institutions, such as the idea that hard work results in success and that actors are self-constituted, autonomous individuals. By contrast, for the reasons that I present below, stories from marginalized perspectives cannot pass as "general truths" and are readily recognized as creative and personal constructions.

18. Labor, community, and human rights groups have needed to collect their own anecdotal evidence on these and related social problems precisely because official research institutions have not pursued the relevant research. See, for instance, Amnesty International (2001), Arendt (OT, 279, 437), Butterfield (2001), Di Chiro (1996), Greider (2000, 12–16), Hanney and Crouse (1999), Lajoie (1999), Lyderson (1998), National Labor Committee (1999), Roy (1999, ix, 16; 2001, 26–27), Service Employees International Union (1987), and Schlosser (2001). In her attempt to offer a Third World perspective on Western science, Sandra Harding also remarks on her need to turn to nontraditional sources that "feel lighter in weight, more fragile, in their evidential underpinnings" (1991, 221). Moreover, when large research institutions do address the problems of marginalized groups, they tend to employ an operational language that represses the critical content that people express in their own stories of their problems (Marcuse [1964] 1991, 109–14).

19. See, for instance, my analysis of Delany (1993) and Zinn (1995) in chapter four and Barrios ([1977] 1986) in chapter five.

20. See, for instance, Howard Zinn's critique of Samuel Morison's history of Columbus (Zinn 1995, 7–8) and my critique of Gerhard Weinberg's account of the bombing of Nagasaki and Hiroshima (Stone-Mediatore 2000, 103).

21. S. Mohanty (1997, 205) describes experience as "raw material" for constructing our identities. Others who treat experience not as a foundation but still as a starting point for critical insight include Harding (1991, 123–24), Hennessy (1993a, 67–94; 1993b), hooks, (1989, 105–11), Moya (1997), Mohanty (1982; 1991a, 33–39), and Panjabi (1997).

22. See, for instance, Bar On (1993, 95), Hennessy (1995, 142), and Janack (1997, 137).

Chapter 1

1. Arendt BPF, 261.

2. Philosophers who affirm the intellectual value of narrative include Benhabib (1992, 126–29), Carr (1986 [1991], 1–72), Disch (1994, 106–40), Lauritzen (1997), Nelson (1995), Nussbaum (1995), and Ricoeur (TNi, 54–64, 74–75, 78–81). Theorists who pursue their work through telling stories include Nelson (1995, 25–26), Ranney (2003), Stewart (1991), Trinh (1989), and the legal theorists discussed by Disch (1994, 10n).

3. On the way that enlightenment epistemology opposes literary narration to "true" representation and the associated disparagement of stories and literary language in the human sciences, see, for instance, Barthes (1989, 3–4 and 139), Benhabib (1992, 206), Mink (1987, 42–44), Gadamer ([1960] 1991, 552–68), Stewart (1991), and Trinh (1989). Analytic philosophy of history does address the epistemological value of narrative; however, as Mink (1987, 42–48) and White (1984, 24–25) note, this field tends to study narrative as a means to scientific explanation rather than narrative as a distinct intellectual practice.

4. As noted in the introduction, I use the term "narrative" to refer to the objectifiable text that can be analyzed in terms of its component parts. I use the term "story" to

refer to that same text in a broader sense: the text as a subjectively meaningful phenomenon whose meaning is realized in its reception by specific, historically located communities.

5. I address the narrative representation of both past and present political phenomena, for the analyses of narration presented by Arendt, Barthes, and White apply to the narrative representation of all past and present events. (I specify my use of "historical" and "political" in my discussion of terms in this chapter.)

6. This follows the definition of "narrative" in the texts I address by Barthes and White as well as the concepts of narrative presented by Mink (1987, 43–58, 200–01) and Ricoeur (TNi, ix–xi, 44, 54–57; 1991, 7–11).

7. Marcuse's analysis of "the functionalization of language" is also particularly helpful for analyzing the way that seemingly realist texts produce meaning on the level of the individual sentence. The functionalization of language refers to the reduction of abstract, ideal-oriented concepts, such as "progress," "development," and "freedom," to mere technical concepts that refer directly to concrete realities. When social and moral concepts are reduced to technical terms, or what Marcuse calls "operational concepts," the concepts no longer provoke us to reflect on historical possibilities and to evaluate existing realities in terms of those possibilities but instead serve only to identify current institutions that go by that name ([1964] 1991, 84–119). Such operational concepts are prevalent in realist historiography, for, ironically, it is precisely the concreteness of the term that gives the impression of objectivity even while that same concreteness imposes a particular slant on social values and historical phenomena. For instance, when a recent history book describes U.S. investments in Latin America as "aid" and tells us that "the emphasis had been on private investment and free trade" (Coerver and Hall 1999, 115), it takes for granted the perspective of North American investors that conditional loans constitute "aid" and that unrestricted international trade constitutes "freedom." When it tells us that, in return for such loans, "the Latin American nations agreed to follow sound economic policy and to eliminate obstacles to progress" (Coerver 1999, 116), it takes for granted the International Monetary Fund's identification of policies that restrict consumer demand (e.g., restricted internal credit, devaluation of local currency, cutting of government subsidies) with "sound economics," and it presumes that integration into the neoliberal economy is equivalent to "progress." (For a very different perspective on the same phenomena, see Galeano 1973, chapter 5.)

8. *The New Shorter Oxford English Dictionary,* 4th. ed. (1993) defines "casualty" as "Chance" and "A chance occurrence; an accident, a mishap, a disaster."

9. Zinn makes this comment with respect to Samuel Eliot Morison's classic history of Christopher Columbus (Zinn 1995, 8).

10. Barthes (1989, 133) divides these "units of content" into *existents* (kinds of people and places) and *occurents* (kinds of actions and social events). In order to relate Barthes's analysis to narrative elements as generally understood, I call these units of content "actor-units" (or "character-units"), "action-units," and "event-units."

11. I present a fuller analysis of Morison's text in Stone-Mediatore 2000, 96–97.

12. On this limitation in White's analysis, see also Carr (1986, 121; 1986 [1991], 19).

13. In his earlier essays, White sometimes suggests that narratives offer a kind of knowledge. For instance, he says that the "style" of narratives has a cognitive value that can be judged in terms of "the richness of metaphors" (1966, 130), and that we can improve our knowledge by aggregating multiple narratives, each of which

offers partial perspectives (1975, 66). In these remarks, however, White does not clearly distinguish the aim of narrative knowledge from the aim of more complete representation. Nor does he reconcile these remarks with his own concern that narration, even when consistent with facts, distorts reality.

14. As various critics have argued, Arendt's distinction between the social and the political realms risks obscuring the political character of economic and domestic life; however, as Disch (1994, 61–67) and Bernstein (1986) observe, we can also interpret Arendt's distinction not as a distinction between clearly separate areas of life but as a distinction between issues that call for public debate and issues that require only administration. In this interpretation, the question of an issue's "political" status is itself open to discussion.

15. Vollrath also identifies two notions of "the political" in Arendt. He argues that the first addresses "genuine" political action and the second addresses totalitarianism (Vollrath 1977, 167). In my view, however, Arendt's second notion of "the political" is not specific to totalitarianism but is a more general concern for all sorts of actions, violent actions included, that call for public debate. Ricoeur (AS, 66) also interprets Arendt's notion of "the political" in this broader sense.

16. Ricoeur also addresses the sense in which narrative discourse is related to action and yet is more than a "copy" of action. He explains that while narrative discourse is informed by our understanding of action and its elements (e.g., actors, goals, motives), narrative is also shaped by the rules of composition, the structure of a text, and the ways that a text allows for the integration of action into a whole. Thus, when we compare action to its imitation, narrative, this is not a "vicious circle" but rather a comparison of certain aspects of lived temporality to aspects of discursively structured temporality (TNi, 54–60).

17. Arendt does not address institutionally determined differences of perspective, but her concept of plurality invites attention to such differences. Chapters three through six extend Arendt's theory of storytelling to address systematically determined differences of perspective.

18. Arendt here anticipates feminist analysis of the interconnections between "private" and "public" life. She does not address the power hierarchies that structure so-called private life, but she does indicate the imbrication of the two spheres when she observes that even "the smallest act" can have widespread repercussions and that public phenomena consist of a plurality of experiences in individual lives. I return to the imbrication of personal and public life from a feminist perspective in chapter five.

19. Ricoeur describes human life as having an *inchoate narrativity* that is not as tightly structured as a written narrative and yet still calls out for narration (TNi, 75). Carr is not as concerned with distinguishing between the status of written and lived narratives; he argues that human experience "apart from its representation" has narrative structure ([1986] 1991, 18–52, 72; 1986).

Carr sharply contrasts his own position from Ricoeur's. In Carr's view, life and narrative form a continuity, but Ricoeur presents a "discontinuity" (Carr 1984, 362, 365–370; [1986] 1991 10–15). Carr seems to me to exaggerate his differences with Ricoeur, focusing one-sidedly on Ricoeur's analysis of the literary and creative sources of narrative and downplaying Ricoeur's discussions of the complex interrelations between experience and literary narrative (Ricoeur TNi, 54–64, 74–75, 78–81). When Ricoeur distinguishes between the written and the lived story, he does not, as Carr claims, consider narrative to be "alien from the 'real world'" (Carr [1986] 1991, 15). Rather, Ricoeur distinguishes narrative and life in order to address their interrelations. Ricoeur's thesis is more complex but ultimately consistent with Carr's notion of a continuity between life and narrative, for Ricoeur concludes that human life "calls for narrative" and that "literature would be incomprehensible if it did not give a configuration to what was already a figure in human action" (TNi, 64, 75).

If Carr reads Ricoeur as too focused on "discontinuity" between life and literature, this seems to me related to Carr's oversimplification of Ricoeur's notion of "being-as." Ricoeur describes narrative as having a "being-as" status, something between being and not-being that (with the work of reading) enables us to more fully experience aspects of our world that cannot be directly described (TNi, 80; TNiii, 154–155). Carr, however, interprets Ricoeur's "being-as" as simply what the world "is not" (Carr [1986] 1991, 15).

20. In his response to White, Carr also overlooks this crucial question raised by White's analysis (Carr 1984, 365; [1986] 1991, 19).

21. Arendt's descriptions of work and storytelling underscore the kinship between the two: She describes work as a "reification" of materials and an endowing of materials with "solidity" (HC, 136–144); she describes storytelling as a "solidifying" of lived phenomena in words and as a "reification" of the living story (HC, 182, 184). Elsewhere, she includes the historiographer among those people who qualify as "*homo faber* in his highest capacity" (HC, 173).

22. Nora (1984), Burke (1989), and Wieseltier (1993) also address the importance to historiography of a certain kind of remembrance. They call this "social memory" and examine the ways that it is pursued in everyday social and cultural practices.

23. Edward Casey (1987) corroborates Arendt's description of human memory insofar as he describes the latter as a process that does not merely retrieve stored information but actively organizes and creates the past in terms of present concerns and a received language. In his comprehensive study of remembrance, Casey points out that not all remembrance has narrative structure. This does not contradict Arendt's analysis, but it does indicate that Arendt treats only a very specific kind of remembrance: remembrance that treats phenomena of public concern and that seeks to understand these as whole events.

24. Both Arendt and Ricoeur address similarities as well as differences between historical narration and schematism. When Arendt describes how we bring sensible phenomena under general concepts, she draws on Kant's theory of schematism; however, she turns instead to Kant's theory of aesthetic judgment and his analysis of the exemplary particular in order to address the judgment of historical phenomena (LK 80–85). Ricoeur emphasizes that narration, like schematism, combines empirical elements (characters and circumstances) with intellectual elements (themes) (TNi, ix-x, 68); however, he later notes that a narrative configuration of human time differs from schematism of the physical world (TNi, 244).

25. In his later works, Ricoeur avoids the term "referent" in order to acknowledge the reader's role in creating the meaning that the text projects (TNiii, 158–79).

26. Socrates tells Crito to "Look at it this way" when he wants Crito to consider certain implications of his possible escape from jail (Plato 1981, 52). "This way" of looking is made possible by a story (in this case, a hypothetical story that is told as if the events had happened) in which the laws are made into characters. The entire subsequent analysis depends on this way of looking at the situation and thus remains only one narrative-dependent way of viewing the situation, not an absolute truth. Still, this narrative perspective serves to bring into relief for Crito some very

important (though certainly not all) aspects of the situation. (Thanks to Brian Klug for pointing out the relevance of this passage to my work.)

27. Arendt does not analyze understanding in *The Life of the Mind*, probably because she considered understanding to be a practical, not strictly mental, activity. Nevertheless understanding is closely related to the mental capacities that she analyzed in that book. Like *judgment*, understanding treats the meaning of particular phenomena for a specific historical community (Arendt LK, 13–14, 72–74; UP 377, 383–86). Like *thinking*, understanding does not seek certain agreement with objects but is concerned with the intangible existential meanings of phenomena. Whereas thinking leaves the experienced world to reflect on these meanings, understanding brings thought to bear on the particulars of experience (Arendt TH 14–16, 42–45, 92–124, 207–11; TM). Judgment and thinking could be viewed as intellectual activities that we employ at various moments within the broader, endless project of trying to understand our world.

28. Arendt's analysis also indicates key differences (differences that Ricoeur does not address) between text interpretation and the interpretation of a political phenomenon. For instance, whereas the written text is a bounded literary object, the political phenomenon is not a discrete entity but consists of a "boundless" chain of actions. Moreover, the actions that make up a political phenomenon present themselves to the storyteller in terms of various kinds of signs, including physical after effects of the event (which function as indices), records of such effects, and processed memories of perceptual and emotional experiences. As the storyteller gathers these elements together, she must decide which of the virtually infinite "signs" of the action to include as part of her "text." Thus, no "objective structure of signs" exists as such before the storyteller determines the parameters of her "text." As a consequence, any particular interpretation of where the event begins and ends must be open to critical examination. In addition to its mixed assortment of signs and amorphous boundaries, the political phenomenon is also a distinct kind of "text" in another way: It calls for a specifically *narrative* interpretation. When it is interpreted, the narrative interpretation of the phenomenon then functions as an objectifiable text that informs subsequent stories that a community tells of its history and identity.

29. I capitalize what Ricoeur calls "Tradition" in the dogmatic sense in order to highlight its distinction from the nondogmatic appeal to one tradition among many.

30. Ricoeur also remarks on the capacity of storytelling to endow inherently "frail" human action with "durability" (AS, 67–71).

31. Carr discusses this thesis in Husserl (Carr 1987, 78–79).

32. This function of storytelling in confirming and helping people to confront obscure phenomena also accounts for the role of storytelling in enabling people to cope with suffering. Both Arendt and Susan Griffin remark on the way in which pain that cannot be articulated, and that is therefore experienced only privately, has the effect of making someone feel alienated from the common world. Both also suggest people can better endure their pain and overcome their alienation when they tell stories of their suffering (Griffin 1992; Arendt BPF, 262; HC, 15, 50).

Chapter 2

1. Kant 1988b, 55. Reprinted with the permission of Cambridge University Press.

2. See, for instance, Benhabib (1992, 3–17, 26–38, 49–51, 130–32, 148–70), Lloyd (1984, 64–85), Kheel (1985), Derrida (1983), Gadamer ([1960] 1991, 270–82, 555–68), and Horkheimer and Adorno (1998).

3. Arendt makes clear that "forgiving has so little to do with understanding that it is neither its condition nor its consequence" (UP, 377). The rest of this chapter explains why understanding historical actions is compatible with moral condemnation.

4. To be precise, storytelling does not aim toward "judgment" in the conventional sense of pronouncing an evaluation but rather toward *understanding* (in the sense I explain in chapter one). Nevertheless, as I explain in this chapter, Arendtian "storytelling" constitutes a responsible approach to evaluating political events. On the close relation between judgment and understanding, see also Arendt (LK, 13–15, 72–74; UP, 379–83) and my discussion of storytelling and Kant's principles of judgment in chapter three.

5. Benhabib (1992) seeks a philosophical account of how we can legitimate moral and political claims. She seeks a post-Enlightenment model of legitimation that can justify feminist claims and can disentangle feminism (as she understands it) from a relativist postmodernism. Mohanty (1997) also seeks a way of overcoming postmodern relativism and critically evaluating knowledge claims; however, he focuses on the social practices and arrangements that produce knowledge with a view to elucidating the kind of practices and arrangements that are most conducive to understanding the factors that condition our lives. He seeks to disentangle a relativistic affirmation of "differences" from a politically powerful multiculturalism that addresses historically specific social relations.

6. On the individual level, this idea of the inclusive judging community serves as a hypothetical vision that guides our thinking: Insofar as we imagine ourselves to belong to such a community, we consider others' views and reason in a manner accountable to others. On a social level, this community indicates the actual social conditions that a society must establish in order to produce more objective knowledge (Benhabib 1992, 28–38, 40–45; S. Mohanty 1997, 242–50).

   Both Benhabib and Mohanty develop their arguments by drawing on Kant's notion of enlarged thought, developed in his third *Critique,* and Kant's notion of the public character of reason, developed in his first *Critique* and political writings. I return to these Kantian themes in chapter three.

7. Satya Mohanty, in his analysis of Toni Morrison's *Beloved* (1997, 216–29), examines some of these interpretive practices, in particular, the remembering practices through which formerly colonized peoples can critically reinterpret their identities. My own work focuses more specifically on the role that narration plays in our attempt to understand and judge political events.

8. Arendt's book *The Origins of Totalitarianism* addresses both Nazism and Stalinism as manifestations of twentieth-century totalitarianism. Because events in her German homeland were her original concern, and in order to narrow the scope of my analysis, I focus in this chapter on her study of Nazism.

9. On Arendt's criticism of the appeal to universal principles to judge Nazism, see also Arendt (NT, 328–29, 360; [1964] 1994, 10–11; BPF, 239–43). On the way that Arendt's experience of Nazism influenced her criticism of Enlightenment morality, see also Disch (1994, 14–17) and Kohn (1994, xi).

   In their critique of "universal" principles, some contemporary critics make the further point that, when liberals appeal to supposedly universal principles, such as "color-blindness," "tolerance," or "privacy," their apparent neutrality conceals the uneven effects that such principles have whenever they are applied in contexts of social inequality. See, for instance, Disch (1994, 213–15) and Mackinnon (1989, 184–234).

10. From her first reflections on her book *The Origins of Totalitarianism,* Arendt makes clear that she pursues a "rather unusual approach . . . to the whole field of political and historical sciences as such" (AR, 77); however, only later does she describe herself as a "storyteller" or use the term "storytelling" to describe political inquiry. See, for instance, Arendt HC, 50, 184–192; Arendt [1964] 1994; and Arendt, "Action and the Pursuit of Happiness," paper delivered at the annual meeting of the American Political Science Association, September 1960 (cited in Vollrath 1977, 160).

11. Arendt proposes this title in a memo to Mary Underwood (cited in Disch 1994, 122).

12. See, for instance, criticism by Abel (1963, 224), Jay (Botstein and Jay 1978, 361), and Voegelin (1953, 68–76).

13. For criticism of this metaphor, see Voegelin (1953).

14. In fact, Arendt suggests that the radical destruction of human dignity is a genuine danger today. In a prescient remark, she observes that the death camps are "as much of an attraction as a warning" for contemporaries (OT, 459). Death factories are a seeming attraction insofar as they present "the swiftest solution to the problem of overpopulation, of economically superfluous and socially rootless masses." They are a warning insofar as they indicate the dangerous implications of social practices that refuse dignity and legal equality to all people, that confuse the victims of social ills with the problems, and that instead of addressing the source of social problems try to destroy the victims. (We might consider, for instance, attempts to rid cities of homeless people by outlawing their existence, to address growing welfare rolls by simply cutting people off welfare, and to exclude refugees and noncitizens from legal rights. See, for instance, Hayter 2002; Roy 2001, 20–23; and Ireland 1999.)

15. Note that Arendt invokes the Enlightenment term "dignity," as this seems to be the best word she can find to communicate the mode of being that she values. Nevertheless, this appeal to an Enlightenment moral concept is not inconsistent with her attempt to test Enlightenment categories. Even while she appeals to "dignity," she does not pursue a mere immanent critique that holds Western institutions to their own values. Instead (in accord with the tradition of hermeneutics) she allows the complexities and strangeness of historical phenomena to test her received categories, but she also recognizes that those categories cannot but provide the initial framework in which she understands the world. Thus Arendt continues to rely on certain Enlightenment values to express her moral vision, while she also tests and extends the meaning of those values in her attempt to make sense of historical phenomena.

16. Kant, "Was heisst: Sich im Denken orientieren?," cited in Arendt LK, 41.

17. On Kant's discussions of the public character of reason, see Arendt (LK, 39–50), Kant (1951, 135–40; 1988a, 126–30) and S. Mohanty (1997, 3, 249).

18. Kant 1988b, 54. Reprinted with the permission of Cambridge University Press.

19. Arendt's radical suggestion regarding the community-situatedness of "individual thought" has roots in undervalued elements within the Enlightenment tradition. Not only Kant (in the passages cited above) but another champion of "individual thinking," John Stuart Mill, situates "individual thought" within a community. Mill argues that the person whose judgment we should most respect is the person who "has kept his mind open to criticism" and who listens "to what can be said about [a subject] by persons of every variety of opinion" (1956, 25). Significantly, Mill also identifies as fundamental to individual freedom the freedom to associate

with others (1956, 16). Mill again implicitly situates individual thinking within the relations between people, when, in his dedication to Harriet Taylor, he tells us that "the work belongs as much to her as to me" (1956, 1).

Chapter 3

1. For instance, factually accurate stories may stifle discussion or distort an event's human significance by naturalizing social facts, by categorizing and arranging material in a way that obscures certain aspects of the phenomenon, or by inundating readers with a plethora of accurate but distracting information. See, for instance, Zinn (1995, 7–8), Stone-Mediatore (2000, 103), White (1978, 84–99, 105–15), and my analysis in chapter one of histories by Samuel E. Morison and Gerhard Weinberg.
2. Arendt also highlights the nonelitist character of Kant's spectator-judge when she reminds us that, for Kant, good judgment does not require genius but only basic common sense "which we have to presuppose in everyone" (Kant, cited in Arendt LK, 70). In addition, Arendt implicitly situates Kant's spectator-judge within an actual, rather than abstract, community of judges when she translates Kant's term for an intersubjective judgment, *allgemein,* as "general" rather than "universal." (On this translation, see Beiner 1982, 163n.) On the way that Arendt appropriates Kant's theory of judgment while distancing herself from Kant's two-world metaphysics, see also Benhabib 1992, 32.
3. The legitimate concern behind Kant's directive that we imagine possible other perspectives rather than collect the actual perspectives of real people is vividly (and comically) illustrated by what I call "the Jay Leno phenomenon." When the late-night talk-show host Jay Leno quizzes people on the street about basic historical and cultural issues, the responses he receives highlight the astounding ignorance of people of all walks of life. Leno's interviews present a clear (even if exaggerated) illustration of Kant's point: that merely surveying a variety of people and tallying the results will not necessarily lead to an intelligent judgment. Sandra Harding expresses a similar concern when she emphasizes the need for intellectual responsibility in her theory of the feminist standpoint (1991, 283).
4. In *Perpetual Peace,* Kant argues that a peaceful federation of states implies a right *not* to conquer and plunder but to visit other lands and to be received hospitably. This hospitality is not simply an option among friends but is a practical necessity for people who share one earth and "must necessarily tolerate one another's company" (Kant 1988a, 106).
5. Kant did believe that adherence to "publicness" eventually leads to world peace, but he maintained that the validity of this principle rests on strictly a priori grounds, independently of any empirical consequences (1988a, 121–30).
6. Arendt here anticipates the connection between engaged storytelling and the imaginative perspective taking of Kantian judgment; she suggests that her openly subjective style can be understood in terms of Kant's notion of the imagination (AR, 79).
7. Arendt belies this structural difference between aesthetic and political judgment when she tries to apply reflective judgment to a slum. Arendt intends to follow Kant's maxim of reflective judgment. However, whereas Kant instructs us to imagine the perspective that others might have on a given object, Arendt does *not*

imagine other people's standpoints on the slum. Nor does she imagine how someone in the standpoint of a slum might perceive an object. Instead, she "represent[s] to [her]self how [she] would feel if [she] had to live there," that is, she imagines the experience of *living within* the phenomenon to be judged. She never acknowledges this detour from Kant's version of enlarged thought. (See Arendt, Lecture course at the New School, "Some Questions of Moral Philosophy," Fourth Session, March 24, 1965 [Hannah Arendt Papers, Library of Congress, Container 40, p. 024648, cited in Beiner 1982, 108].)

8. Taylor 1993, 58. © 1993 Hypatia, Inc. Reprinted with the permission of Indiana University Press.

9. Many critics agree that, although social locations do not define our essential nature, they do profoundly affect our experience of who we are. Thus social identities cannot simply be shed like a false skin but must be reckoned with as part of "the social and historical dimensions of our innermost selves" (S. Mohanty 1997, 221). See also Mohanty (1982), Moya (1997), and hooks (1995).

10. Disch 1994, 170. This critical remark refers to Arendt's Kant lectures. While Disch is critical of the lectures, she finds in Arendt's letters and literary essays a conception of enlarged thought that is more sensitive to the alterity of others (1994, chapter six). I likewise find a difference-sensitive enlarged thought in Arendt's historical work, which I examine in chapter two.

11. Elaborating on Marx's theory of ideology, Smith explains how the basic categories of academic and popular discourses, categories such as "home" and "action," reflect the perspective of dominant social groups; however, such categories seem neutral when they are widely distributed by the groups that dominate cultural and social life (1987, 2–9, 50–57, 74–78).

12. Wardell Yotoghan, a long-time resident of Cabrini Green and the co-chair of the Coalition to Save Public Housing, explained that Cabrini Green residents opposed the city's development plan, in part, because they did not believe that the city's promised rent vouchers would provide realistic opportunities for alternative housing and, in part, because they had formed attachments to the Cabrini Green community. Apparently, their complaints about the neighborhood did not stop them from experiencing the area as a locus of community and community action (Committee on New Priorities Public Forum on Public Housing, Chicago, May 21, 1997).

13. This results in what Gadamer calls the hermeneutic circle: Even when a critic seeks to address the specific details of a phenomenon, the critic can identify and grasp together these details only in light of a tradition-given discursive framework Gadamer argues that his recognition of the hermeneutic circle and the human finitude that this circle implies does not constitute a political position; it simply describes the essential structure of human understanding ([1960] 1991, 573).

14. Campus Watch seems to share information and to be associated with the more public group, the American Council of Trustees and Alumni (ACTA). ACTA presents itself as dedicated to the "free exchange of ideas on campus," but, together with Campus Watch, encourages surveillance of teachers who promote ideas that it considers unpatriotic. See the groups' websites, www.campus-watch.org and www.goacta.org and the ACTA publication, "Defending Civilization: How Our Universities Are Failing America and What Can Be Done about It."

15. This narrative strategy, in which one pursues understanding of another by relating elements in the other's situation to elements in one's own world, resembles what Nelson calls "stories of humility." Nelson recognizes similar effects in such stories:

Such stories "put faces on people," thereby allowing us to resist "the tendency to homogenize difference" and, instead, to "deal with difference in a manner that is attentive to individuals." Nelson also recognizes that, when someone tells such a story, she "not only puts a face on the Other, but also faces herself" (1995, 30–31).

16. Carole Taylor (1993, 71) also values this sort of cautious perspective taking. Taylor argues that a narrator can avoid oversimplifying the perspective that she presents and overestimating her own authority only if she makes explicit her own discursive work, a strategy that both Arendt and Griffin practice.

17. Showalter argues that the term itself, "shell-shock," disguises the "feminine" sense of powerlessness and speechlessness that this experience entails (1985, 172–75).

18. Seyla Benhabib also investigates how Kant's principles of judgment might be translated into political guidelines. She suggests that a public space exhibits enlarged thought if it has a "public ethos of democratic participation," that is, a civic culture that invites and protects the publicizing of diverse perspectives (1992, 140–141).

19. Elsewhere, Arendt theorizes this historical responsibility that is implicit in her historical work. She explains that, when we judge historical events or actions, we risk making decisions about right and wrong and we risk exposing our beliefs to public scrutiny. We also risk inserting ourselves in the world as engaged historical actors responsible for the course of events. We can avoid this risk by refraining from judging; for instance, we can mechanically follow orders or social norms, or we can claim that we cannot judge others because "we weren't there." When we do so, however, we forgo any moral basis for principled action in the present. We also leave events in an "unmastered past," neglecting our responsibility to learn from history. By contrast, when we take the initiative to judge past events, we own up to our responsibility as thinking and acting beings, for we recognize that we are not passive recipients of history but can evaluate and respond to the possibilities that history presents (Arendt BPF, 10–15; LK, 5; [1963] 1965, 296–297; and Arendt, "The Jew as Pariah," cited in Beiner 1982, 99–100).

Chapter 4

1. Some of the material in this chapter first appeared in "Chandra Mohanty and the Revaluing of Experience," *Hypatia* (summer 1998).

2. Even while they draw on women's experience to develop their theories, Hartsock and Mackinnon recognize the dangers of naive appeals to experience (Hartsock 1983, 288, 303; Mackinnon 1989, 99–125). Smith sometimes uses language that seems to naturalize experience and that raises red flags for contemporary readers; for instance, she sometimes refers to "actual experience" or to "a world experienced at a level prior to knowledge or expression" (Smith 1987, 49 and 50). Nevertheless, Smith's point is not to invoke an empiricist notion of self-evident experience but only to underscore the phenomenological fact that we have experiences that, even if embedded in social relations and mediated by cultural texts, are not spoken, named, or recognized in dominant representations of the world.

3. For instance, Harding values the experience that one gains by struggling against oppression (1991, 126–27, 282, 287); Mohanty values experience as a strategically chosen historical location (1982, 39–42); and Haraway reclaims visual experience as a self-consciously embodied, critically positioned phenomenon (1988, 582–87).

4. To be fair to Scott, she directs her criticism specifically to appeals to experience that presume experience to be a source of transparent, self-evident meaning (1991, 778). In one place, she recognizes that experience can also "upset what has been taken for granted" (1991, 793); however, she never investigates this critical import of experience. In her critique of histories of experience, she presumes that all such histories use experience in a problematic, positivist manner.

5. Butler rightly warns against making generalizations about poststructuralism based on the work of one critic (1992, 5–7). In highlighting Scott's work, I do not mean to imply that all poststructuralist-oriented scholars share her position on experience. Nor do I deny the value of poststructuralist tools for analyzing critically our foundational concepts and methods. I focus on Scott simply because she follows to its radical conclusions the poststructuralist approach of treating experience as a discursive phenomenon and thus reveals the insights and the dangers of this sort of approach to experience.

6. As I explain in the introduction, endnote number five, I mean by *discourse* socially reproduced signifying systems that yield meaning through rules for identifying and opposing terms and rules for conceptualizing basic aspects of existence such as subjectivity, agency, and historical change. In her effort to overcome the metaphysical opposition between language and reality, Scott sometimes claims to use the term "discourse" broadly to encompass both language systems and social life, "not only ways of thinking but ways of organizing lives, institutions, societies" (1987, 40; see also Scott 1988, 54–55, 94; 1991, 778–779). When she analyzes experience, however, she ends up using the term more narrowly to refer to representational practices and conceptual systems. Scott's identification of "discourse" with "rhetoric" anticipates this narrower usage (1988, 4). She never acknowledges her narrower use of the term and, as a result, she overlooks the limitations of discourse analysis. On Scott's unwitting narrowing of the term "discourse," see also Hennessy (1993a, 112–113, 122–23) and Stansell (1987, 26–28).

7. Foucault analyzes the discursive constitution of subjectivity within his investigation of the conditions that make possible the human sciences. He argues that "discursive formations" (or, later, "power-knowledge apparatuses") underlie the human sciences insofar as they make certain domains of life into objects of study and regulation. Discursive formations consist of an ensemble of social institutions, technologies, and rules for forming verifiable statements. When Foucault addresses the power-knowledge apparatus, he includes here discursive practices as well as extradiscursive "plays of power," that is, institutions and learned behavior that issue from and condition discursive forms. Foucault does not try to distinguish discursive from nondiscursive practices (or ideas from institutions) because his concern is with the ensemble of epistemological and institutional practices that *work together* in specific historical contexts to produce particular historical effects. See, for instance, Foucault ([1969] 1972, 35–38, 48–55, 117; 1980, 196–98, 131–133; 1984, 334–335). On the significance of Foucault's transition to "apparatus," see also Rawlinson (1987, 385–387).

   Foucault prefers the term "discourse" to "ideology" because the latter implies a truth outside of ideology, a subject whose pre-existing consciousness ideology distorts. "Ideology," in other words, implies that ideas are secondary to a material infrastructure (Foucault 1980, 50, 118)

   I appreciate Foucault's concern to address the joint operation of discursive and extradiscursive practices; however, I distinguish discursive practices, specifically narration, from extradiscursive labor, property, and state relations in order to examine how these mutually affect each other. (On the need to distinguish between discursive and extradiscursive practices in order to examine the interrelations between these, see also Hennessy 1993a, xv–xvi, 6–8, 31–32, 87–91; 1993b, 20–26.) I also appreciate Foucault's concern not to reduce knowledge practices to a mere "superstructure"; however, I still find Marx's term, "ideology," useful insofar as this term emphasizes that ideas are produced by social institutions and serve specific social interests.

8. Although Scott sometimes recognizes the possibility of combining the narration of experience with discourse analysis (e.g., Scott 1988, 27) and some of her own histories work toward this goal, she is clear in her critique of experience (1991) that the narration of experience is incompatible with discourse analysis. On the opposition that Scott presents between these two projects, see also Canning (1994, 375).

9. Scott presents this analysis of Delany in two parts: at the beginning of the essay, she criticizes Delany's presumably empiricist project; at the end she reinterprets the "identity" presented in the text as a discursive production. She does not explain the connection between the two readings, but the most logical one seems to be that the later reading tells us what Delany is "really doing," despite his empiricist intentions.

10. Galeano 1989, 220. This and subsequent translations are my own.

11. Canning (1994), Stansell (1987), and Alcoff (unpublished paper, cited in Moya 1997, 127) present similar criticisms of Scott.

12. Kaplan's work (1982 and 1990) exemplifies the kind of work that Scott credits with having established the importance of gender in organizing social life but also criticizes as reproducing existing definitions of women, gender, and politics (Scott 1988, 4, 19–22, 24). In some respects, Kaplan's work fits Scott's description. In her later essay on "women's political cultures," for instance, Kaplan takes for granted "women's experience" insofar as she appeals to such experience to explain what she calls a characteristically female political consciousness. She also presupposes a narrow conception of politics insofar as she addresses how marginalized groups can affect the formal political process. At the same time, however, in the process of investigating specific popular-class women's struggles, she transforms precisely those categories—"identity" and "politics"—that Scott claims are naturalized by histories of experience. She describes, for instance, the formation of nonfoundationalist collective "identities" that have emerged from women's articulation of their common interests in specific situations. She also describes women's political movements that have challenged the logic of separate "private" and "public" spheres in their attempts to address politics to everyday difficulties, such as the Chilean women whose motto was "Democracy in The Country and In the Home" (Chilean Women for Life, cited in Kaplan 1990, 264).

13. See, for instance, Tilly (1989). Despite their disagreement over future strategies, Tilly and Scott coincide in their sharp and sweeping criticisms of histories of experience.

14. Delany 1993, 176

15. Even while Foucault criticizes theories that attempt to define freedom based on a supposedly universal structure of subjectivity, he does support "practices of freedom," that is, the continuous exposure and modification of the concrete technologies and procedures that regulate our everyday lives (Foucault 1984, 245–246). On Foucault's notion of "practices of freedom," see also Rawlinson (1987, 390–392) and Sawicki (1996, 170–176).

16. Marcuse 1991 [1964], 98.

17. These examples are from, respectively, Countee Cullen, Richard Wright, a woman participating in the Montgomery bus boycott, and Margaret Wright, all cited in Zinn 1995.

18. Satya Mohanty makes a similar point in his powerful analysis of Toni Morrison's book *Beloved*. Mohanty specifically addresses the problem of how members of formerly colonized groups can reclaim an identity beyond the terms of colonialism. Examining how Morrison's characters come to terms with their shared past, Mohanty explains that the stories we tell (or do not tell) of our past inform our understanding of our own identities, for they lead us to appreciate (or to neglect) "the social and historical dimensions of our innermost selves" (1997, 221). Thus, we can expand our sense of our own identity through telling stories that help us to establish kinship with forgotten past communities. Especially for those of us who belong to colonized groups, however, we can do so only with psychologically difficult work in which we come to terms, both emotionally and conceptually, with aspects of ourselves and our past that we may not have consciously acknowledged, and often cannot confront, without a supportive community (Mohanty 1997, 217–27). (I address this latter point further in chapter five.)

19. Arundhati Roy, interview (Barsamian 2001). Used with permission of The Progressive Magazine, 409 E. Main St., Madison, WI 53703, www.progressive.org.

20. Gramsci's term "hegemonic" describes conceptual paradigms whose influences are so strong that they appear to us as if they were general truths and even affect our own understandings of ourselves. Representations of the world that achieve hegemony are never completely stable and self-sufficient because they are forged through ongoing ideological struggles. Thus hegemonic representations include within them elements of various, competing discourses. They can be revised and recast when we use them in ways that reveal their limits and contradictions (Gramsci 1995, 12–13, 57–60, 210–12, 333–35, 365–66, 416). Postcolonial feminists have found this term particularly useful for addressing the effects of colonialist and neocolonialist ideologies. See, for instance, Hennessy (1993a, 76–79), Alexander and Mohanty (1997b, xxii and xxx), and Panjabi (1997, 152).

21. I here borrow Roy's technique of putting the past tense in parentheses.

22. My claim that somatic experience can exceed and resist language practices does not presume that bodily experience is somehow outside of language but only that such experience, even while it is influenced by our interpretations, is also shaped by an extradiscursive material and biophysical world whose effects exceed, inform, and sometimes react against language practices. Canning (1994, 373–96), Griffin (1997), and Wilkerson (2000, 254–68) also address this sort of resistant bodily experience.

23. Such an investigation of the relations between language practices and social institutions (which I pursue in chapter five) differs in emphasis from Foucault's analysis of discursive formations. Nevertheless, it seems to me compatible with his project, for even while Foucault focuses on "noneconomic" discursive forms of power, he acknowledges that discursive formations are "enmeshed in" relations of domination and exploitation (Foucault 1980, 89; see also Foucault, "The Subject and Power," 213, cited in Sawicki 1996, 171).

   Scott sometimes recognizes that we must "situate and contextualize" language in relation to an extradiscursive "reality" (1988, 40; 1991, 783, 795); however, Scott never explicates all she lumps together under "reality." She also dismisses this reality when she rejects as positivist any attempt to relate people's experience to materially defined social positions. For instance, Scott (1987a, 43) claims that

Christine Stansell embraces "seemingly positivist history"; however, Stansell (1987, 28) only claims that historians should "see speaking and writing as entering into continuing and dialectical relation with many social practices" when speakers and writers are subject to structurally conditioned material constraints. On Scott's inadequate attention to the interrelations between language and social institutions, see also Varikas (1995, 95–98), Stansell (1987, 20–22, 24–29), Fox-Genovese (1991, 157), and Hennessy (1993a, 123–125).

24. For instance, the emerging discourse of "global justice" begins to articulate the worldview that is implicit in social movements that are not against global community per se but that seek more democratic, more environmentally responsible, and more just forms of global community. (See my discussion of such movements in relation to transnational feminism in chapter five). Nevertheless, the discourse of global justice movements remains fragmented and under the influence of ruling discourses that equate current neoliberal institutions with "globalization" per se. As a result, global justice advocates sometimes present their position as "antiglobalization" or "anti-free trade," thus unwittingly accepting the ruling logic that equates globalization with current transnational institutions and "freedom" with current trade laws.

25. Interestingly, Scott implicitly recognizes (even though she does not theorize) an extradiscursive experience that drives Delany's writing. She finds that the motivation for Delany to reclaim and reinterpret his sexuality lay in something she calls intriguingly his "subjective perceptual clarity," but she never explicates (1991, 794). She also implicitly acknowledges a subjective experience that is incongruent with received discursive categories when she tells us that Delany finds that "the available social categories aren't sufficient for [his] story" (Scott 1991, 795). However, Scott cannot theorize these extralinguistic experiences or their influence on Delany's writing. As a result, her reading leaves us with a paradox: On the one hand, Delany's bathhouse experience is constituted through his interpretation of that event; on the other hand, the interpretation is itself motivated and informed by Delany's extradiscursive experiences. Scott cannot resolve the paradox because she refuses to recognize an experience beyond language and thus cannot theorize the mutual interrelations between experience and language.

Chapter 5

1. Barrios ([1977] 1986, 230). This and subsequent translations are my own.

2. Unlike the other theorists mentioned here, Barrios has little formal education and is not familiar with postcolonial or poststructuralist theory. Nonetheless, her testimony (1977 [1986]) offers a rich account of how cultural representations of "women" and "worker" have obstructed many women's understanding of their own experiences while they have obscured the relation between those experiences and broader systems of domination. She also demonstrates how people who have been oppressed can use reflection on their experiences (and the experiences of others who share similar struggles) as a means of developing a critical analysis of their situation.

3. I use the term "Third World women" not as a neutral name for a self-evident or naturally existing group but, rather, as an explicitly strategic term; this term highlights the common interests with respect to transnational institutions and the

potential political alliance among women across the globe who live in, or who have ancestry from, formerly colonized countries. On the strategic value use of the term "Third World women," see also Alexander and Mohanty [hereafter A and M] (1997b), Mohanty (1991a, 2–7; 1997, 7–8, 27–28), Johnson-Odim (1991), and Panjabi (1997, 152).

Any strategic use of the term "Third World women" should also recognize the dangers and limits of this term. For instance, like any identity category, the term can be misread and reappropriated as an essentialist and objectifying category that effaces the differences among people within that category (Mohanty 1991b, 53–56; Narayan 1998; Panjabi 1997, 152).

4. Mohanty defines "colonization" as "a relation of structural domination, and a suppression—often violent—of the heterogeneity of the subject(s) in question" (1991b, 42). Such colonization can occur on economic, legal, cultural, and psycho-logical levels. Contemporary forms of neocolonialism are a legacy of earlier political colonialism but are also characterized by a "recolonization" unique to contemporary capitalism (Mohanty 1991b, 52–57; A and M 1997b, xxi–xxvi).

5. Transnational feminism is closely related to Third World feminism, as both foreground the concerns of the world's most marginalized women. I will reserve the latter term to designate work that is produced specifically by and for Third World women, i.e., women who have historical ties to colonized social groups. I use the popular term "global feminism" to refer more generally to all feminist practices that speak to the concerns of women across the globe.

6. In order to avoid reinscribing the "public/private" dichotomy, Panjabi (1997, 155) uses the terms "microsocial" and "macrosocial." Panjabi's terms allow us to distinguish between those realms of life that are more intimate and those realms of life that are more public, while they recognize the socially conditioned character of both of these realms.

7. For transnational feminist uses of this term, see, for instance, Panjabi (1997, 156) and Mohanty (1991a, 13–16, 34, 39).

8. Some of the concrete steps for more democratic, publicly accountable global institutions that these organizations advocate include the following: that transnational trade agreements include provisions to strengthen wage and environmental stan-dards; that dispute bodies (which are now governed by government and corporate representatives and closed to the public) allow community and labor groups to present complaints; that dispute bodies include on their governing boards members of labor, environmental, and other community groups; and that dispute bodies be empowered to enforce the punishments necessary to hold corporations accountable to community-determined standards. See, for instance, A and M (1997b, xxvii–xlii), Anderson (1998; 1999), Borosage (1999), Coalition for Justice in the Maquiladoras (1999), Economic Policy Institute (1997), Greider (2000), Kamel and Hoffman (1999, 111–15), Nichols (1999), U.S./Cuba Labor Exchange (1997, 19–27).

9. For critical analysis of neoliberal accounts of globalization, see, for instance, Anderson et al. (1998, 7), Borosage (1999), Kamel (1990), Ranney (2003), Instituto del Tercer Mundo (1999, 62–76), and U.S./Cuba Labor Exchange (1997, 8–10).

10. Micklethwait and Wooldridge justify the current global division of labor on the grounds that "[t]he more people specialize in what they do best, the more productivity is improved. . . . The whole point of engaging in trade is to allocate resources to the country that can use them best, even if that activity is linking Chinese hands with American consumers . . . producers also benefit from doing what they do best rather than what can be done better by others" (2000, 111–12).

Are we to presume that manual labor is what Chinese people "do best" while Americans are naturally suited to consumption?

11. Eduardo Galeano 1989, 217.

12. Norma Alarcón 1990, 363. From *Making Face/Making Soul.* Copyright © 1990, ed. Gloria Anzaldúa. Reprinted by permission of Aunt Lute Books.

13. For instance, when CNN anchorwoman Greta Van Sustren was interviewing a guest female physician from Afghanistan, she commented that the Taliban seemed to have enforced their severe repression against Afghani women without any resistance from the women (December 17, 2001, "The Point," CNN). The guest corrected her.

14. I have encountered in my own experience the dangers of this sort of cultural caricaturing. As part of a faculty study group on globalization, I raised concerns about the working conditions endured by women, children, and other workers in Third World countries. Ironically, I was met with the response that my concern for women's and workers' rights was biased toward "Western values" and "insensitive to Third World cultures," as if respect for people's basic health and safety were inherently "Western values" and diametrically opposed to "Third World cultures." Such "sensitivity to other cultures," when it is not accompanied by attention to *all of the people in those cultures,* including marginalized groups, becomes a guise for cultural reductionism and a convenient rationale for ignoring social problems.

    A more subtle example of the oversimplifying of "traditional culture" occurs in Michael Ignatieff (2001). Ignatieff clearly seeks to advance the cultural and political agency of Third World women, but even his sophisticated analysis of the relevance of human rights across cultures often presumes homogeneous and static "traditional cultures." For instance, when he claims that, "it is for the women themselves to decide how to adjudicate between tribal and Western wisdom," he recognizes Third World women as agents but he also presumes that their choice for women's rights must be a choice for "Western wisdom" (2001, 112). Similarly, when he writes that, "[i]n traditional societies, harmful practices can be abandoned only when the whole community decides to do so," he expresses the legitimate concern that an individual cannot easily take a stand alone against his or her dominant culture; however, he presumes that cultural dissent and critique is a "Western" practice that is difficult only for people in "traditional cultures" (2001, 113).

15. For a few of the many examples of activism on the part of Third World women, see, for instance, Barrios ([1977] 1986), Di Chiro (1996), Flanders (2001), Ford-Smith (1997), Gilliam (1991), Kaplan (1982, 1990), Kamel (1990, 40–75), Mohanty (1997, 24–29), and Onishi (2002).

16. Mohanty (1991a, 29–30) presents additional examples of these sort of stereotypes.

17. On these political activities, see, for instance, Ford-Smith (1997), Instituto del Tercer Mundo (1999, 28–29, 394), Kaplan (1990), Mohanty (1991a, 19), Barrios ([1977]1986), Greider (2000, 16), Roy (1999), and Shriver (1994). See also Martin Luther King (1963, 22–25) on the way that commonplace notions of "peace" can mask hidden tensions.

18. For instance, Ford-Smith (1997) describes how she had difficulties obtaining funding for her women's political theater group in Jamaica because international aid agencies claimed that the group produced no "product."

19. Feminist theorists have focused on the difficult resistant agency of people who are multiply oppressed; however, people of any social position face similar obstacles to expressing their agency when they attempt to challenge powerful social institutions.

Consider, for instance, Alice Hertz, a North American who sought to express her protest against the arms race and her solidarity with the Vietnamese people killed by the American military (Ryan 1994). Like the widow Bhuvaneswari Bhaduri, whose suicide Spivak describes (1988, 307–08), Hertz lived in a world hostile to, and unable to understand, her aims. In particular, Hertz's aim confounded the logic of self-interest and national identity that war narratives presuppose. Also like Bhaduri, Hertz determined that she could best express her protest only by killing herself. Both women's gestures were interpreted by the general public as senseless suicides. Their acts are politically meaningful only when narrators such as Spivak or Ryan create a new narrative context that renders intelligible those projects that cannot be spoken within prevailing discourses.

Or consider the spring 1998 protest by Ohio State University students when Madeleine Albright spoke on their campus in defense of the Clinton administration's plans to bomb Iraq. The protest was portrayed by the mainstream media as an unruly disruption of the dialogue. The "disruption" assumes a different significance, however, when we consider the power inequalities that structured the "dialogue": Not only did Albright have the advantage of speaking as an expert and speaking in accord with a commonplace military logic, but planners had arranged things so that the "discussion" would entertain only pregiven questions by invited groups, including a military history class and the ROTC (see, for instance, Pollitt 1998). This arrangement effectively limited debate to a military discursive framework (for instance, a focus on military strategy and an identification of "the Americans" and "the Iraqis" as homogeneous units) while it ensured that the widely broadcasted event would "demonstrate" the supposed public support for the administration's policy. The disruption, even if it did not express a clear position, did defy the pretense of consensus and register public protest against the terms of the debate.

20. Anzaldúa (1990a, xxvii). From *Making Face/Making Soul*. Copyright © 1990, ed. Gloria Anzaldúa. Reprinted by permission of Aunt Lute Books.

21. This phrase is a paraphrase of Varikas (1995, 99).

22. On feminist consciousness-raising in North America, see, for instance, hooks (1989, 24–26, 109–11) and Mackinnon (1989, 83–105). Kaplan (1982) describes a similar kind of consciousness-raising in her study of the political activities of early-twentieth-century Barcelonian popular-class women. When the women shared their stories about the ways that their abilities to nurture their families had been disrupted, their informal "gossiping" eventually forged a women's community consciousness and activism that succeeded in bringing their "private" concerns into political discussion.

23. See, for instance, Mohanty (1991a, 35) and Sommer (1988).

24. On the importance of experience-based, geographically specific pluralist identities, as opposed to the abstract pluralist identities espoused in much poststructuralist theory, see also A and M (1997b, xvii–xviii), S. Mohanty (1997, 230–34), and Moya (1997).

25. Satya Mohanty describes identity similarly. Identities, he says, both grow out of and organize experience. Thus identities are not self-evident representations or mere fictions but are rather "ways of making sense of our experiences" (1997, 216, 230). Mohanty is particularly concerned with the production of "noncolonial identities." He argues that a person whose heritage is tied to slavery or to a colonized country can reclaim her identity from colonialist narratives by reckoning with forgotten or repressed elements of her past and by extending her historical imagination so as to

gain a new understanding of her community and, in turn, a new sense of herself (1997, 217–228). Barrios and Anzaldúa illustrate two possible ways that this might be done.

26. Anzaldúa (1983; 1990a, xxiv-xxv), hooks (1989, 8), and Kadi (1996, 39–56) each describe how internalized social prejudices have inhibited them, even after they were successful writers, from identifying as "knowers." They each use experience-based writing to help them overcome these internalized obstacles. Alcoff (1995, 110), Collins (1986, 518–19), and S. Mohanty (1997, 227) also address the empowering effects of marginalized people telling their own stories.

27. On the emotionally difficult and collective character of memory, especially for people with a colonized heritage, see also A and M (1997b, xxii, xxvii-xxviii, xxxviii), Anzaldúa (1983), S. Mohanty (1997, 222–29), and Panjabi (1997).

28. For instance, Micklethwait and Wooldridge claim that Mexicans complain about the superior productivity of North Americans while the latter complain that Mexican workers are cheap (2000, 111). The authors claim that these (alleged) complaints are ungrounded because they misunderstand the benefits of moving industry to where resources are cheapest. The authors take for granted the "superior productivity" of North Americans and "cheapness" of Mexicans, thus perpetuating the stereotype of Mexicans as less productive than North Americans.

29. Mohanty (1991a, 35–38; 1997, 4–5), Foucault (1980, 220), and Panjabi (1997) also address the way that everyday resistant activities can point to alternative forms of social relations. In her study of Jaya Mitra's and Alicia Partnoy's prison memoirs, Panjabi describes how Mitra (imprisoned in India in the early 1970s) and Partnoy (imprisoned in Argentina in the late 1970s) present extreme cases of state manipulation of women's bodies, sexualities, and everyday subsistence; however, both writers also foreground the way that the communities of support formed by imprisoned women countered the dominant social relations with nurturing, communicative, ethically guided interpersonal relations whose values were more flexible and bonds stronger than those of the Indian and the Argentinean states with their technical rules and abstract values.

Chapter 6

1. Harding 1991, 102. Reprinted from Sandra Harding: *Whose Science? Whose Knowledge?: Thinking from Women's Lives*. Copyright © 1991 Cornell University. Used by permission of the publisher, Cornell University Press.

2. See, for instance, Liu (1994), Mohanty (1990; 1991b), Narayan (1997, chapter 2), and Taylor (1993). The journal *Rethinking Schools* also regularly addresses the problem of how to teach effectively socially and culturally marginalized perspectives.

3. On these dangers, see, for instance, Alarcón (1990), Anzaldúa (199a, xxi), Harding (1991, 246–47), hooks (1994, 62), Kadi (1996), and Taylor (1993).

4. In accord with my reading of Harding, I use the term "standpoint" to refer to the understanding that one develops upon viewing the world from a particular socially defined subject-position. I use the term "perspective" to refer to the view of the world that is available from historically specific people's lives. The two are related but distinct: The critical standpoint is a function of objectively defined subject-positions, but such a standpoint is made possibly only by viewing the world from the perspective of particular people's lives.

5. Rosemary Hennessy recognizes the incomplete treatment of this issue by standpoint theorists when she asks, "What exactly is the material relation between a feminist perspective and its starting point, between theory and lives?" (1993b, 16; see also Hennessy 1993a, 71; 1993b 15–16; 1995, 39–43). I address a specific aspect of this problem: the relation between one person's lived experience and *another person's* knowledge.

6. On the inadequacy of conventional theory to marginalized experiences, see, for instance, Alarcón (1990, 356–64), Anzaldúa (1990a, xviii-xxvii), hooks (1994, 61–64), Mohanty (1991a, 32–38; 1991b), Smith (1987, 55–60), Trinh (1989), and the introduction to this book. Authors such as Alarcón (1990), Anzaldúa (1990a; 1990b), hooks (1994), Mohanty (1991b, 64–66), and Smith (1987, 105–225) also investigate how we might revise our approach to "theory" so that theory is more responsive to those who are excluded from institutionalized discourses.

7. On this last possibility, I have in mind a report that the pension plan, TIAA-CREF, has holdings in Talisman Energy, which is one of three transnational energy corporations that sends "hundreds of millions of dollars annually to the Khartoum regime, which is spending close to $1 million per day on its genocidal war" in the Sudan, partly in an effort to remove people who live in oil-rich regions (Reeves 2001).

8. Hennessy (1995, 142) also makes this criticism of Harding.

9. Some standpoint theorists avoid these dangers. Harding (1991), for instance, avoids mystifying epistemic privilege by defining epistemic privilege in terms of a standpoint that is achieved through struggle, as opposed to an innate quality of a particular group. She also makes clear that the feminist standpoint (and other critical standpoints) are not the exclusive privilege of a particular group but are achievements that are possible for anyone, so long as that person is willing to learn from the insights of others, to struggle against relations of domination, and to grapple with their own prejudices.

10. Bar On also warns that when standpoint theorists claim epistemic privilege for a particular group, they presuppose an essentialist identity for the group or they idealize certain practices that they associate with the group. Standpoints including Collins (1997), Harding (1991, 123, 127, 286–87), and Moya (1997; 2000, 18) have responded to these sort of criticisms.

11. Janack also presents an illuminating discussion of how decisions about epistemological authority should address ethical traits, such as trustworthiness (1997, 136–37).

12. Nancy Hartsock confirms that standpoint theory does not simply serve predefined goals but enables us to approach our goals intelligently. Hartsock may seem to advocate a strictly political approach to standpoint thinking when she says that "the criteria for privileging some knowledges over others are ethical and political rather than purely 'epistemological'" (1997, 372). However, she also claims that knowledge that begins from marginalized standpoints "offer[s] possibilities for envisioning more just social relations" and for developing the political consciousness and collective agency that is necessary to work toward those visions (Hartsock 1997, 373). Insofar as it contributes to realizing a more just world, standpoint thinking is a political practice; however, insofar as it offers *possibilities for envisioning* a more just world, it is also a *way of knowing* that allows people to rethink, in a critical, collective, and historically efficacious manner, their visions of themselves and their worlds.

On the limitation of approaches that endorse the side of "the victim" without examining the meaning of "democracy," "justice," and other values in the context of specific historical situations, see also Howard (1996, 312–15).

13. For instance, Bar On (1993) and Heckman (1997) attribute these claims to feminist standpoint theory.

14. Harding, Hartsock, Smith, and Collins locate the space for critique in what Harding calls "the gap" or Smith calls "the line of fault" between the standpoint available from privileged lives and that available from oppressed lives (Collins 1986, 526; Smith 1987, 49–51; Harding 1991, 276; Hartsock 1983; Hennessy 1993b, 27–28). In a slightly different vein, Hennessy locates the "inaugural space for critique" in "cracks" within dominant beliefs themselves, that is, in incoherences that arise from the not-entirely successful attempts of those beliefs to "seal over" social contradictions. While their emphases differ, standpoint theorists agree that criticism is enabled by gaps in received beliefs, gaps that are symptoms of social contradictions that ultimately manifest themselves in subjective experience, in "the very fabric of many women's lived reality" (Hennessy, 1993b, 27).

15. In the case of acronyms, such as "PAP," the abbreviated format adds to the dehumanizing effect, for the abbreviation allows us to forget the content of the terms that have been abbreviated (Marcuse [1964] 1991, 94). As Roy puts it, "PAPs soon cease to be people" (1999, 32).

16. Throughout the Western tradition, qualities such as open-mindedness and self-reflexivity have been affirmed as both epistemological and ethical virtues. For instance, in the *Apology,* Socrates describes human wisdom in terms of integrity, humility, and caring about the "most important things," while he makes clear that the philosophers' "examined life" is also an ethical life that involves living in accord with one's sense of right and constantly seeking to improve oneself and one's city, even in the face of death (Plato 1981). Kant associates "enlightened thought" with the courage to take responsibility for one's own beliefs and the political capacity to participate in a free republic (1988b). He also makes clear that "enlarged thought" has less to do with "a man's natural gifts" or intellect than with his willingness to consider others' standpoints (1951, 137). Mill similarly describes intelligence in terms of the character traits, humility and open-mindedness (1956, 25). Certainly, the specific character traits that are affirmed as epistemologically valuable traits warrant critical examination, for gender, race, and class prejudices often influence the kind of traits that are associated with reason (Lloyd 1984, Janack 1997, Kadi 1996, and Kheel 1985). Nevertheless, the idea that epistemological traits are not strictly epistemological but are also ethical traits may be an idea that feminist epistemologists can productively reclaim.

References

Abel, Lionel. 1963. The aesthetics of evil. *Partisan Review* 30.

Adams, Carol J. 1995. *Neither man nor beast: Feminism and the defense of animals*. New York: Continuum.

Alarcón, Norma. 1990. The Theoretical subject(s) of *This bridge called my back* and Anglo-American feminism. In *Making face, Making soul hacienda caras: Creative and critical perspectives by feminists of color*, ed. G. Anzaldúa. San Francisco: Aunt Lute Books.

Alcoff, Linda. 1995. Speaking for others. In *Who can speak?* See Roof and Wiegman 1995.

Alexander, M. Jacqui. 1997. Erotic autonomy as a politics of decolonization: An anatomy of feminist and state practice in the Bahamas tourist economy. In *Feminist genealogies, colonial legacies, democratic futures*. See Alexander and Mohanty 1997a.

Alexander, M. Jacqui and Mohanty, Chandra Talpade, eds. 1997a. *Feminist genealogies, colonial legacies, democratic futures*. New York: Routledge.

———. 1997b. Introduction: Genealogies, legacies, movements. In *Feminist genealogies, colonial legacies, democratic futures*. See Alexander and Mohanty 1997a.

Amnesty International. 2001. Women sexually assaulted under INS detention to be deported. *Amnesty Now* 26 (3).

Anderson, Sarah, John Cavanagh, Karen Hansen Kuhn, and David Ranney. 1996. *NAFTA's first two years: The Myths and the reality*. Ontario: Common Frontiers.

Anderson, Sarah, Alberto Arroyo, Peter Bakvis, Patty Barrera, John Dillon, Karen Hansen, and David Ranney. 1998. *Alternatives for the Americas: Building a people's hemispheric agreement*. Ontario: Common Frontiers.

Anderson, Sarah, John Cavanaugh with Thea Lee. 1999. We can fight. We can win. *The Nation* 269 (19).

Anderson, Sarah, John Cavanagh, and David Ranney. 1999. NAFTA: Trinational fiasco. In *The maquiladora reader*. See Kamel and Hoffman 1999.

Anzaldúa, Gloria. 1983. *Speaking in tongues: A Letter to Third World women writers*. In *This bridge called my back*. See Moraga and Anzaldúa 1983.

————. 1988. Tlilli, tlapalli: The Path of the red and black ink. In *Multicultural Literacy*. See Simonson and Walker 1988.

————. 1990a. Haciendo caras, una entrada. In *Making Face, making soul haciendo caras*. See Anzaldúa 1990c.

————. 1990b. La conciencia de la mestiza: Towards a new consciousness. In *Making face, making soul haciendo caras*. See Anzaldúa 1990c.

————. ed. 1990c. *Making face, making soul haciendo caras: Creative and critical perspectives by feminists of color*. San Francisco: Aunt Lute Books.

Arendt, Hannah. [1951] 1979. *The origins of totalitarianism*. New York: Harcourt Brace Jovanovich.

————. 1953a. Understanding and politics. *Partisan Review* 20: 377–392.

————. 1953b. A reply. *Review of Politics* 15: 76–85.

————. 1958. *The human condition*. Chicago: University of Chicago.

————. [1954] 1968. *Between past and future: Eight exercises in political thought*. New York: Penguin.

————. [1955] 1968. *Men in dark times*. New York: Harcourt Brace Jovanovich.

————. [1963] 1965. *Eichmann in Jerusalem: A Report on the banality of evil*, enlarged ed. New York: Viking Press.

————. 1965. "Some questions of moral philosophy." Lecture course at the New School (March 24). In the Hannah Arendt Papers, Library of Congress, Container 40, p. 024648, cited in Beiner 1982.

————. [1964] 1994. What remains? The language remains: A conversation with Gunter Gaus. Trans. Joan Stambaugh. In *Essays in understanding*, ed. Jerome Kohn. New York: Harcourt, Brace & Company.

————. 1971. Thinking and moral considerations. *Social Research* 38.

————. [1971] 1978. *Thinking*. In *The life of the mind*. New York: Harcourt Brace Jovanovich.

Bann, Stephen. 1981. Towards a critical historiography: Recent work in philosophy of history. *Philosophy* 56.

————. 1982. *Lectures on Kant's political philosophy*, ed. Ronald Beiner. Chicago: University of Chicago Press.

————. 1994 The difficulties of understanding. In *Essays in understanding*, ed. Jerome Kohn. New York: Harcourt, Brace & Company.

————. 1994 The nature of totalitarianism. In *Essays in understanding*, ed. Jerome Kohn. New York: Harcourt, Brace & Company.

Bar On, Bat-Ami. 1993. Marginality and epistemic privilege. In *Feminist epistemlogies*, ed. Linda Alcoff and Elizabeth Potter. New York: Routledge.

Barrios de Chungara, Domitila. [1977] 1986. *"Si me permiten hablar . . . " testimonio de Domitila una mujer de las minas de Bolivia*, ed. Moema Viezzar. Mexico City: Siglo Veintiuno.

Barroso, Carmen and Bruschini, Cristina. 1991. Building politics from personal lives: Discussions on sexuality among poor women in Brazil. In *Third world women and the politics of feminism*. See Mohanty, Russo, and Torres, 1991.

Barsamian, David. 2001. Interview with Arundhati Roy. *The Progressive* (April).

Barthes, Roland. 1989. *The rustle of language*. Trans. Richard Howard. Berkeley: University of California Press.

Bauzá, Vaness. 1994. Puerto Rico: The Covert campaign to sterilize women. *Ms.* (September/October): 14.

Beiner, Ronald. 1982. Interpretative essay. In *Lectures on Kant's political philosophy*, ed. Ronald Beiner. Chicago: University of Chicago.

Benhabib, Seyla. 1988. Judgment and the moral foundations of politics in Arendt's thought. *Political Theory* 16 (1).

———. 1990. Hannah Arendt and the redemptive power of narrative. *Social Research* 57.

———. 1992. *Situating the self: Gender, community and postmodernism in contemporary ethics*. New York: Routledge.

Benjamin, Walter. 1968. The storyteller. In *Illuminations*, ed. H. Arendt. Trans. Harry Zohn. New York: Schocken Books.

Bernstein, Richard. 1986. Rethinking the social and political. In *Philosophical Profiles*. Philadelphia: University of Pennsylvania Press.

———. 1991. *Beyond objectivism and relativism: Science, hermeneutics, and praxis*. Philadelphia: University of Pennsylvania Press.

Borosage, 1999. The Battle in Seattle. *The Nation* 269 (19).

Botstein, Leo and Jay, Martin. 1978. Hannah Arendt: Opposing views. *Partisan Review* 45: 349–380.

Burke, Peter. 1989. History as social memory. In *Memory: History culture and the mind*, ed. Thomas Butler. London: Basil Blackwell.

Butler, Judith. 1990. Gender trouble, feminist theory, and psychoanalytic discourse. In *Feminism/postmodernism*, ed. Linda Nicholson. New York: Routledge.

———. 1992. Contingent foundations: Feminism and the question of "postmodernism." In *Feminists theorize the political*. See Butler and Scott 1992a.

———. 2002. Guantánamo limbo. *The Nation* (April 1).

Butler, Judith and Joan Wallach Scott, eds. 1992a. *Feminists theorize the political.* New York: Routledge.

———. 1992b. Introduction. In *Feminists theorize the political.* See Butler and Scott 1992a.

Butterfield, Fox. 2001. When the police shoot, who's counting? *New York Times,* 29 April.

Caffentzis, George. 2001. Oil and the Islamists. *The New Internationalist* 341 (December).

Canning, Kathleen. 1994. Feminist history after the linguistic turn: Historicizing discourse and experience. *Signs.* 19 (2).

Cantrell, Carol. 1994. Women and language in Susan Griffin's *Women and nature: The roaring inside her. Hypatia* 9(3).

Carr, David. 1984. Review of *Temp et récit tome 1. History and Theory* 23: 357–70.

———. 1986. Narrative and the real world: An argument for continuity. *History and Theory* 25: 117–31.

———. [1986] 1991. *Time, narrative, and history.* Bloomington: Indiana University Press.

———. 1987. *Interpreting Husserl.* Boston: Martinus Nijhoff.

Casey, Edward. 1987. *Remembering.* Bloomington: Indiana University Press.

Chevigny, Bell, Myra Jehlen, and Judith Walkowitz. 1989. Patrolling the borders: Feminist historiography and the new historicism. *Radical History Review* 43.

Chow, Rey. 1991. Violence in the other country. In *Third World women and the politics of feminism.* See Mohanty, Russo, and Torres 1991.

Coalition for Justice in the Maquiladoras. 1999. *Maquiladora standards of conduct.* In *The maquiladora reader.* See Kamel and Hoffman 1999.

Collins, Patricia Hill. 1986. Learning from the outsider within: The sociological significance of black feminist thought. *Social Problems* 33.

———. 1997. Comment of Heckman's "Truth and Method: Feminist Standpoint Theory Revisited": Where's the power? *Signs* 22 (2).

Coerver, Don and Linda Hall. 1999. *Tangled destinies: Latin America and the United States.* Albuquerque: University of New Mexico Press.

Correa, Sonia and Rosalind Petchesky. 1994. Exposing the numbers game: Feminists challenge the population-control establishment. *Ms.* (September/October): 10, 13, and 15–17.

Cutting-Gray, Joanne. 1993. Hannah Arendt, feminism, and the politics of alterity: "What will we lose if we win?" *Hypatia* 8 (1): 35–54.

de Beauvoir, Simone. [1949] 1989. *The second sex*. Trans H. M. Parshely. New York: Random House.

de Bolla, Peter. [1986]. Disfiguring history. *Diacritics* 16.

de Certeau, Michel. 1986. History: Science and fiction. In *Heterologies: Discourse on the other*. Trans. Brian Massumi. Minneapolis: University of Minnesota Press.

Delany, Samuel. 1993. *The motion of light in water: Sex and science fiction writing in the east village, 1957–1965*. New York: Masquerade Books.

Derrida, Jaques. 1983. The principle of reason: The university in the eyes of its pupils. *Diacritics* 13.

Di Chiro, Giovanni. 1996. Nature as community. *Uncommon ground: Rethinking the human place in nature*. New York: Norton.

Disch, Lisa. 1994. *Hannah Arendt and the limits of philosophy*. New York: Cornell University Press.

Economic Policy Institute. 1997. *The Failed experiment: NAFTA after three years*. Washington, D.C.: The Economic Policy Institute.

Fields, Barbara. 1982. Ideology and race in American history. In *Region, race and reconstruction: Essays in honor of C. Vann Woodward*, ed. J. Morgan Kousser and James McPherson. New York: Oxford University Press.

———. 1989. Categories of analysis? Not in my book. *Viewpoints*. American Council of Learned Societies Occasional Paper no. 10.

Flanders, Laura. 2001. Afghan feminists speak out. *The Progressive* 65:11.

Fox-Genovese, Elizabeth. 1991. *Feminism without illusions: A Critique of individualism*. Chapel Hill: University of North Carolina.

Ford-Smith, Honor. Ring ding in a tight corner: Sistren, collective democracy, and the organization of cultural production. In *Feminist genealogies, colonial legacies, democratic futures*. See Alexander and Mohanty 1997a.

Foucault, Michel. [1963] 1994. *The birth of the clinic*. Trans. A. M. Sheridan Smith. New York: Vintage.

———. [1969] 1972. *The Archeology of knowledge*. Trans. A. M. Sheridan Smith. New York: Pantheon.

———. [1975] 1979. Discipline and punish. Trans. Alan Sheridan. New York: Random House.

———. [1976] 1990. *The history of sexuality*. Vol. 1. Trans. Robert Hurley. New York: Random House.

————. 1980. *Power/knowledge: Selected interview and other writings 1972–1977*, ed. Colin Gordon. New York: Pantheon.

————. 1984. Preface to *The History of sexuality*. Vol. 2. Trans. and ed. Paul Rabinow. In *The Foucault reader*. New York: Random House.

Frazier, Nancy. 1989. *Unruly practices: Power, discourse, and gender in contemporary social theory*. Minneapolis. University of Minneapolis Press.

Gadamer, Hans-Georg. [1960] 1991. *Truth and method*. Trans. Joel Weinshemer and Donald Marshall. New York: Crossroad Publishing.

————. 1980. Practical philosophy as a model of the human sciences. *Research in Phenomenology 9*.

Galeano, Eduardo. 1973. *Open veins of Latin America: Five Centuries of the Pillage of a Continent*. Trans. Cedric Belfrage. New York: Monthly Review Press.

————. 1988. *Memory of fire: Century of the wind*. Trans. Cedric Belfrage. New York: Pantheon.

————. 1989. Defense de la palabra. In *Nosotros decimos no: cronicas (1963/1988)*. Mexico, D.F.: Siglo Veintiuno.

George, Susan. 2002. Another world is possible. *The Nation* (February 18).

Gilliam, Angela. 1991. Women's equality and national liberation. In *Third World women and the politics of feminism*. See Mohanty, Russo, and Torres 1991.

Gordon, Colin. 1980. Afterword. In Michel Foucualt, *Power/knowledge: Selected interviews and other writings 1972–1977*, ed. Colin Gordon. New York: Pantheon.

Gramsci, Antonio. 1995. *Selections from the prison notebooks*. Trans. and ed. Quintin Hoare and Geoffrey Smith. New York: International Publishers.

Grant, Judith. 1987. I feel therefore I am: A critique of female experience as the basis for feminist epistemology. In *Feminism and epistemology: Approaches to research in women and politics*, ed. Maria Falco. New York: Haworth.

Greider, William. 1997. *One world, ready or not: The Manic logic of global capitalism*. New York: Simon and Schuster.

————. 2000. Global agenda. *The Nation* 270 (4).

Griffin, Susan. 1992. *A chorus of stones: The private life of war*. New York: Doubleday.

————. 1997. Ecofeminism and meaning. In *Ecofeminism: Women, Culture, Nature*, ed. Karen Warren. Bloomington: Indiana University Press.

Hanney, Suzanne and Crouse, Charity. 1999. Partnerships with the poor. *Streetwise.* (August 3–16): 1 and 3.

Haraway, Donna. 1988. Situated knowledges: The science question in feminism and the privilege of partial perspective. *Feminist Studies* 14: 575–599.

———. 1990. A Manifesto for cyborgs: Science, technology, and socialist feminism in the 1980s. In *Feminism/Postmodernism,* ed. Linda Nicholson. New York: Routledge.

Harding, Sandra. 1987. Conclusion: Epistemological questions. In *Feminism Methodology,* ed. Sandra Harding. Bloomington: Indiana University Press.

———. 1991. *Whose science? whose knowledge?: Thinking from women's lives.* New York: Cornell University Press.

———. 1995. Subjectivity, experience, and knowledge: An epstimelogy from/for rainbow coalition politics. In *Who can speak?* See Roof and Wiegman 1995.

———. 1997. Comment on Heckman's "Truth and Method: Feminist Standpoint Theory Revisited": Whose standpoint needs the regimes of truth and reality. *Signs* 22 (2): 382–291.

Hartsock, Nancy. 1983. The Feminist standpoint: Developing the ground for a specifically feminist historical materialism. In *Discovering reality,* ed. Sandra Harding and Merrill Hintikka. Dordrecht: Reidel Publishing.

———. 1997. Comment on Heckman's "Truth and Method: Feminist Standpoint Theory Revisited": Truth or justice? *Signs* 22 (2).

Hayter, Theresa. 2002. The new common sense. *The New Internationalist* 350.

Hebert, H. Josef. 1993. Government conceals nuclear radiation tests. *Indiana Daily Student.* December 8.

Heckman, Susan. 1997. Truth & method: Feminist standpoint theory revisited. *Signs* 22 (2).

Hennessy Rosemary. 1993a. *Materialist feminism and the politics of discourse.* New York: Routledge.

———. 1993b. Women's lives/feminist knowledge: Feminist standpoint as ideology critique. *Hypatia* 8 (1).

———. 1995. Subjects, knowledges, . . . and all the rest: Speaking for what? In *Who can speak?,* ed. J. Roof and R. Wiegman. Urbana: University of Illinois Press

Higham, John. 1963. *The reconstruction of American history.* London: Hutchinson & Co.

———. 1970. *Writing American history: Essays in modern scholarship.* Bloomington: Indiana University Press.

Holt, Stull. 1940. The idea of scientific history in America. *Journal of the History of Ideas* 1 (3): 352–362.

hooks, bell. 1989. *Talking back: Thinking feminist, thinking black.* Boston: South End Press.

———. 1994. *Teaching to transgress.* New York: Routledge.

———. 1995. Postmodern blackness. In *The truth about the truth,* ed. Walter Anderson. New York: Putnam.

Horkheimer, Max and Adorno, Theodor. 1998. *The dialectic of Enlightenment.* Trans. John Cumming. New York: Continuum.

Howard, Dick. 1994. Towards a politics of judgment. *Constellations* 1 (2): 286–305.

———. 1996. *Political judgments.* Maryland: Rowman & Littlefield.

Ignatieff, Michael. 2001. The attack on human rights. *Foreign Affairs* (November/December).

Instituto del Tercer Mundo. 1999. *The World guide 1999/2000.* Oxford: New International Publications.

Ireland, Doug. 1999. America's disappeared. *The Nation* (July 12).

Janack, Marianne. 1997. Standpoint epistemology without the "standpoint"?: An Examination of epistemic privilege and epistemic authority. *Hypatia* 12 (2): 125–39.

Jaquet, Janine. 1998. The Media nation: TV. *The Nation* (June 8): 23–28.

Jehl, Douglas. 1999. Arab honor's price: A Woman's blood. *The New York Times*, 20 June: 1 and 9.

Johnson-Odim, Cheryl. 1991. Common themes, different contexts: Third World women and feminism. In *Third World women and the politics of feminism.* See Mohanty, Russo, and Torres 1991.

Kadi, Joanna. 1996. *Thinking class: Sketches from a cultural worker.* Boston: South End Press.

Kamel, Rachel. 1990. *The Global factory: Analysis and action for a new economic era.* Packard Press.

Kamel, Rachael and Anya Hoffman, eds. 1999. *The maquiladora reader: Cross-border organizing since NAFTA.* Philadelphia: American Friends Service Committee.

Kant, Immanuel. 1951. *Critique of judgment.* Trans. J. H. Bernard. New York: MacMillan.

———. 1965. *Critique of pure reason.* Trans. Norman Kemp Smith. New York: St. Martin's Press.

———. 1988a. *Perpetual peace.* In *Kant's political writings,* ed. Hans Reiss. Trans. H. B. Nisbet. New York: Cambridge University Press.

———. 1988b. What is enlightenment? In *Kant's political writings*, ed. Hans Reiss. Trans. H. B. Nisbet. New York: Cambridge University Press.

Kaplan, Temma. 1982. Female consciousness and collective action: The Case of Barcelona, 1910–1918. *Signs* 7: 545–566.

———. 1990. Community and resistance in women's political cultures. *Dialectical Anthropology* 15: 259–267.

Kermode, Frank. 1992. Whose history is bunk? *New York Times Book Review*, 23 February: 1 and 33.

Kernaghan, Charles. 1999. Public Lecture at Ohio Wesleyan University. October.

Kheel, Marti. 1985. The liberation of nature: A circular affair. *Environmental Ethics* 7.

King, Martin Luther, Jr. 1963. Letter from a Birmingham jail. Reprinted in *A. J. Muste Memorial Institute Essay Series No. 1*. New York: A. J. Muste Memorial Institute.

Kohn, Jerome. 1994. Introduction. *Essays in understanding*, ed. Jerome Kohn. New York: Harcourt, Brace & Company.

Kuklick, Bruce. 1969. The mind of the historian. *History and Theory* 8 (3): 313–331.

Kurzweil, Edith. 1992. The changing curriculum: Then and now. *Partisan Review* 2: 249–261.

LaCapra, Dominick. 1985. *History and criticism*. New York: Cornell University Press.

Lajoie, Ron. 1999. In the land of the free. *Amnesty International USA newsletter* (fall): 6.

Lasch, Christopher. 1983. Introduction. *Salmugundi* 60. Special Issue on Hannah Arendt, ed. Christopher Lasch.

Lauritzen, Paul. 1997. Hear no evil, see no evil, think no evil: Ethics and the appeal to experience. *Hypatia* 19 (2): 83–104.

Liu, Tessie. 1994. Teaching the differences among women from a historical perspective: Rethinking race and gender as social categories. New York: Routledge.

Lloyd, Genevieve. 1984. *The man of reason*. Minneapolis: University of Minnesota.

Lorde, Audre. 1984. *Sister outsider*. Freedom, CA: The Crossing Press.

Luban, D. 1983. Explaining dark times: Hannah Arendt's theory of theory. *Social Research* 50.

Lugones, Maria. 1987. Playfulness, "world"-traveling, and loving perception. *Hypatia* 2 (2): 3–18.

————. 1997. Strategies of the street-walker/estratégias de la callejera. Paper presented at the Eastern Meeting of the Society for Women in Philosophy. Chicago, Illinois.

Lyderson, Kari. 1998. Residents protest oil refinery. *Streetwise* (November 10–23): 1 and 20.

Mackinnon, Catherine. 1989. *Toward a feminist theory of the state.* Cambridge: Harvard University Press.

Manning, Steve. 1999. How corporations are buying their way into America's classrooms. *The Nation* (September 27): 11–18.

Marcuse, Herbert. [1964] 1991. *One-dimensional man.* Boston: Beacon Press.

Martin, Biddy. 1982. Feminism, criticism, and Foucault. *New German Critique* 27: 3–30.

Marx, Karl. 1997. *Writing of the young Marx on philosophy and society.* Trans. and ed. Loyd Easton and Kurt Guddat. Indianapolis: Hackett.

McChesney, Robert. 1999. The New global media. *The Nation* 269 (18) (November 29).

Micklethwait, John and Adrien Wooldridge. 2000. *A future perfect: The challenge and hidden promise of globalization.*

Mill, John Stuart. 1956. *On liberty.* Upper Saddle River: Prentice-Hall.

Mines, Luke. 1998. Globalization in the classroom. *The Nation* (June 1): 22 and 24.

Mink, Louis. 1978. Narrative as a cognitive instrument. In *The writing of history,* ed. Robert Canary and Henry Kozicki. Madison: University of Wisconsin Press.

————. 1987. *Historical understanding.* Ithaca: Cornell University Press.

Moberg, David. 2000. For Unions, Green's not easy. *The Nation* 270 (7) (February 21).

Mohanty, Chandra Talpade. 1982. Feminist encounters: Locating the politics of experience. *Copyright* 1: 30–44.

————. 1990. On race and voice: Challenges for a liberal education in the 1990s. *Cultural Critique* (winter 1989–1990).

————. 1991a. Cartographies of struggle: Third world women and the politics of feminism. In *Third world women and the politics of feminism.* See Mohanty, Russo, and Torres 1991.

————. 1991b. Under western eyes: Feminist scholarship and colonial discourses. In *Third world women and the politics of feminism.* See Mohanty, Russo, and Torres 1991.

————. 1997. Women workers and capitalist scripts: Ideologies of domination, common interests, and the politics of solidarity. In *Feminist genealogies, colonial legacies, democratic futures*. See Alexander and Mohanty 1997a. New York: Routledge.

Mohanty, Chandra, Ann Russo, and Lourdes Torres, eds. 1991. *Third world women and the politics of feminism*. Bloomington: Indiana University Press.

Mohanty, Satya. 1997. *Literary theory and the claims of history*. Ithaca: Cornell University Press.

Moraga, Cherríe and Gloria Anzaldúa eds. 1983. *This bridge called my back: Writings by radical women of color*. New York: Kitchen Table, Women of Color Press.

Morison, Samuel Eliot. 1951. Faith of a historian. *The American Historical Review* 56 (2): 261–275.

————. 1965. *The Oxford history of the American people*. New York: Oxford University Press.

Morrison, Toni. 1987. *Beloved*. New York: Knopf.

Moya, Paula. 1997. Postmodernism, "realism," and the politics of identity: Cherríe Moraga and Chicana feminism. In *Feminist genealogies, colonial legacies, democratic futures*. See Alexander and Mohanty 1997a.

————. 2000. Introduction: Reclaiming identity. In *Reclaiming identity,* ed. Paula Moya and Michael Hames-García. Berkeley: University of California Press.

Mura, David. 1988. Strangers in the village. See Simonson and Walker 1988.

Narayan, Uma. 1997. *Dislocating Cultures: Identities, Traditions, and Third World Feminism*. New York: Routledge.

————. 1998. Essence of culture and a sense of history: A Feminist critique of cultural essentialism. *Hypatia* 13(2)

National Labor Committee. 1999. Testimony of Jiovanni Fuentes, Blanca Ruth Palacios, and Lorena Moran del Carmen presented to the United States Congress. New York: National Labor Committee.

Nazma, Sk. n.d. Testimony of Sk. Nazma. National Labor Committee Bangladesh Worker Tour. New York: National Labor Committee.

Nelson, Hilde Lindemann. 1995. Resistance and insubordination. *Hypatia* 10 (2):23–40.

Nichols, John. Raising a Ruckus. 1999. *The Nation* 269(19).

Nora, Pierre. (1984). *Les lieux de memoire*. Paris: Gallimard.

Novick, Peter. 1988. *That noble dream: The "objectivity question" and the American historical profession*. Chicago: Cambridge University Press.

Nussbaum, Martha. 1995. *Poetic justice: The literary imagination and public life*. Boston: Beacon Press.

Okin, Susan. 1998. Sexual orientation, gender, and families: Dichotomizing differences. *Hypatia* 11 (1).

Onishi, Norimitsu. 2002. Flow of oil wealth skirts Nigerian villange. *New York Times*, 22 December: 1,14.

Palmer, Brian. 1987. Response to Joan Scott. *International Labor and Working Class History* 31: 15–23.

Panjabi, Kavita. 1997. Probing morality and state violence: Feminist values and communicative interaction in prison testimonios in India and Argentina. In *Feminist Genealogies*. See Alexander and Mohanty 1997a.

Phillips, William, ed. 1992. *Partisan Review 2: The changing culture of the university*.

Plato. 1981. *Five dialogues*. Trans. G. M. A. Grube. Indianapolis: Hackett.

Pleites, Julia Esmeralda. 1998. Nike code of conduct: 'Just do it'—or you're fired? *Christian Science Monitor* (November 25).

Pollitt, Katha. 1998. Hello, Columbus. *The Nation* (March 3).

Polter, Julie. 1995. The Enola Gay: History's fallout. *Sojourners* May/April: 13.

Ranney, David. 2003. *Global decisions, local collisions: Urban life in the new world order*. Philadelphia: Temple University Press.

Rawlinson, Mary. 1987. Foucault's strategy: Knowledge, power, and the specifity of truth. *The Journal of Medicine and Philosophy* 12: 371–395.

Reeves, Eric. 2001. Rapacious instincts in Sudan. *The Nation* (June 4).

Ricoeur, Paul. 1971. The model of the text: Meaningful action considered as a text. *Social Research* 38.

———. 1974. *The conflict of interpretations*, ed. Don Ihde. Evanston: Northwestern University Press.

———. 1980. Narrative time. *Critical Inquiry* 7.

———. 1983. Action, story and history: On re-reading *The Human Condition*. *Salmagundi* 60.

———. [1983] 1984. *Time and narrative*. Vol. 1. Trans. Kathleen Blamey and David Pellauer. Chicago: Unversity of Chicago Press.

———. [1984] 1985. *Time and narrative*. Vol. 2. Trans. Kathleen Blamey and David Pellauer. Chicago: University of Chicago Press.

———. [1985] 1988. *Time and narrative*. Volume 3. Trans. Kathleen Blamey and David Pellauer. Chicago: University of Chicago Press.

———. 1991. *From text to action*. Trans. Kathleen Blamey and John Thompson. Evanston: Northwestern University Press.

Rodney, Walter. 1982. *How Europe underdeveloped Africa*. Washington, D.C.: Howard University Press.

Roof, Judith and Robin Wiegman, eds. 1995. *Who can speak?* Urbana: University of Illinois Press.

Rowbotham, Sheile. 1974. *Hidden from history*. New York: Pantheon.

Roy, Arundhati. 1999. *The cost of living*. New York: Random House.

———. 2001. *Power politics*. Cambridge: South End Press.

Ruiz, Vicki and Ellen Carol DuBois. 1994a. Introduction to the second edition. In *Unequal Sisters*. See Ruiz and DuBois 1994b.

Ruiz, Vicki and Ellen Carol DuBois, eds. 1994b. *Unequal sisters: A Multicultural reader in U.S. women's history*. New York: Routledge.

Ryan, Cheyney. 1994. The one who burns herself for peace. *Hypatia* 9 (2).

Said, Edward. 2001. The clash of ignorance. *The Nation* (October 22).

Sawicki, Jana. 1996. Feminism, Foucault, and "subjects" of power and freedom. In *Feminist interpretations of Foucault*, ed. S. Hekman. University Park: University of Pennsylvania Press.

Schlosser, Eric. 2001. The chain never stops. *Mother Jones* (July/August).

Scott, Joan Wallach. 1987a. A reply to criticism. *International Labor and Working Class History* 32.

———. 1987b. On language, gender, and working-class history. *International Labor and Working Class History* 31.

———. 1988. *Gender and the politics of history*. New York: Columbia University.

———. 1991. The evidence of experience. *Critical Inquiry* 17.

Service Employees International Union. 1987. *Health and safety problems of video display terminal (VDT) workers*. Washington, D.C.: Service Employees International Union.

Shenk, David. 1999. Money + science = ethics problems on campus. *The Nation* (March 22): 11–18.

Shohat, Ella. 1997. Post-Third-Worldist culture: Gender, nation, and the cinema. In *Feminist Genealogies*. See Alexander and Mohanty 1997a.

Showalter, Elaine. 1985. *The female malady: Women, madness, and English culture 1830–1980*. New York: Penguin Books.

Shriver, Jeff. 1994. A Faith to move mountains: Shaking the foundations of power in Mexico. *Sojourners* (May).

Simonson, Rick and Scott Walker. 1988. *Multicultural Literacy: Opening the American mind*. Saint Paul: Greywolf Press.

Smith, Dorothy. 1987. *The everyday world as problematic: A feminist sociology.* Boston: Northeastern University Press.

———. 1997. Comment of Hekman's "Truth and Method: Feminist Standpoint Theory Revisited." *Signs* 22 (2).

Sommer, Doris. 1988. Not just a personal story: Women's testimonios and the plural self. In *Life/lines: Theorizing women's autobiography*, ed. Bella Brodski and Celeste Schenke. Ithaca: Cornell University Press.

Spivak, Gayatri. 1988. Can the subaltern speak? In *Marxism and the interpretation of culture*, ed. C. Nelson and L. Grossberg. Urbana: University of Illinois Press.

———. 1990. *The Postcolonial critic: Interviews, strategies, and dialogues*, ed. Sarah Harasyn. New York: Routledge.

Stansell, Christine. 1987. A response to Joan Scott. *International Labor and Working Class History* 32: 24–29.

Stewart, Kathleen. 1991. On the politics of cultural theory: A case for "contaminated" cultural critique. *Social Research* 58 (2): 389–412.

Stone-Mediatore, Shari. 1996. Review of *Hannah Arendt and the Limits of Philosophy*, by Lisa Jane Disch. *Hypatia* 11 (3).

———. 1998. Chandra Mohanty and the revaluing of experience. *Hypatia* 13 (2).

———. 2000. Hannah Arendt and Susan Griffin: Toward a feminist metahistory. In *Presenting women philosophers*, ed. Sara Ebenreck and Cecile Tougas. Philadelphia: Temple University Press.

Taylor, Carole Anne. 1993. Positioning subjects and objects: Agency, narration, relationality. *Hypatia* 8 (1): 55–80.

Tilly, Louise. 1989. Gender, women's history, and social history. *Social Science History* 13: 439–62.

Trinh Min-ha. (1989). Grandma's story. In Trinh Min-ha, *Women, native, other*. Bloomington: Indiana University.

U.S./Cuba Labor Exchange. 1997. *International workers meeting confronting neoliberalism and the global economy.* Redford: U.S./Cuba Labor Exchange.

Van Sertima, Ivan, ed. 1986. *Blacks in science: Ancient and modern.* New Brunswick: Transaction.

Varikas, Eleni. 1995. Gender, experience and subjectivity: The Tilly-Scott disagreement. *New Left Review* 211: 89–101.

Voegelin. Eric. 1953. The Origins of Totalitarianism. *Review of Politics* 15: 68–76.

Vollrath, E. 1977. Hannah Arendt and the method of political thinking. *Social Research* 44.

Walkowitz, Judith, Dubois, Ellen, Buhle, Mari-Jo, Kaplan, Temma, Lerner, Gerda, and Smith-Rosenberg, Caroll. 1980. Politics and culture in women's history: A symposium. *Feminist Studies* 6 (1): 26–64.

Wallace, Michael. 1987. Reagan's abuse of history. *Tikun* 2 (1).

Weed, Elizabeth. 1989. Introduction: Terms of reference. In *Coming to terms: Feminism, theory, politics,* ed. E. Weed. New York: Routledge.

Weinberg, Gerhard. 1994. *A world at arms: A global history of World War II*. Boston: Cambridge University Press.

White, Hayden. 1966. The burden of history. *History and Theory* 5 (2): 112–134.

———. 1973. The politics of contemporary philosophy of history. *Clio* 3: 35–53.

———. 1975. Historicism, history and the figurative imagination. *History and Theory* 14: 48–67.

———. 1978. *The tropics of discourse*. Baltimore: John Hopkins.

———. 1980. The value of narrativity in the representation of reality. *Critical Inquiry* 7: 5–27.

———. 1982. The politics of historical intepetation: Discipline and de-sublimation. *Critical Inquiry* 1982: 113–137.

———. 1984. The question of narrative in contemporary historical theory. *History and Theory* 23: 1–33.

Wieseltier, Leon. 1993. After memory. *The New Republic* (May 3).

Wilkerson, William. 2000. Is there something you need to tell me? Coming out and the ambiguity of experience. In *Reclaiming Identity*, ed. Paula Moya and Michael Hames-García. Berkeley: University of California Press.

Yotoghan, Wardell. 1997. Public statement by the Coalition to Save Public Housing. Presented at the Committee on New Priorities forum on public housing. Chicago, May 21.

Zake, Ieva. 2001. Trope analysis of women's political subjectivity: Women secretaries and the issue of sexual harrassment in Latvia. *Feminist Theory* 2 (3).

Zinn, Howard. 1995. *A people's history of the United States*. New York: Harper & Row.

Index

Academic discourse, "neutral" categories of, 180–181
Acronyms, dehumanizing effects of, 215n. 15
Action
  Barrios and Anzaldúa's treatment of, 143
  as collective phenomenon, 153–154
  constellations of, 28, 154
  dominant notions of, 154
  historical, obstacles to, 142
  narrative, 138–140
  renarrating, 152–155
Action-units, 22, 197n. 10
  assumptions contained in, 22
Activism. *See also* Resistance movements
  narration of, 8, 141–142
  of Third World women, 211n. 15
Actors
  Barrios and Anzaldúa's treatment of, 143
  discrete identities of, 167
  Enlightenment concept of, 136
  narrative, 135–138
Actor-units, 21–22, 197n. 10
  assumptions contained in, 21
  unconventional, in resistance movements, 140–141
Aesthetic judgment
  Kant's concept of, 199n. 24
  versus political judgment, 203n. 7
  validity in, 70
African history, Western science and, 186–188
Agency
  Anzaldúa's struggle for, 150–151

avoiding problematic categories of, 143
  collective, 151–152
  community situatedness of, 151–152
  individual, in Enlightenment thought, 150
  obstacles to expression of, 211n. 19
  renarrating, 150–152
  social preconditions of, 139
  thwarted, nonrecognition of, 139–140
Alarcón, Norma, 135
  on preconceived narrative frameworks, 167
Albright, Madeleine, protest against, 212n. 19
Alexander, Jacqui, on internalized prejudice, 150
Alienation, citizen, as pre-totalitarian element, 53
American Council of Trustees and Alumni, 204n. 14
Amnesty International, use of stories by, 4
Antisemitism
  Himmler's, 84
  as human response *versus* natural instinct, 52–53
Anzaldúa, Gloria, 12–13, 126, 142, 166
  challenges to dominant beliefs, 167
  and connection between historical events and everyday life, 157–158
  cultural confusion of, 145
  metaphors of, 145
  narrative construction of, 164
  narrative experimentation of, 184–185
  and narration as resistance, 11